LEARNING WITH
Uncertainty

T0330716

LEARNING WITH
Uncertainty

XIZHAO WANG
JUNHAI ZHAI

CRC Press
Taylor & Francis Group
Boca Raton London New York

CRC Press is an imprint of the
Taylor & Francis Group, an **informa** business

CRC Press
Taylor & Francis Group
6000 Broken Sound Parkway NW, Suite 300
Boca Raton, FL 33487-2742

First issued in paperback 2020

ISBN 13: 978-0-367-57417-8 (pbk)
ISBN 13: 978-1-4987-2412-8 (hbk)

Library of Congress Cataloging-in-Publication Data

Names: Wang, Xizhao, author. | Zhai, Junhai, author.
Title: Learning with uncertainty / Xizhao Wang, Junhai Zhai.
Description: Boca Raton : CRC Press, [2016] | Includes bibliographical references and index.
Identifiers: LCCN 2016030316| ISBN 9781498724128 (acid-free paper) | ISBN 9781498724135 (e-book)
Subjects: LCSH: Machine learning. | Fuzzy decision making. | Decision trees.
Classification: LCC Q325.5 .W36 2016 | DDC 006.3/1--dc23
LC record available at https://lccn.loc.gov/2016030316

**Visit the Taylor & Francis Web site at
http://www.taylorandfrancis.com**

**and the CRC Press Web site at
http://www.crcpress.com**

Contents

Preface

Learning is an essential way for humans to gain wisdom and furthermore for machines to acquire intelligence. It is well acknowledged that learning algorithms will be more flexible and more effective if the uncertainty can be modeled and processed during the process of designing and implementing the learning algorithms.

Uncertainty is a common phenomenon in machine learning, which can be found in every stage of learning, such as data preprocessing, algorithm design, and model selection. Furthermore, one can find the impact of uncertainty processing on various machine learning techniques; for instance, uncertainty can be used as a heuristic to generate decision tree in inductive learning, it can be employed to measure the significance degree of samples in active learning, and it can also be applied in ensemble learning as a heuristic to select the basic classifier for integration. This book makes an initial attempt to systematically discuss the modeling and significance of uncertainty in some processes of learning and tries to bring some new advancements in learning with uncertainty.

The book contains five chapters. Chapter 1 is an introduction to uncertainty. Four kinds of uncertainty, that is, randomness, fuzziness, roughness, and nonspecificity, are briefly introduced in this chapter. Furthermore, the relationships among these uncertainties are also discussed in this chapter. Chapter 2 introduces the induction of decision tree with uncertainty. The contents include how to use uncertainty to induce crisp decision trees and fuzzy decision trees. Chapter 2 also discusses how to use uncertainty to improve the generalization ability of fuzzy decision trees. Clustering under uncertainty environment is discussed in Chapter 3. Specifically, the basic concepts of clustering are briefly reviewed in Section 3.1. Section 3.2 introduces two types of clustering, that is, partition-based clustering and hierarchy-based clustering. Validation functions of clustering are discussed in Section 3.3 and feature-weighted fuzzy clustering is addressed in next sections. In Chapter 4, we first present an introduction to active learning in Section 4.1. Two kinds of active learning techniques, that is, uncertainty sampling and query by committee, are discussed in Section 4.2. Maximum ambiguity–based active learning is presented in Section 4.3. A learning approach for support vector machine is presented in Section 4.4. Chapter 5 includes five sections. An introduction to ensemble learning is reviewed in Section 5.1.

Bagging and boosting, multiple fuzzy decision trees, and fusion of classifiers based on upper integral are discussed in the next sections, respectively. The relationship between fuzziness and generalization in ensemble learning is addressed in Section 5.5.

Taking this opportunity, we deliver our sincere thanks to those who offered us great help during the writing of this book. We appreciate the discussions and revision suggestions given by those friends and colleagues, including Professor Shuxia Lu, Professor Hongjie Xing, Associate Professor Huimin Feng, Dr. Chunru Dong, and our graduate students, Shixi Zhao, Sheng Xing, Shaoxing Hou, Tianlun Zhang, Peizhou Zhang, Bo Liu, Liguang Zang, etc. Our thanks also go to the editors who help us plan and organize this book.

The book can serve as a reference book for researchers or a textbook for senior undergraduates and postgraduates majored in computer science and technology, applied mathematics, automation, etc. This book also provides some useful guidelines of research for scholars who are studying the impact of uncertainty on machine learning and data mining.

Xizhao Wang
Shenzhen University, China

Junhai Zhai
Hebei University, China

Symbols and Abbreviations

Symbols

A	The set of conditional attributes
A_{ij}	The jth fuzzy linguistic term of the ith attribute
$Bel(\cdot, \cdot)$	Belief function
$bpa(\cdot, \cdot)$	Basic probability assignment function
C	The set of decision attributes
$(C) \int f \, d\mu$	Choquet fuzzy integral
$D(\cdot \parallel \cdot)$	KL-divergence
$DP(\cdot)$	Decision profile
F_{α}	The α cut-set of fuzzy set F
$H^{\dagger}$	Moore–Penrose generalized inverse of matrix H
I	Index set
$k(\cdot, \cdot)$	Kernel function
$p_{ij}^{(l)}$	The relative frequency of A_{ij} regarding to the lth class
POS_P^Q	The positive region of P with respect to Q
$P_{\theta}(y\vert x)$	Given x, the posterior probability of y under the model θ
R^d	d dimension Euclidean space
$\underline{R}(X)$	Lower approximation of X with respect to R
$\overline{R}(X)$	Upper approximation of X with respect to R
S_B	Scatter matrix between classes
S_W	Scatter matrix within class
$(S) \int f \, d\mu$	Sugeno fuzzy integral
U	Universe
u_{ij}	The membership of the ith instance with respect to the jth class
$(U) \int f \, d\mu$	Upper fuzzy integral
$V(y_i)$	The number of votes of y_i
x_i	The ith instance

$[x]_R$ Equivalence class of x with respect to R
y_i The class label of x_i
β Degree of confidence
γ_P^Q The significance of P with respect to Q
$\delta_{ij}^{(w)}$ The weighted similarity degree between the ith and jth samples
$\mu_A(x)$ Membership function

Abbreviations

AGNES	AGglomerative NESting
BIRCH	Balanced iterative reducing and clustering using hierarchies
CF	Certainty factor
CNN	Condensed nearest neighbors
CURE	Clustering Using REpresentatives
DDE	Dynamic differential evolution
DE	Differential evolution
DES	Differential evolution strategy
DIANA	DIvisive ANAlysis
DT	Decision table
ELM	Extreme learning machine
FCM	Fuzzy C-means
F-DCT	Fuzzy decision tree
FDT	Fuzzy decision table
F-ELM	Fuzzy extreme learning machine
F-KNN	Fuzzy K-nearest neighbors
FLT	Fuzzy linguistic term
FRFDT	Fuzzy rough set–based decision tree
GD	Gradient descent
GD-FWL	Gradient descent–based feature weight learning
IBL	Instance based learning
K-NN	K-nearest neighbors
LS-SVM	Least square support vector machine
MABSS	Maximum ambiguity based sample selection
MEHDE	Hybrid differential evolution with multistrategy cooperating evolution
MFDT	Multiple fuzzy decision tree
QBC	Query by committee
ROCK	RObust Clustering using linKs
SMTC-C	Similarity matrix's transitive closure
SVM	Support vector machine
WFPR	Weighted fuzzy production rules

Chapter 1

Uncertainty

Uncertainty is a common phenomenon in machine learning, which can be found in every phase of learning, such as data preprocessing, algorithm design, and model selection. The representation, measurement, and handling of uncertainty have a significant impact on the performance of a learning system. There are four common uncertainties in machine learning, that is, randomness [1], fuzziness [2], roughness [3], and nonspecificity [4]. In this chapter, we mainly introduce the first three kinds of uncertainty, briefly list the fourth uncertainty, and give a short discussion about the relationships among the four uncertainties.

1.1 Randomness

Randomness is a kind of objective uncertainty regarding random variables, while entropy is a measure of the uncertainty of random variables [5].

1.1.1 Entropy

Let X be a discrete random variable that takes values randomly from set $\mathcal{X}$, its probability mass function is $p(x) = Pr(X = x)$, $x \in \mathcal{X}$, denoted by $X \sim p(x)$. The definition of entropy of X is given as follows [5].

Definition 1.1 The entropy of X is defined by

$$H(X) = -\sum_{x \in \mathcal{X}} p(x) \log_2 p(x). \tag{1.1}$$

We can find from (1.1) that the entropy of X is actually a function of p; the following example can explicitly illustrate this point.

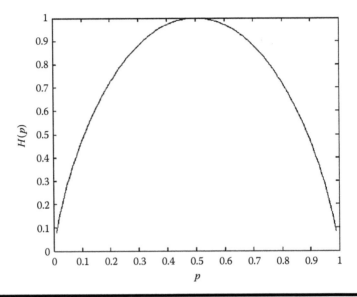

Figure 1.1   The relationship between entropy H(p) and p.

Example 1.1 Let $\mathcal{X} = \{0, 1\}$, and $Pr(X = 1) = p$, $Pr(X = 0) = 1 - p$. According to Equation (1.1), the entropy of X is

$$H(X) = -p \times \log_2 p - (1 - p) \times \log_2(1 - p). \tag{1.2}$$

Obviously, $H(X)$ is a function of p. For convenience, we denote $H(X)$ as $H(p)$. The graph of the function $H(p)$ is shown in Figure 1.1. We can see from Figure 1.1 that $H(p)$ takes its maximum at $p = \frac{1}{2}$.

Example 1.2 Table 1.1 is a small discrete-valued data set with 14 instances. For attribute $X = Outlook$, $\mathcal{X} = \{\text{Sunny}, \text{Cloudy}, \text{Rain}\}$, we can find from Table 1.1 that $Pr(X = \text{Sunny}) = p_1 = \frac{5}{14}$, $Pr(X = \text{Cloudy}) = p_2 = \frac{4}{14}$, $Pr(X = \text{Rain}) = p_3 = \frac{5}{14}$. According to (1.1), we have

$$H(Outlook) = -\frac{5}{14} \log_2 \frac{5}{14} - \frac{4}{14} \log_2 \frac{4}{14} - \frac{5}{14} \log_2 \frac{5}{14} = 1.58.$$

Similarly, we have

$$H(Temperature) = -\frac{4}{14} \log_2 \frac{4}{14} - \frac{6}{14} \log_2 \frac{6}{14} - \frac{4}{14} \log_2 \frac{4}{14} = 1.56.$$

$$H(Humidity) = -\frac{7}{14} \log_2 \frac{7}{14} - \frac{7}{14} \log_2 \frac{7}{14} = 1.00.$$

Table 1.1 A Small Data with 14 Instances

x	Outlook	Temperature	Humidity	Wind	y (PlayTennis)
x_1	Sunny	Hot	High	Weak	No
x_2	Sunny	Hot	High	Strong	No
x_3	Cloudy	Hot	High	Weak	Yes
x_4	Rain	Mild	High	Weak	Yes
x_5	Rain	Cool	Normal	Weak	Yes
x_6	Rain	Cool	Normal	Strong	No
x_7	Cloudy	Cool	Normal	Strong	Yes
x_8	Sunny	Mild	High	Weak	No
x_9	Sunny	Cool	Normal	Weak	Yes
x_{10}	Rain	Mild	Normal	Weak	Yes
x_{11}	Sunny	Mild	Normal	Strong	Yes
x_{12}	Cloudy	Mild	High	Strong	Yes
x_{13}	Cloudy	Hot	Normal	Weak	Yes
x_{14}	Rain	Mild	High	Strong	No

$$H(Wind) = -\frac{8}{14}\log_2\frac{8}{14} - \frac{6}{14}\log_2\frac{6}{14} = 0.99.$$

$$H(PlayTennis) = -\frac{5}{14}\log_2\frac{5}{14} - \frac{9}{14}\log_2\frac{9}{14} = 0.94.$$

It is worth noting that the probability mentioned earlier is approximated by its frequency, that is, the proportion of a value in all cases.

1.1.2 Joint Entropy and Conditional Entropy

Given two random variables X and Y, suppose that $(X, Y) \sim p(x,y)$. The joint entropy of X and Y can be defined as follows.

Definition 1.2 The joint entropy of (X, Y) is defined as

$$H(X, Y) = -\sum_{x \in \mathcal{X}} \sum_{y \in \mathcal{Y}} p(x, y) \log_2 p(x, y). \tag{1.3}$$

Given a random variable X, we can define the conditional entropy $H(Y|X)$ of a random variable Y.

Definition 1.3 Suppose $(X, Y) \sim p(x, y)$, $H(Y|X)$ is defined as

$$H(Y|X) = - \sum_{x \in \mathcal{X}} p(x) H(Y|X = x)$$

$$= - \sum_{x \in \mathcal{X}} p(x) \sum_{y \in \mathcal{Y}} p(y|x) \log_2 p(y|x)$$

$$= - \sum_{x \in \mathcal{X}} \sum_{y \in \mathcal{Y}} p(x, y) \log_2 p(y|x). \tag{1.4}$$

It is necessary to note that generally $H(Y|X) \neq H(X|Y)$, but $H(X) - H(X|Y) = H(Y) - H(Y|X)$.

1.1.3 Mutual Information

Given two random variables X and Y, the mutual information of X and Y, denoted by $I(X; Y)$, is a measure of relevance of X and Y. We now give the definition of mutual information.

Definition 1.4 The mutual information of X and Y is defined as

$$I(X; Y) = H(X) - H(X|Y). \tag{1.5}$$

We can find from (1.5) that $I(X; Y)$ is the reduction of the uncertainty of X due to presentation of Y. By symmetry, it also follows that

$$I(X; Y) = H(Y) - H(Y|X). \tag{1.6}$$

Theorem 1.1 The mutual information and entropy have the following relationships [5]:

$$I(X; Y) = H(X) - H(X|Y); \tag{1.7}$$

$$I(X; Y) = H(Y) - H(Y|X); \tag{1.8}$$

$$I(X; Y) = H(X) + H(Y) - H(X, Y); \tag{1.9}$$

$$I(X; Y) = I(Y, X); \tag{1.10}$$

$$I(X; X) = H(X). \tag{1.11}$$

Example 1.3 Given Table 1.1, let $X = Outlook$, $Y = PlayTennis$, then the mutual information of X and Y is

$$H(Y|X) = -\sum_{x \in \mathcal{X}} p(x) \sum_{y \in \mathcal{Y}} p(y|x) \log_2 p(y|x)$$

$$= -Pr(X = Sunny) \left[Pr(Y = Yes|X = Sunny) \right.$$
$$\times \log_2 Pr(Y = Yes|X = Sunny) \right]$$
$$- Pr(X = Sunny) \left[Pr(Y = No|X = Sunny) \right.$$
$$\times \log_2 Pr(Y = No|X = Sunny) \right]$$
$$- Pr(X = Cloudy) \left[Pr(Y = Yes|X = Cloudy) \right.$$
$$\times \log_2 Pr(Y = Yes|X = Cloudy) \right]$$
$$- Pr(X = Cloudy) \left[Pr(Y = No|X = Cloudy) \right.$$
$$\times \log_2 Pr(Y = No|X = Cloudy) \right]$$
$$- Pr(X = Rain) \left[Pr(Y = Yes|X = Rain) \right.$$
$$\times \log_2 Pr(Y = Yes|X = Rain) \right]$$
$$- Pr(X = Rain) \left[Pr(Y = No|X = Rain) \right.$$
$$\times \log_2 Pr(Y = No|X = Rain) \right]$$

$$= -\frac{5}{14} \left(\frac{2}{5} \log_2 \frac{2}{5} + \frac{3}{5} \log_2 \frac{3}{5} \right)$$
$$- \frac{4}{14} \left(\frac{4}{4} \log_2 \frac{4}{4} + \frac{0}{4} \log_2 \frac{0}{4} \right)$$
$$- \frac{5}{14} \left(\frac{3}{5} \log_2 \frac{3}{5} + \frac{2}{5} \log_2 \frac{2}{5} \right)$$
$$= -(0.35 + 0 + 0.35) = 0.7.$$

Similarly, we can calculate the mutual information $I(Temperature; PlayTennis)$, $I(Humidity; PlayTennis)$, and $I(Wind; PlayTennis)$, which are 0.15, 0.05, and 0.03, respectively. Because $I(Sunny; PlayTennis)$ is maximal, we can conclude that *Sunny* is the most significant attribute with respect to *PlayTennis*.

For the case of continuous random variable, the corresponding concepts can be found in Chapter 8 of Reference 5.

1.2 Fuzziness

Fuzziness is a kind of cognitive uncertainty due to the absence of strict or precise boundaries of concepts [6–10]. In the real world, there are many vague concepts, such as young, hot, and high. These concepts can be modeled by fuzzy sets that can be represented by their membership functions [2,11]. In this section, regarding a fuzzy set, we briefly review the definition, properties, operations, and measures of fuzziness. The details can be found in [2,11].

1.2.1 Definition and Representation of Fuzzy Sets

In classical set theory, the characteristic function of a set assigns a value of either 1 or 0 to each element in the set. In other words, for every element, it either belongs to the set or does not belong to the set. Let U be a set of objects, called the universe, and $A \subseteq U$; the characteristic function of A is defined as follows:

$$\mu_A(x) = \begin{cases} 1 & \text{if } x \in A; \\ 0 & \text{if } x \notin A. \end{cases} \tag{1.12}$$

If we extend the values of $\mu_A(x)$ from $\{0, 1\}$ to interval $[0, 1]$, then we can define a fuzzy set A. In order to distinguish between classical sets and fuzzy sets, we use $\widetilde{A}$ to represent a fuzzy set. In the following, we present the definition of fuzzy set.

Definition 1.5 Let U be a universe and $\widetilde{A}$ be a mapping from U to $[0, 1]$, denoted by $\mu_{\widetilde{A}}(x)$. If $\forall x \in U$, $\mu_{\widetilde{A}}(x) \in [0, 1]$, then $\widetilde{A}$ is said to be a fuzzy set defined on U; $\mu_{\widetilde{A}}(x)$ is called the membership degree of element x belonging to $\widetilde{A}$.

The set of all fuzzy sets defined on U is denoted by $\mathcal{F}(U)$; $\varnothing$ (the empty set) is a fuzzy set whose membership degree for any element is zero.

For a given fuzzy set $\widetilde{A}$ defined on U, $\widetilde{A}$ is completely characterized by the set of pairs [11,12]

$$\widetilde{A} = \{(x, \mu_{\widetilde{A}}(x)), x \in U\}. \tag{1.13}$$

If U is a finite set $\{x_1, x_2, \ldots, x_n\}$, then fuzzy set $\widetilde{A}$ can be conveniently represented by

$$\widetilde{A} = \frac{\mu_{\widetilde{A}}(x_1)}{x_1} + \frac{\mu_{\widetilde{A}}(x_2)}{x_2} + \cdots + \frac{\mu_{\widetilde{A}}(x_n)}{x_n}. \tag{1.14}$$

When U is not finite, we can write (1.14) as

$$\widetilde{A} = \int_{\widetilde{A}} \frac{\mu_{\widetilde{A}}(x)}{x}. \tag{1.15}$$

1.2.2 Basic Operations and Properties of Fuzzy Sets

Definition 1.6 Let $\tilde{A}, \tilde{B} \in \mathcal{F}(U)$. If $\forall x \in U$, we have $\tilde{A}(x) \le \tilde{B}(x)$. Then we say that $\tilde{B}$ includes $\tilde{A}$; in other words, $\tilde{A}$ is included in $\tilde{B}$, denoted by $\tilde{A} \subseteq \tilde{B}$ or denoted by $\tilde{B} \supseteq \tilde{A}$.

Definition 1.7 Let $\tilde{A}, \tilde{B} \in \mathcal{F}(U)$. If $\forall x \in U$, we have $\tilde{A}(x) = \tilde{B}(x)$. Then we say that $\tilde{B} = \tilde{A}$. If $\tilde{A}$ is included in $\tilde{B}$, but $\tilde{A} \ne \tilde{B}$, then we say that $\tilde{B}$ truly includes $\tilde{A}$; in other words, $\tilde{A}$ is truly included in $\tilde{B}$, denoted by $\tilde{A} \subset \tilde{B}$, or denoted by $\tilde{B} \supset \tilde{A}$.

Theorem 1.2 Let $\tilde{A}, \tilde{B}, \tilde{C} \in \mathcal{F}(U)$. Then the following properties hold:

(1) $\varnothing \subseteq \tilde{A} \subseteq U$.
(2) $\tilde{A} \subseteq \tilde{A}$.
(3) $\tilde{A} \subseteq \tilde{B}, \tilde{B} \subseteq \tilde{A} \Rightarrow \tilde{A} = \tilde{B}$.
(4) $\tilde{A} \subseteq \tilde{B}, \tilde{B} \subseteq \tilde{C} \Rightarrow \tilde{A} \subseteq \tilde{C}$.

Definition 1.8 Let $\tilde{A}, \tilde{B} \in \mathcal{F}(U)$. We define the union $\tilde{A} \cup \tilde{B}$, the intersection $\tilde{A} \cap \tilde{B}$, and the complement $\tilde{A}^c$ as follows, respectively:

$$(\tilde{A} \cup \tilde{B})(x) = \tilde{A}(x) \vee \tilde{B}(x) = \max\{\tilde{A}(x), \tilde{B}(x)\};$$
$$(\tilde{A} \cap \tilde{B})(x) = \tilde{A}(x) \wedge \tilde{B}(x) = \min\{\tilde{A}(x), \tilde{B}(x)\};$$
$$\tilde{A}^c(x) = 1 - \tilde{A}(x).$$

Theorem 1.3 Let $\tilde{A}, \tilde{B}, \tilde{C} \in \mathcal{F}(U)$. Then the following laws hold:

(1) $\tilde{A} \cup \tilde{A} = A, \tilde{A} \cap \tilde{A} = A$.
(2) $\tilde{A} \cup \tilde{B} = \tilde{B} \cup \tilde{A}, \tilde{A} \cap \tilde{B} = \tilde{B} \cap \tilde{A}$.
(3) $\tilde{A} \cup (\tilde{B} \cup \tilde{C}) = (\tilde{A} \cup \tilde{B}) \cup \tilde{C}, \tilde{A} \cap (\tilde{B} \cap \tilde{C}) = (\tilde{A} \cap \tilde{B}) \cap \tilde{C}$.
(4) $\tilde{A} \cup (\tilde{B} \cap \tilde{C}) = (\tilde{A} \cup \tilde{B}) \cap (\tilde{A} \cup \tilde{C}), \tilde{A} \cap (\tilde{B} \cup \tilde{C}) = (\tilde{A} \cap \tilde{B}) \cup (\tilde{A} \cap \tilde{C})$.
(5) $\tilde{A} \cup (\tilde{A} \cap \tilde{B}) = \tilde{A}, \tilde{A} \cap (\tilde{A} \cup \tilde{B}) = \tilde{A}$.
(6) $(\tilde{A}^c)^c = \tilde{A}$.
(7) $\tilde{A} \cup \varnothing = \tilde{A}, \tilde{A} \cap \varnothing = \varnothing, \tilde{A} \cup U = U, \tilde{A} \cap U = \tilde{A}$.
(8) $(\tilde{A} \cup \tilde{B})^c = \tilde{A}^c \cap \tilde{B}^c, (\tilde{A} \cap \tilde{B})^c = \tilde{A}^c \cup \tilde{B}^c$.

The proof can be found in [13].

1.2.3 Fuzzy Measures

The fuzziness of a fuzzy set can be measured with fuzzy entropy. Luca and Termini pointed out that fuzzy entropy must satisfy the following properties [14].

Theorem 1.4 Let $H(\widetilde{A})$ be a fuzzy entropy defined on fuzzy set $\widetilde{A}$. $H(\widetilde{A})$ must satisfy the following properties:

(1) $\forall \widetilde{A} \in \mathcal{F}(U)$, $H(\widetilde{A}) = 0$, if and only if $\widetilde{A}$ is a classical set.
(2) $\forall \widetilde{A} \in \mathcal{F}(U)$, $H(\widetilde{A}) = 1$, if and only if $\forall x \in U$, $\mu_{\widetilde{A}}(x) = 0.5$.
(3) $\forall \widetilde{A}, \widetilde{B} \in \mathcal{F}(U)$, if $\mu_{\widetilde{A}}(x) \leq \mu_{\widetilde{B}}(x)$, when $\mu_{\widetilde{A}}(x) \geq \frac{1}{2}$ and $\mu_{\widetilde{A}}(x) \geq \mu_{\widetilde{B}}(x)$, when $\mu_{\widetilde{A}}(x) \leq \frac{1}{2}$, then $H(\widetilde{A}) \geq H(\widetilde{B})$.
(4) $\forall \widetilde{A} \in \mathcal{F}(U)$, $H(\widetilde{A}) = H(\widetilde{A}^c)$.

Many fuzzy entropies have been defined by different researchers. A short survey of fuzzy entropy can be found in [15] or in [16]. In the following, we introduce three fuzzy entropies commonly used in practice.

Definition 1.9 (Zadeh fuzzy entropy [2]) Let $\widetilde{A}$ be a fuzzy set defined on U. $P = \{p_1, p_2, \ldots, p_n\}$ is a probability distribution of U, $U = \{x_1, x_2, \ldots, x_n\}$, $\mu_{\widetilde{A}}(x_i)$ is the membership function of $\widetilde{A}$, and the fuzzy entropy of $\widetilde{A}$ is defined as follows:

$$H(\widetilde{A}) = -\sum_{i=1}^{n} \mu_{\widetilde{A}}(x_i) p_i \log_2 p_i. \tag{1.16}$$

Definition 1.10 (Luca–Termini fuzzy entropy [14]) Let $\widetilde{A}$ be a fuzzy set defined on U. $U = \{x_1, x_2, \ldots, x_n\}$, $\mu_{\widetilde{A}}(x_i)$ is the membership function of $\widetilde{A}$, and the fuzzy entropy of $\widetilde{A}$ is defined as follows:

$$H(\widetilde{A}) = -\frac{1}{n}\sum_{i=1}^{n} \left[\mu_{\widetilde{A}}(x_i) \log_2 \mu_{\widetilde{A}}(x_i) + (1 - \mu_{\widetilde{A}}(x_i)) \log_2 (1 - \mu_{\widetilde{A}}(x_i))\right]. \tag{1.17}$$

Definition 1.11 (Kosko fuzzy entropy [17]) Let $\widetilde{A}$ be a fuzzy set defined on U. $U = \{x_1, x_2, \ldots, x_n\}$, $\mu_{\widetilde{A}}(x_i)$ is the membership function of $\widetilde{A}$, and the fuzzy entropy of $\widetilde{A}$ is defined as follows:

$$H(\widetilde{A}) = \frac{\sum_{i=1}^{n} \left[\mu_{\widetilde{A}}(x_i) \wedge \mu_{\widetilde{A}^c}(x_i)\right]}{\sum_{i=1}^{n} \left[\mu_{\widetilde{A}}(x_i) \vee \mu_{\widetilde{A}^c}(x_i)\right]}. \tag{1.18}$$

1.3 Roughness

Roughness is originally proposed by Pawlak [3] in order to represent the inadequacy of knowledge. To introduce roughness, we first review some fundamental concepts of rough sets.

Rough set theory [3] was developed on the foundation of indiscernible relation, which is actually an equivalence relation. In the framework of classification, the objects processed by rough set theory are represented as decision tables.

Definition 1.12 A decision table DT is a four tuple $DT = (U, A \cup C, V, f)$, where $U = \{x_1, x_2, \ldots, x_n\}$ called universe is a set of objects; $A = \{a_1, a_2, \ldots, a_d\}$ is a set of conditional attributes, each attribute taking discrete values; C is a class label variable, taking values in $\{1, 2, \ldots, k\}$; V is the Cartesian product of conditional attributes; and f is an information function, $f : U \times A \to V$.

Given a discrete-valued decision table DT and a binary relation R on U, we have the following basic definitions.

Definition 1.13 R is called an equivalence relation if it satisfies the following conditions:

(1) $\forall x \in U, xRx$.
(2) $\forall x, y \in U$, if xRy, then yRx.
(3) $\forall x, y, z \in U$, if xRy and yRz, then xRz.

Definition 1.14 $\forall x \in U$. The equivalence class of x is defined as follows:

$$[x]_R = \{y | (y \in U) \wedge (yRx)\}. \tag{1.19}$$

Definition 1.15 $\forall X \subseteq U$. The lower approximation and the upper approximation of X with respect to R are defined as

$$\underline{R}(X) = \{x | (x \in U) \wedge ([x]_R \subseteq X)\} \tag{1.20}$$

and

$$\overline{R}(X) = \{x | (x \in U) \wedge ([x]_R \cap X) \neq \varnothing\}. \tag{1.21}$$

Definition 1.16 $\forall X \subseteq U$. The approximate accuracy and the roughness of R are defined as

$$\alpha_R(X) = \frac{|\underline{R}(X)|}{|\overline{R}(X)|} \tag{1.22}$$

and

$$\beta_R(X) = 1 - \alpha_R(X) = \frac{|\overline{R}(X) - \underline{R}(X)|}{|\overline{R}(X)|}. \tag{1.23}$$

1.4 Nonspecificity

Nonspecificity [4] is also called ambiguity, which is another type of cognitive uncertainty. It results from choosing one from two or more unclear objects. For example, an interesting film and an expected concert are holding at the same time. In this situation, it is hard for those who love both film and music to decide which one should be attended. This uncertainty is associated with a possibility distribution that was proposed by Zadeh [18].

Let X be a classical set and let $\mathscr{P}(X)$ denotes the power set of X. A possibility measure is a function π [19]:

$$\pi : \mathscr{P}(X) \to [0, 1] \tag{1.24}$$

that has the following properties [19]:

(1) $\pi(\varnothing) = 0$.
(2) $A \subseteq B \Longrightarrow \pi(A) \leq \pi(B)$.
(3) $A_1 \subseteq A_2 \subseteq \cdots \Longrightarrow \pi\left(\bigcup_{i\in I} A_i\right) = \sup_{i\in I} \pi(A_i)$,

where I is an index set.

Any possibility measure can be uniquely determined by a possibility distribution function $f : X \to [0, 1]$ via the formula $\pi(A) = \sup_{x\in A} f(x)$, where $A \subset X$.

Definition 1.17 The possibility distribution π is called a normalized possibility distribution if and only if $\max_{x\in X} \pi(x) = 1$.

The nonspecificity or ambiguity of a possibility distribution π is defined as follows.

Definition 1.18 Let $X = \{x_1, x_2, \ldots, x_n\}$ and let $\pi = \{\pi(x)|x \in X\}$ be a normalized possibility distribution on X. The measure of nonspecificity or ambiguity is defined as follows [4]:

$$g(\pi) = \sum_{i=1}^{n} (\pi_i^* - \pi_{i+1}^*) \ln i, \qquad (1.25)$$

where $\pi^* = \{\pi_1^*, \pi_2^*, \ldots, \pi_n^*\}$ is the permutation of the possibility distribution $\pi = \{\pi(x_1), \pi(x_2), \ldots, \pi(x_n)\}$, sorted so that $\pi_i^* \geq \pi_{i+1}^*$, for $i = 1, 2, \ldots, n$, and $\pi_{n+1}^* = 0$.

Ambiguity expresses the possible uncertainty of choosing one from many available objects. Obviously, the larger the set of possible alternatives is, the bigger the ambiguity is. The ambiguity will attain its maximum when all the μ_i are equivalent, that is, all the $\mu_i^* = 1 (1 \leq i \leq n)$ but $\mu_{n+1}^* = 0$. It will be full specificity, that is, no ambiguity exists, when only one alternative is possible, that is, only one μ_i is equal to 1 but all others equal to zero.

1.5 Relationships among the Uncertainties

Entropy is to measure the uncertainty caused by randomness. Fuzziness is to measure the uncertainty of a linguistic term, which is usually represented by a fuzzy set. Roughness is to measure the uncertainty of representing knowledge associated with a target concept. Given equivalence relation R (i.e., the so-called knowledge) and a target concept X, the bigger the boundary region of X with respect to R is, the bigger the roughness of R is. Ambiguity is to measure the nonspecificity when we choose one from many available choices. In the following, we discuss the relationships among randomness, fuzziness, and ambiguity [20].

In the framework of classification, for a given set of samples or instances, entropy measures the impurity of a crisp set; fuzziness measures the distinction between the set and its complement; ambiguity measures the amount of uncertainty associated with the set of possible alternatives. Clearly, the significance of the three uncertainties is different. The entropy of the sample set is associated with the proportions of the number of samples from every class, which denotes the class impurity of the set. Usually, entropy is restricted to be used for a crisp set. The fuzziness of a sample set is associated with the membership degree of every sample to any class. Fuzziness denotes the sharpness of the border of every fuzzy subset that is formed according to the partition based on classes. Particularly, there is no fuzziness for a crisp set. The ambiguity of a sample set, similar to fuzziness, is associated with the membership degree of every sample to any class. But ambiguity describes the uncertainty associated with the situation resulting from the lack of specificity in describing the best or the most representative one. It emphasizes the uncertainty of possibility of choosing one from many available choices. Next, we discuss the relationship between entropy and fuzziness and the relationship between fuzziness and ambiguity in detail.

1.5.1 Entropy and Fuzziness

Entropy is defined on a probability distribution $E_0 = (p_1, p_2, \ldots, p_n)$, where $\sum_{i=1}^{n} p_i = 1$ and $0 \leq p_i \leq 1$ for each i ($1 \leq i \leq n$). Fuzziness is defined on a possibility distribution B, that is, a fuzzy set $B = (\mu_1, \mu_2, \ldots, \mu_n)$, where $0 \leq \mu_i \leq 1$ for each i ($1 \leq i \leq n$). Since a probability distribution is a possibility distribution, we can consider the fuzziness of a probability distribution E_0. We now analyze the relationship between entropy and fuzziness based on a probability distribution $E_0 = (p_1, p_2, \ldots, p_n)$.

As a special case, when E_0 is a two-dimensional probability distribution, that is, $E_0 = (p_1, p_2)$, according to (1.1) and (1.17), we have

$$\begin{aligned} Entropy(E_0) &= -p_1 \ln p_1 - p_2 \ln p_2 \\ &= -p_1 \ln p_1 - (1 - p_1) \ln p(1 - p_1) \end{aligned} \tag{1.26}$$

and

$$Fuzziness(E_0) = 2(-p_1 \ln p_1 - (1 - p_1) \ln p(1 - p_1)). \tag{1.27}$$

Obviously, $Fuzziness(E_0) = 2Entropy(E_0)$.

Suppose that $E_0 = (p_1, p_2, \ldots, p_n)$ is an n-dimensional probability distribution. We now discuss their monotonic properties and extreme-value points. Noting that $\sum_{i=1}^{n} p_i = 1$, we assume that, without losing generality, p_1 is the single variable and $p_2, \ldots, p_n$ are $n - 2$ constants with $\sum_{i=2}^{n} p_i = c$ and $p_n = 1 - c - p_1$. Then, (1.1) and (1.17) degenerate, respectively, to

$$Entropy(E_0) = -p_1 \ln p_1 - (1 - p_1) \ln p(1 - p_1) + A \tag{1.28}$$

and

$$\begin{aligned} Fuzziness(E_0) &= Entropy(E_0) - (1 - p_1) \ln p(1 - p_1) \\ &\quad - (p_1 + c) \ln(p_1 + c) + B, \end{aligned} \tag{1.29}$$

where A and B are two constants that are independent on p_1. By solving

$$\frac{d}{dp_1} Entropy(E_0) = 0 \tag{1.30}$$

and

$$\frac{d}{dp_1} Fuzziness(E_0) = 0, \tag{1.31}$$

we can obtain that both *Entropy*(E_0) and *Fuzziness*(E_0) with respect to the variable p_1 attain the maximum at $p_1 = \frac{1-c}{2}$ and monotonically increase when $p_1 < \frac{1-c}{2}$ and monotonically decrease when $p_1 > \frac{1-c}{2}$. It indicates that the entropy and fuzziness for a probability distribution have the same monotonic characteristics and extreme-value points. Furthermore, noting that $\sum_{i=2}^{n} p_i = c$ and the symmetry of variables $p_1, p_2, \ldots, p_n$, we conclude that the entropy and fuzziness of an n-dimensional probability distribution attain their maximum at

$$p_1 = p_2 = \cdots = p_n = \frac{1}{n}. \tag{1.32}$$

Roughly speaking, the fuzziness is an extension of the entropy.

When $n = 3$, the entropy and the fuzziness of $E_0 = (p_1, p_2, p_3)$ are depicted in Figure 1.2a and b, which are 3D contour plot of entropy and fuzziness. From Figure 1.2a and b, we can see that the entropy of $E_0 = (p_1, p_2, p_3)$ is similar to the fuzziness of $E_0 = (p_1, p_2, p_3)$. They all attain their maximum at $p_1 = p_2 = 0.33$ and minimum at three points $p_1 = p_2 = 0$, or $p_1 = 0, p_2 = 1$, or $p_1 = 1, p_2 = 0$.

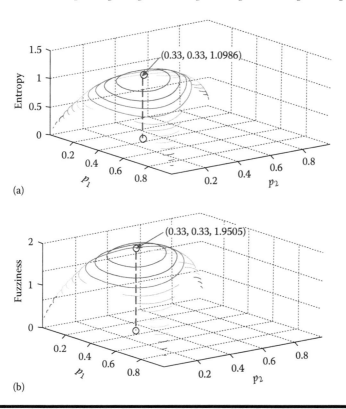

Figure 1.2 (a) Entropy of $E_0 = (p_1, p_2, p_3)$. (b) Fuzziness $E_0 = (p_1, p_2, p_3)$.

1.5.2 Fuzziness and Ambiguity

Both of the fuzziness and ambiguity are defined on a fuzzy set. For a general possibility distribution $B = (\mu_1, \mu_2, \ldots, \mu_n)$ of which the fuzziness is defined as (1.17), we derive by solving

$$\frac{\partial}{\partial \mu_1} Fuzziness(B) = \frac{\partial}{\partial \mu_2} Fuzziness(B)$$

$$= \cdots = \frac{\partial}{\partial \mu_n} Fuzziness(B) = 0 \tag{1.33}$$

that $Fuzziness(B)$ attains its maximum at

$$\mu_1 = \mu_2 = \cdots = \mu_n = 0.5. \tag{1.34}$$

It is easy to check that $Fuzziness(B)$ attains its minimum (zero) only at $\mu_i = 0$ or $\mu_i = 1$ for each i $(1 \leq i \leq n)$. The monotonic feature of the $Fuzziness(B)$ is simple, that is, $Fuzziness(B)$ monotonically increases in $(0.0, 0.5)$ and monotonically decreases in $(0.5, 1.0)$ for each μ_i $(1 \leq i \leq n)$.

The ambiguity of $B = (\mu_1, \mu_2, \ldots, \mu_n)$ is defined as (1.25). According to [19], $g(B) = Ambiguity(B)$ is a function with monotonicity, continuity, and symmetry. Its maximum is attained at $\mu_1 = \mu_2 = \cdots = \mu_n = 1$, and its minimum is attained in cases where only one μ_j $(1 \leq j \leq n)$ is not zero.

Combining the above analysis on $Fuzziness(B)$ and $Ambiguity(B)$, we can think that the essential difference between the two uncertainties exists. When $n = 2$, the fuzziness and ambiguity of $B = (\mu_1, \mu_2)$ can degenerate, respectively, to

$$Fuzziness(B) = -\mu_1 \ln \mu_1 - (1 - \mu_1) \ln(1 - \mu_1)$$

$$- \mu_2 \ln \mu_2 - (1 - \mu_2) \ln(1 - \mu_2). \tag{1.35}$$

and

$$Ambiguity(B) = \begin{cases} (\mu_1/\mu_2) \times \ln 2 & \text{if } 0 \leq \mu_1 < \mu_2; \\ \ln 2 & \text{if } \mu_1 = \mu_2; \\ (\mu_2/\mu_1) \times \ln 2 & \text{others.} \end{cases} \tag{1.36}$$

The pictures of $Fuzziness(B)$ in (1.35) and $Ambiguity(B)$ in (1.36) are depicted in Figure 1.3a and b. From Figure 1.3a, we can see that the plot of fuzziness of $B = (\mu_1, \mu_2)$ is plane symmetric and the symmetrical planes are $\mu_1 = 0.5$ and $\mu_2 = 0.5$, respectively. Fuzziness of $B = (\mu_1, \mu_2)$ attains its maximum at $(0.5, 0.5)$ and attains its minimum at four endpoints, $(0, 0)$, $(0, 1)$, $(1, 0)$, and $(1, 1)$. In Figure 1.3b, the surface above the plane $z = 0$ is the ambiguity of $B = (\mu_1, \mu_2)$. The lines in the plane $z = 0$ are the contours of the ambiguity of $B = (\mu_1, \mu_2)$. From the contours, we can see that the points with the same values of μ_1/μ_2 are with the same ambiguity. The more the contour approaches the line $\mu_1 = \mu_2$, the more the ambiguity is.

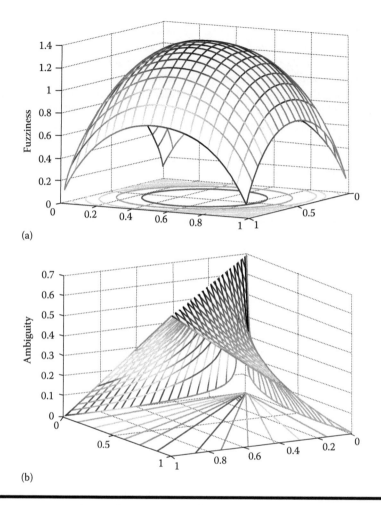

Figure 1.3 (a) Fuzziness of $B = (\mu_1, \mu_2)$. (b) Ambiguity of $B = (\mu_1, \mu_2)$.

References

1. V. R. Hogg, A. T. Craig. *Introduction to Mathematical Statistics*. New York: Pearson Education, 2004.
2. L. A. Zadeh. Fuzzy sets. *Information and Control*, 1965, 8:338–353.
3. Z. Pawlak. Rough sets. *International Journal of Information and Computer Sciences*, 1982, 11:341–356.
4. Y. Yuan, M. J. Shaw. Induction of fuzzy decision trees. *Fuzzy Sets and Systems*, 1995, 69(2):125–139.
5. T. M. Cover, J. A. Thomas. *The Elements of Information Theory*, 2nd edn. John Wiley & Sons, Inc., Hoboken, NJ, 2006.

6. A. Colubi, G. Gonzalez-Rodriguez. Fuzziness in data analysis: Towards accuracy and robustness. *Fuzzy Sets and Systems*, 2015, 281:260–271.
7. R. Coppi, M. A. Gil, H. A. L. Kiers. The fuzzy approach to statistical analysis. *Computational Statistics & Data Analysis*, 2006, 51(1):1–14.
8. R. Seising. On the absence of strict boundaries—Vagueness, haziness, and fuzziness in philosophy, science, and medicine. *Applied Soft Computing*, 2008, 8(3):1232–1242.
9. Q. Zhang. Fuzziness–vagueness–generality–ambiguity. *Journal of Pragmatics*, 1998, 29(1):13–31.
10. G. J. Klir. Where do we stand on measures of uncertainty, ambiguity, fuzziness, and the like? *Fuzzy Sets and Systems*, 1987, 24(2):141–160.
11. D. Dubois, H. Prade. *Fuzzy Sets and Systems: Theory and Applications*. Cambridge, UK: Academic Press, Inc. A Division of Harcourt Brace & Company, 1980.
12. G. J. Klir, B. Yuan. *Fuzzy Sets and Fuzzy Logic: Theory and Applications*. New Jersey: Prentice Hall PTR, 1995.
13. B. Q. Hu. *Foundations of Fuzzy Theory*. Wuhan, China: Wuhan University Press, 2004.
14. A. D. Luca, S. Termini. A definition of a nonprobabilistic entropy in the setting of fuzzy set theory. *Information Control*, 1972, 20(4):301–312.
15. J. D. Shie, S. M. Chen. Feature subset selection based on fuzzy entropy measures for handling classification problems. *Applied Intelligence*, 2007, 28(1):69–82.
16. H. M. Lee, C. M. Chen, J. M. Chen, Y. L. Jou. An efficient fuzzy classifier with feature selection based on fuzzy entropy. *IEEE Transactions on Systems, Man, and Cybernetics-Part B: Cybernetics*, 2001, 31(3):426–432.
17. B. Kosko. Fuzzy entropy and conditioning. *Information Sciences*, 1986, 40(2): 165–174.
18. L. A. Zadeh. Fuzzy sets as a basis for a theory of possibility. *Fuzzy Sets and Systems*, 1978, 1(1):9–34.
19. M. Higashi, G. J. Klir. Measures of uncertainty and information based on possibility distributions. *International Journal of General Systems*, 1982, 9(1):43–58.
20. X. Z. Wang, L. C. Dong, J. H. Yan. Maximum ambiguity-based sample selection in fuzzy decision tree induction. *IEEE Transactions on Knowledge and Data Engineering*, 2012, 24(8):1491–1505.

Chapter 2

Decision Tree with Uncertainty

Supervised learning, which can be categorized into classification and regression problems, is the central part of the machine learning field. Over the past several decades, designing an effective learning system and promoting the system's performance have been the most important tasks in supervised learning. How to model and process the uncertainty existing in the learning process has become a key challenge in learning from data. Uncertainty processing has a very significant impact on the entire knowledge extraction process.

Many theories and methodologies have been developed to model and process different kinds of uncertainties. Focusing on the decision tree induction, this chapter will discuss the impact of uncertainty modeling and processing on the learning process. We introduce the target concept learned with the decision tree algorithm, some popular decision tree learning algorithms including widely used ID3 and its fuzzy version, the induction of fuzzy decision tree based on rough fuzzy techniques, and, more importantly, the relationship between the generalization ability of fuzzy decision tree and the uncertainty in the learning process.

2.1 Crisp Decision Tree

In this section, we first introduce the ID3 algorithm, which is the original version for learning decision trees from discrete-valued data sets [1,2]. Then we extend it to the case of learning decision trees from continuous-valued data sets.

2.1.1 ID3 Algorithm

ID3 algorithm uses information gain as a heuristic to greedily select the extended attributes. The input of ID3 algorithm is a data set, that is, a decision table (DT), in which the conditional attributes are with discrete values. Table 2.1 is a small decision table with 14 instances [2]. The output is a decision tree in which internal nodes correspond to the selected attributes, the branches correspond to a set of the values of the selected attributes, and the leaf nodes correspond to classes. Figure 2.1 is a decision tree learned from the data set given in Table 2.1. The learned decision tree can be transformed into a set of if-then rules. The details of the ID3 algorithm are presented in Algorithm 2.1.

Each path from root to leaf node in the learned decision tree can be transformed into an if-then rule; the number of rules is the number of leaf nodes in decision tree. Finally, the learned decision tree can be transformed into a set of if-then rules.

Suppose that the instances in data set S are classified into m categories $C_1, C_2, \ldots, C_m$. The numbers of instances in C_i ($1 \leq i \leq m$) and in S are denoted by $|C_i|$ and $|S|$, respectively. Obviously, the proportion of instances belonging to C_i is

Table 2.1 A Small Sample of Data Set with 14 Instances

Day	Outlook	Temperature	Humidity	Wind	PlayTennis
D_1	Sunny	Hot	High	Weak	No
D_2	Sunny	Hot	High	Strong	No
D_3	Overcast	Hot	High	Weak	Yes
D_4	Rain	Mild	High	Weak	Yes
D_5	Rain	Cool	Normal	Weak	Yes
D_6	Rain	Cool	Normal	Strong	No
D_7	Overcast	Cool	Normal	Strong	Yes
D_8	Sunny	Mild	High	Weak	No
D_9	Sunny	Cool	Normal	Weak	Yes
D_{10}	Rain	Mild	Normal	Weak	Yes
D_{11}	Sunny	Mild	Normal	Strong	Yes
D_{12}	Overcast	Mild	High	Strong	Yes
D_{13}	Overcast	Hot	Normal	Weak	Yes
D_{14}	Rain	Mild	High	Strong	No

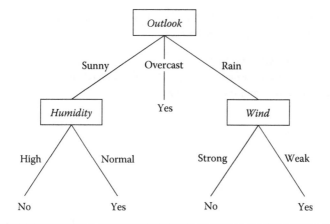

Figure 2.1   The decision tree learned from the data set in Table 2.1.

Algorithm 2.1: ID3 Algorithm

Input: A decision table with discrete-valued attributes.
Output: A decision tree.
1 For each attribute A, compute its information gain.
2 Select extended attribute A^* with maximum information gain.
3 Partition the data set into k subsets according to the values of A^*, where k is the number of values of A^*.
4 For each subset, if the class labels of the instances are same, then obtain a leaf node with the label; otherwise, repeat the above process.
5 Output a decision tree.

$$p_i = \frac{|C_i|}{|S|} \quad (1 \leq i \leq m). \tag{2.1}$$

In the following, we present the related definitions used in ID3 algorithm.
The entropy of S is defined as

$$Entropy(S) = -\sum_{i=1}^{m} p_i \log_2(p_i). \tag{2.2}$$

The information gain of attribute A with respect to S is defined as

$$Gain(S, A) = Entropy(S) - \sum_{v \in Value(A)} \frac{|S_v|}{|S|} Entropy(S_v), \tag{2.3}$$

where S_v is the subset of instances for which the attribute A takes value v.

For the data set given in Table 2.1, the steps of constructing a decision tree with ID3 algorithm are illustrated as follows.

Step 1: Select the extended attribute.

First, for each conditional attribute A, calculate its information gain. When $A = Outlook$, the information gain of Outlook is

$$Gain(S, Outlook) = Entropy(S) - \sum_{v \in \{Sunny, Overcast, Rain\}} \frac{|S_v|}{|S|} Entropy(S_v)$$

$$= Entropy(S) - \left[\frac{5}{14} Entropy(S_{Sunny}) + \frac{4}{14} Entropy(S_{Overcast}) \right.$$

$$\left. + \frac{5}{14} Entropy(S_{Rain}) \right],$$

where

$$Entropy(S) = -\left(\frac{9}{14} \log_2 \frac{9}{14} + \frac{5}{14} \log_2 \frac{5}{14} \right) = 0.94$$

$$Entropy(S_{Sunny}) = -\left(\frac{2}{5} \log_2 \frac{2}{5} + \frac{3}{5} \log_2 \frac{3}{5} \right) = 0.97$$

$$Entropy(S_{Overcast}) = -\left(\frac{4}{4} \log_2 \frac{4}{4} + \frac{0}{4} \log_2 \frac{0}{4} \right) = 0$$

$$Entropy(S_{Rain}) = -\left(\frac{3}{5} \log_2 \frac{3}{5} + \frac{2}{5} \log_2 \frac{2}{5} \right) = 0.97$$

Hence,

$$Gain(S, Outlook) = 0.246.$$

Similarly, we have

$$Gain(S, Temperature) = 0.151$$
$$Gain(S, Humidity) = 0.048$$
$$Gain(S, Wind) = 0.029$$

Because the information gain of conditional attribute *Outlook* is the maximum, *Outlook* is selected as the extended attribute.

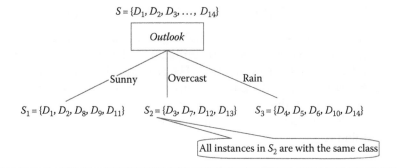

Figure 2.2   Partition data set with attribute *Outlook*.

Step 2: Partition the data set of instances.

The conditional attribute *Outlook* is selected as the extended attribute for the root of the decision tree. According to its values, the data set of instances is partitioned into three subsets. From Figure 2.2, we see

$$S_1 = \{D_1, D_2, D_8, D_9, D_{11}\}$$

$$S_2 = \{D_3, D_7, D_{12}, D_{13}\}$$

$$S_3 = \{D_4, D_5, D_6, D_{10}, D_{14}\}$$

Because the instances in subset S_2 have the same class (*Yes*), a leaf node is then generated. Since the instances in subset S_1 (or S_3) do not belong to the same class, repeat Step 1. Finally, a decision tree shown in Figure 2.1 is generated.

Step 3: Transform the learned decision tree into a set of if-then rules.

There are five leaf nodes in the generated decision tree; hence, we can obtain the following five if-then rules:

1. If (*Outlook* = Sunny and *Humidity* = High), then *Play Tennis* = No.
2. If (*Outlook* = Sunny and *Humidity* = Normal), then *Play Tennis* = Yes.
3. If (*Outlook* = Overcast), then *Play Tennis* = Yes.
4. If (*Outlook* = Rain and *Wind* = Strong), then *Play Tennis* = No.
5. If (*Outlook* = Rain and *Wind* = Weak), then *Play Tennis* = Yes.

When we obtain a decision tree, we can use it to test new instances (unseen instance), that is, predict the class label of new instance. For example, given a new instance D_{15} = (Rain, Hot, High, Strong), the path matched with this unseen instance is $Outlook \xrightarrow{\text{Rain}} Wind \xrightarrow{\text{Strong}}$ No. Hence, the predicted class label of D_{15} is No.

2.1.2 Continuous-Valued Attributes Decision Trees

Based on the idea of discretization, the ID3 algorithm can be directly extended to handle data sets with continuous-valued attributes. In this section, we introduce an algorithm that has similar steps with ID3. The presented algorithm uses Gini index [3–5] as heuristic to select the extended attributes. In the following, we first give some notations used in this algorithm, and then present the algorithm, and finally use an example to illustrate the process of constructing decision tree for continuous-valued attributes.

Definition 2.1 Given a threshold value T for a continuous-valued attribute A, the instances satisfying the condition $A \leq T$ are assigned to the left branch, while the instances satisfying the condition $A > T$ are assigned to the right branch. The threshold value T is called a cut-point.

Given a data set S with N instances, A is a continuous-valued attribute. In general, the cut-points corresponding to A are determined in the following way. The instances are first sorted by increasing value of the attribute A, and the midpoint between each successive pair of values of A in the sorted sequence is considered as a cut-point. Thus, for each continuous-valued attribute A, totally there are $N - 1$ cut-points denoted by $T_1, T_2, \ldots, T_{N-1}$, where we suppose that any successive pair of values are different.

Definition 2.2 Given a cut-point T_i ($1 \leq i \leq N - 1$), if the corresponding pair of instances belong to different classes, then T_i is called imbalance cut-point; otherwise, T_i is called balance cut-point.

Definition 2.3 Let the instances in data set S be classified into m categories $C_1, C_2, \ldots, C_m$. The numbers of instances in C_i ($1 \leq i \leq m$) and in S are denoted by $|C_i|$ and $|S|$. The proportion of instances belonging to C_i is $p_i = |C_i|/|S|$ ($1 \leq i \leq m$). The Gini index of S is defined as

$$Gini(S) = 1 - \sum_{i=1}^{m} p_i^2. \tag{2.4}$$

Definition 2.4 Given a set S of instances, a continuous-valued attribute A, and a cut-point T with respect to A, let $S_1 \subset S$ be the subset of instances whose values of

---

Algorithm 2.2: A Decision Tree Algorithm for Continuous-Valued Attributes

---

Input: A decision table with continuous-valued attributes.

Output: A binary decision tree.

1 For each attribute A, select its optimal cut-point T and add T to the candidate cut-point set.

2 Select the optimal cut-point T^* from the candidate cut-point set; the corresponding attribute A^* is selected as extended attribute.

3 Partition the data set with the selected cut-point T^* into two subsets, and repeat Step 1 on two subsets, until the halt condition is met. Finally a decision tree is generated.

4 Output a binary decision tree.

A are less than or equal to T and $S_2 \subset S$ be the subset of instances whose values of A are greater than T. The Gini index of the partition induced by T is defined as

$$Gini(A, T, S) = \frac{|S_1|}{|S|} Gini(S_1) + \frac{|S_2|}{|S|} Gini(S_2). \tag{2.5}$$

Definition 2.5 Given a set S of instances, a continuous-valued attribute A, and a cut-point T, the Gini gain of A with respect to cut-point T is defined as

$$Gain(S, T, A) = Gini(S) - Gini(A, T, S)$$

$$= Gini(S) - \frac{|S_1|}{|S|} Gini(S_1) - \frac{|S_2|}{|S|} Gini(S_2). \tag{2.6}$$

Definition 2.6 Given a set S of instances and a continuous-valued attribute A, if the cut-point T^* maximized $Gain(S, T, A)$, that is, $T^* = \text{argmax}_T\{Gain(S, T, A)\}$, then we call T^* as an optimal cut-point.

Fayyad has proved in [3] that the optimal cut-point can only be imbalance cut-point. Based on this conclusion, by extending directly ID3 algorithm, an inductive algorithm for learning decision trees from data sets with continuous-valued attributes can be obtained as Algorithm 2.2.

Similar to ID3, each path in the learned decision tree can be transformed into an if-then rule; the number of rules is the number of leaf nodes in decision tree.

> **Example 2.1** A small continuous-valued data set with 24 instances is given in Table 2.2. We then illustrate the process of using Algorithm 2.2 to generate a decision tree.

Table 2.2   A Small Continuous-Valued Data Set with 24 Instances

No.	Income (A_1)	Area of Grassland (A_2)	Class
1	60	18.4	1
2	85.5	16.8	1
3	64.8	21.6	1
4	61.5	20.8	1
5	87	23.6	1
6	110.1	19.2	1
7	108	17.6	1
8	82.8	22.4	1
9	69	20	1
10	93	20.8	1
11	51	22	1
12	81	20	1
13	75	19.6	2
14	52.8	20.8	2
15	64.8	17.2	2
16	43.2	20.4	2
17	84	17.6	2
18	49.2	17.6	2
19	59.4	16	2
20	66	18.4	2
21	47.4	16.4	2
22	33	18.8	2
23	51	14	2
24	63	14.8	2

For the data set given in Table 2.2, the steps of constructing a decision tree using Algorithm 2.2 are presented as follows.

Step 1: Select the extended attribute.

(1) For attributes A_1 and A_2, calculate their optimal cut-points, and add them into the candidate cut-point set.

Sorting the instances in Table 2.2 according to the values of attribute A_1, we obtain Table 2.3.

The 23 cut-points corresponding to attribute A_1 are given as

$$T_1 = \frac{33 + 43.2}{2} = 38.1, \ldots, T_3 = \frac{47.4 + 49.2}{2} = 48.3,$$

$$T_4 = \frac{49.2 + 51}{2} = 50.1, \ldots, T_{23} = \frac{108 + 110.1}{2} = 109.05. \tag{2.7}$$

where T_1, T_2, T_3, T_6, T_7, T_9, T_{13}, T_{17}, T_{19}, T_{20}, T_{21}, T_{22}, and, T_{23} are 13 balance cut-points, while T_4, T_5, T_8, T_{10}, T_{11}, T_{12}, T_{14}, T_{15}, T_{16}, and T_{18} are 10 imbalance cut-points. The data set S is partitioned into S_1 and S_2 by T_1, because that $Gini(S) = 0.5$, $Gini(S_1) = 0$, and $Gini(S_2) = 1 - \left[\left(\frac{11}{23} \right)^2 + \left(\frac{12}{23} \right)^2 \right] = 0.4991$.

Hence,

$$Gain(S, T_1, A_1) = Gini(S) - Gini(A_1, T_1, S)$$

$$= Gini(S) - \left[\frac{1}{24} Gini(S_1) + \frac{23}{24} Gini(S_2) \right]$$

$$= 0.5 - \left[\frac{1}{24} \times 0 + \frac{23}{24} \times 0.4991 \right]$$

$$= 0.5 - 0.4783 = 0.0217. \tag{2.8}$$

Similarly, the Gini gain of A_1 with respect to other cut-points can be obtained. Finally, calculate $T_{A_1} = \mathrm{argmax}_{1 \le i \le 23} Gini(S, T_i, A_1)$, $T_{A_1} = 84.75$ is the optimal cut-point of A_1, and add it into the candidate cut-point set.

For attribute A_2, repeat the earlier process. The optimal cut-point is $T_{A_2} = 19$; add it into the candidate cut-point set.

Actually, for each attribute, we only need to calculate the Gini gain with respect to imbalance cut-points.

(2) Select cut-point with maximum Gini grain from the candidate cut-point set. The corresponding attribute is selected as extended attribute. In this example, the final optimal cut-point is T_{A_2}, and then the extended attribute is A_2.

Step 2: Partition data set of instances.

Partition S into S_1 and S_2 by the extended attribute A_2 (see Figure 2.3), where $S_1 = \{1, 2, 7, 15, 17, 18, 19, 20, 21, 22, 23, 24\}$, $S_2 = S - S_1$. If the instances in S_i ($1 \le i \le 2$) don't belong to the same class, then repeat Step 1 and Step 2 on S_i ($1 \le i \le 2$). Finally, the obtained decision tree is shown in Figure 2.4.

Table 2.3   The Sorted Data Set (Table 2.2) by A_1

No.	Income (A_1)	Area of Grassland (A_2)	Class
22	33	18.8	2
16	43.2	20.4	2
21	47.4	16.4	2
18	49.2	17.6	2
11	51	22	1
23	51	14	2
14	52.8	20.8	2
19	59.4	16	2
1	60	18.4	1
4	61.5	20.8	1
24	63	14.8	2
3	64.8	21.6	1
15	64.8	17.2	2
20	66	18.4	2
9	69	20	1
13	75	19.6	2
12	81	20	1
8	82.8	22.4	1
17	84	17.6	2
2	85.5	16.8	1
5	87	23.6	1
10	93	20.8	1
7	108	17.6	1
6	110.1	19.2	1

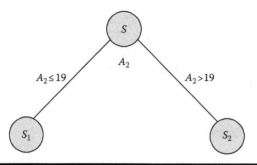

Figure 2.3   The first partition by attribute A_2.

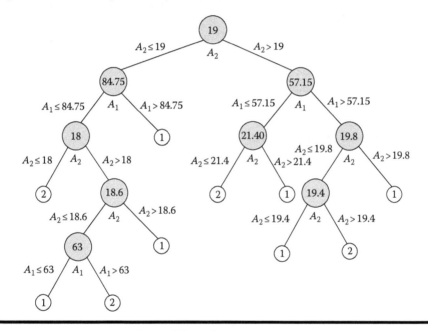

Figure 2.4   Decision tree learned from data set given in Table 2.2.

The learned decision tree can be transformed into a set of if-then rules. Each path in the learned decision tree can be transformed into an if-then rule, and the number of rules is the number of leaf nodes in decision tree. Accordingly, totally 10 if-then rules can be transformed from Figure 2.4.

> ***Rule 1:*** If $A_2 \leq 18$ and $A_1 \leq 84.75$, then the class is 2.
> ***Rule 2:*** If $A_2 \leq 19$ and $A_1 > 84.75$, then the class is 1.
> ***Rule 3:*** If $18.6 < A_2 \leq 19$ and $A_1 \leq 84.75$, then the class is 1.
> ***Rule 4:*** If $A_2 \leq 18.6$ and $A_1 \leq 63$, then the class is 1.
> ***Rule 5:*** If $A_2 \leq 18.6$ and $63 < A_1 \leq 84.75$, then the class is 2.

Rule 6: If $A_2 > 21.4$ and $A_1 \leq 57.15$, then the class is 1.
Rule 7: If $19 < A_2 \leq 21.4$ and $A_1 \leq 57.15$, then the class is 2.
Rule 8: If $A_2 > 19.8$ and $A_1 \geq 57.15$, then the class is 1.
Rule 9: If $19.4 < A_2 \leq 19.8$ and $A_1 > 57.15$, then the class is 2.
Rule 10: If $19 < A_2 \leq 19.4$ and $A_1 > 57.15$, then the class is 1.

2.2 Fuzzy Decision Tree

In this section, we introduce fuzzy ID3 algorithm [6], which is an extension of ID3 for learning fuzzy decision trees [7–11] from a fuzzy decision table (FDT), in which both the conditional attributes and the decision attribute are fuzzy. An FDT can be described in Table 2.4.

In Table 2.4, $A_1, A_2, \ldots, A_d$ are d fuzzy conditional attributes. Each $A_i \ (1 \leq i \leq d)$ consists of a set of fuzzy linguistic terms $FLT_i = \{A_{i1}, A_{i2}, \ldots, A_{is_i}\}$ $(1 \leq i \leq d)$, which are fuzzy sets defined on the space of samples $U = \{x_1, x_2, \ldots, x_n\}$. C denotes a fuzzy decision attribute with a set of fuzzy linguistic terms $FLT_C = \{C_1, C_2, \ldots, C_k\}$, which are also fuzzy sets defined on U. Each fuzzy linguistic term $A_{ij} \ (1 \leq i \leq d; 1 \leq j \leq s_i)$ or $C_l \ (1 \leq l \leq k)$ is considered as a fuzzy set that can be represented as

$$A_{ij} = \frac{x_{ij}^{(1)}}{x_1} + \frac{x_{ij}^{(2)}}{x_2} + \cdots + \frac{x_{ij}^{(n)}}{x_n} \tag{2.9}$$

and

$$C_l = \frac{c_l^{(1)}}{x_1} + \frac{c_l^{(2)}}{x_2} + \cdots + \frac{c_l^{(n)}}{x_n}, \tag{2.10}$$

where $x_{ij}^{(p)} \ (1 \leq i \leq d; 1 \leq j \leq s_i; 1 \leq p \leq n)$ is the conditional membership degree, while $c_l^{(p)} \ (1 \leq l \leq k; 1 \leq p \leq n)$ is the class membership degree. As an illustration, Table 2.5 gives a small FDT with four fuzzy conditional attributes and one fuzzy decision attribute. This FDT is a modification of decision Table 2.1. In fuzzy decision Table 2.5, the four fuzzy conditional attributes and their linguistic terms are

$A_1 = Outlook,\ FLT_1 = \{A_{11}, A_{12}, A_{13}\} = \{Sunny, Cloudy, Rain\},$
$A_2 = Temperature,\ FLT_2 = \{A_{21}, A_{22}, A_{23}\} = \{Hot, Mild, Cool\},$
$A_3 = Humidity,\ FLT_3 = \{A_{31}, A_{32}\} = \{Humid, Normal\},$
$A_4 = Wind,\ FLT_4 = \{A_{41}, A_{42}\} = \{Windy, Not\text{-}Windy\}.$

The fuzzy decision attribute and its linguistic terms are $C = \{Play\}$ and $FLT_C = \{C_1, C_2, C_3\} = \{V, S, W\}$ representing three sports: swimming, volleyball, and weight lifting.

Table 2.4 The Fuzzy Decision Table

x	A_1				A_2				$\cdots$	A_d				C			
	A_{11}	A_{12}	$\cdots$	A_{1s_1}	A_{21}	A_{22}	$\cdots$	A_{2s_2}	$\cdots$	A_{d1}	A_{d2}	$\cdots$	A_{ds_d}	C_1	C_2	$\cdots$	C_k
x_1	$x_{11}^{(1)}$	$x_{12}^{(1)}$	$\cdots$	$x_{1s_1}^{(1)}$	$x_{21}^{(1)}$	$x_{22}^{(1)}$	$\cdots$	$x_{2s_2}^{(1)}$	$\cdots$	$x_{d1}^{(1)}$	$x_{d2}^{(1)}$	$\cdots$	$x_{ds_d}^{(1)}$	$c_1^{(1)}$	$c_2^{(1)}$	$\cdots$	$c_k^{(1)}$
x_2	$x_{11}^{(2)}$	$x_{12}^{(2)}$	$\cdots$	$x_{1s_1}^{(2)}$	$x_{21}^{(2)}$	$x_{22}^{(2)}$	$\cdots$	$x_{2s_2}^{(2)}$	$\cdots$	$x_{d1}^{(2)}$	$x_{d2}^{(2)}$	$\cdots$	$x_{ds_d}^{(2)}$	$c_1^{(2)}$	$c_2^{(2)}$	$\cdots$	$c_k^{(2)}$
$\cdots$	$\cdots$	$\cdots$	$\cdots$	$\cdots$	$\cdots$	$\cdots$	$\cdots$	$\cdots$	$\cdots$	$\cdots$	$\cdots$	$\cdots$	$\cdots$	$\cdots$	$\cdots$	$\cdots$	$\cdots$
x_n	$x_{11}^{(n)}$	$x_{12}^{(n)}$	$\cdots$	$x_{1s_1}^{(n)}$	$x_{21}^{(n)}$	$x_{22}^{(n)}$	$\cdots$	$x_{2s_2}^{(n)}$	$\cdots$	$x_{d1}^{(n)}$	$x_{d2}^{(n)}$	$\cdots$	$x_{ds_d}^{(n)}$	$c_1^{(1)}$	$c_2^{(n)}$	$\cdots$	$c_k^{(n)}$

Table 2.5 A Small Fuzzy Decision Table

x	Outlook			Temperature			Humidity		Wind		Play		
	Sunny	Cloudy	Rain	Hot	Mild	Cool	Humid	Normal	Windy	Not-windy	V	S	W
x_1	1.0	0.0	0.0	0.7	0.2	0.1	0.7	0.3	0.4	0.6	0.0	0.6	0.4
x_2	0.6	0.4	0.0	0.6	0.2	0.2	0.6	0.4	0.9	0.1	0.7	0.6	0.0
x_3	0.8	0.2	0.0	0.0	0.7	0.3	0.2	0.8	0.2	0.8	0.3	0.6	0.1
x_4	0.3	0.7	0.0	0.2	0.7	0.1	0.8	0.2	0.3	0.7	0.9	0.1	0.0
x_5	0.7	0.3	0.0	0.0	0.1	0.9	0.5	0.5	0.5	0.5	1.0	0.0	0.0
x_6	0.0	0.3	0.7	0.0	0.7	0.3	0.3	0.7	0.4	0.6	0.2	0.2	0.6
x_7	0.0	0.0	1.0	0.0	0.3	0.7	0.8	0.2	0.1	0.9	0.0	0.0	1.0
x_8	0.0	0.9	0.1	0.0	1.0	0.0	0.1	0.9	0.0	1.0	0.3	0.0	0.7
x_9	1.0	0.0	0.0	1.0	0.0	0.0	0.4	0.6	0.4	0.6	0.4	0.7	0.0
x_{10}	0.0	0.3	0.7	0.7	0.2	0.1	0.8	0.2	0.9	0.1	0.0	0.3	0.7
x_{11}	1.0	0.0	0.0	0.6	0.3	0.1	0.7	0.3	0.2	0.8	0.4	0.7	0.0
x_{12}	0.0	1.0	0.0	0.2	0.6	0.2	0.7	0.3	0.7	0.3	0.7	0.2	0.1
x_{13}	0.0	0.9	0.1	0.7	0.3	0.0	0.1	0.9	0.0	1.0	0.0	0.4	0.6
x_{14}	0.0	0.9	0.1	0.1	0.6	0.3	0.7	0.3	0.7	0.3	1.0	0.0	0.0
x_{15}	0.0	0.3	0.7	0.0	0.0	1.0	0.2	0.8	0.8	0.2	0.4	0.0	0.6
x_{16}	0.5	0.5	0.0	1.0	0.0	0.0	1.0	0.0	1.0	0.0	0.7	0.6	0.0

Similar to crisp decision tree, each path from root node to leaf node is a fuzzy if-then rule. In the following, we first give some the necessary concepts and then present the fuzzy ID3 algorithm.

Definition 2.7 Let A, B_i $(i = 1, 2, \ldots, m)$ be fuzzy sets defined on U. A fuzzy partition of A is defined as $\{A \cap B_i | i = 1, 2, \ldots, m\}$.

Definition 2.8 Let F be a fuzzy set defined on U. $\forall x \in U$, the significant level α of the membership degree, is defined as follows:

$$\mu_{F_\alpha}(x) = \begin{cases} \mu_F(x) & \text{if } \mu_F(x) \geq \alpha \\ 0 & \text{if } \mu_F(x) < \alpha. \end{cases} \tag{2.11}$$

Definition 2.9 Let $A \to C$ be a fuzzy rule; its degree of confidence β is defined as

$$\beta = S(A, C) = \frac{M(A \cap C)}{M(A)} = \frac{\sum_{x \in X} \min(\mu_A(x), \mu_C(x))}{\sum_{x \in X} \mu_A(x)}. \tag{2.12}$$

The details of fuzzy ID3 are given in Algorithm 2.3.

Example 2.2 Let $\alpha = 0.0$ and $\beta = 0.80$. We construct a fuzzy decision tree from Table 2.5 using fuzzy ID3 algorithm.

Similar to the crisp ID3 algorithm, the fuzzy ID3 algorithm also includes two steps: (1) select extended attribute and (2) partition the FDT.

Step 1: Select extended attribute.

(1) For the first attribute $A_1 = Outlook$
   (1.1) For the fuzzy linguistic terms, *Sunny*, *Cloudy*, and *Rain*, compute their relative frequency with respect to fuzzy decision attributes $V, S,$ and W. We have

$$p_{11}^{(1)} = p_{Outlook,Sunny}^V = \frac{M(Sunny \cap V)}{M(Sunny)} = \frac{3.2}{6.1} = 0.52$$

$$p_{11}^{(2)} = p_{Outlook,Sunny}^S = \frac{M(Sunny \cap S)}{M(Sunny)} = \frac{4.0}{6.1} = 0.66$$

$$p_{11}^{(3)} = p_{Outlook,Sunny}^W = \frac{M(Sunny \cap W)}{M(Sunny)} = \frac{0.7}{6.1} = 0.11$$

Algorithm 2.3: Fuzzy ID3 Algorithm

Input: $FDT = (U, A \cup C, V, f)$.

Output: A fuzzy decision tree T.

1 **for** (*Each fuzzy conditional attribute $A_i (1 \le i \le d)$*) **do**

2   **for** (*Each fuzzy linguistic term $A_{ij}(1 \le i \le d; 1 \le j \le s_i)$*) **do**

3   Compute the relative frequency of A_{ij} regarding C_l as

4

$$p_{ij}^{(l)} = \frac{M\left(A_{ij} \cap C_l\right)}{M\left(A_{ij}\right)}$$

5   Compute fuzzy classification entropy of A_{ij} as

6

$$Entr(A_{ij}) = -\sum_{l=1}^{m} p_{ij}^{(l)} \log_2\left(p_{ij}^{(l)}\right)$$

7   **end**

8 **end**

9 **for** (*Each fuzzy conditional attribute $A_i(1 \le i \le d)$*) **do**

10   Compute A_i's fuzzy classification entropy, which is the weighted average of fuzzy classification entropy for its linguistic terms:

11

$$Entr(A_i) = \sum_{j=1}^{s_i} \left(\frac{M\left(A_{ij}\right)}{\sum_{j=1}^{s_i} M\left(A_{ij}\right)}\right) Entr\left(A_{ij}\right)$$

12 **end**

13 Select extended attribute as follows:

14

$$E_{i0} = \min_{1 \le i \le n}\{Entr(A_i)\}$$

15 **if** (*The degree of confidence β is less than the given threshold*) **then**

16   Partition the fuzzy decision table;

17   Goto 1;

18 **end**

19 Output a fuzzy decision tree T.

(1.2) Compute fuzzy classification entropy of the three linguistic terms of *Outlook*:

$$Entr(A_{11}) = -\frac{3.2}{6.1}\log_2\frac{3.2}{6.1} - \frac{4.0}{6.1}\log_2\frac{4.0}{6.1} - \frac{0.7}{6.1}\log_2\frac{0.7}{6.1} = 1.25.$$

$$Entr(A_{12}) = -\frac{4.5}{6.5}\log_2\frac{4.5}{6.5} - \frac{2.3}{6.5}\log_2\frac{2.3}{6.5} - \frac{2.4}{6.5}\log_2\frac{2.4}{6.5} = 1.43.$$

$$Entr(A_{13}) = -\frac{0.9}{3.4}\log_2\frac{0.9}{3.4} - \frac{0.5}{3.4}\log_2\frac{0.5}{3.4} - \frac{3.1}{3.4}\log_2\frac{3.1}{3.4} = 0.68.$$

(1.3) Compute the fuzzy classification entropy of *Outlook*:

$$Entr(A_1) = \sum_{j=1}^{s_1}\left(\frac{M(A_{1j})}{\sum_{j=1}^{s_1}M(A_{1j})}\right)Entr(A_{1j})$$

$$= \frac{6.1}{6.1+6.5+3.4}\times 1.25 + \frac{6.1}{6.1+6.5+3.4}$$

$$\times 1.43 + \frac{6.1}{6.1+6.5+3.4}\times 0.68$$

$$= 1.20.$$

Similarly, for attributes $A_2 = $ *Temperature*, $A_3 = $ *Humidity*, and $A_4 = $ *Windy*, we have

$$Entr(A_2) = 1.46$$
$$Entr(A_3) = 1.49$$
$$Entr(A_4) = 1.47$$

Obviously,

$$Entr(A_1) = \min_{1\leq k\leq 4}\{Entr(A_k)\}.$$

Hence, *Outlook* is the extended attribute. Based on values of *Outlook*, the root of the tree is divided with three branches shown in Figure 2.5.

Step 2: Fuzzy partition the FDT.

First, calculate the degree of confidence β of Sunny with respect to V, S, and W. According to the following formula,

$$\beta = S(A, C) = \frac{M(A\cap C)}{M(A)} = \frac{\sum_{x\in X}\min(\mu_A(x), \mu_C(x))}{\sum_{x\in X}\mu_A(x)}.$$

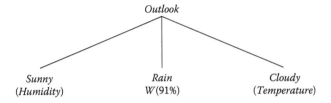

Figure 2.5 The three branches generated by attribute *Outlook*.

We have

$$\beta_{Sunny}^{(V)} = S(Sunny, V) = \frac{M(Sunny \cap V)}{M(Sunny)}$$

$$= \frac{\sum_{x \in X} \min\left(\mu_{Sunny}(x), \mu_V(x)\right)}{\sum_{x \in X} \mu_{Sunny}(x)} = \frac{3.2}{6.1} = 0.52$$

$$\beta_{Sunny}^{(S)} = S(Sunny, S) = \frac{M(Sunny \cap S)}{M(Sunny)}$$

$$= \frac{\sum_{x \in X} \min\left(\mu_{Sunny}(x), \mu_S(x)\right)}{\sum_{x \in X} \mu_{Sunny}(x)} = \frac{4.0}{6.1} = 0.66$$

$$\beta_{Sunny}^{(W)} = S(Sunny, W) = \frac{M(Sunny \cap W)}{M(Sunny)}$$

$$= \frac{\sum_{x \in X} \min\left(\mu_{Sunny}(x), \mu_W(x)\right)}{\sum_{x \in X} \mu_{Sunny}(x)} = \frac{0.7}{6.1} = 0.11.$$

Obviously, they are all less than the threshold $\beta = 0.80$, and therefore, it is necessary to continue partitioning the FDT in this node.

Similarly, for *Cloudy*, we have

$$\beta_{Cloudy}^{(V)} = S(Cloudy, V) = 0.69$$

$$\beta_{Cloudy}^{(S)} = S(Cloudy, S) = 0.35$$

$$\beta_{Cloudy}^{(W)} = S(Cloudy, W) = 0.37$$

Obviously, it is also necessary to continue partitioning the decision table in this node.

For *Rain*, we have

$$\beta_{Rain}^{(V)} = S(Rain, V) = 0.26$$

$$\beta_{Rain}^{(S)} = S(Rain, S) = 0.15$$

$$\beta_{Rain}^{(W)} = S(Rain, W) = 0.91$$

Because $\beta_{Rain}^{(W)} = 0.91 > 0.80$, we obtain a leaf node. For the *Sunny* branch, it is necessary to compute the fuzzy partition of *Sunny* with respect to *Temperature*, *Humidity*, and *Wind*, respectively.

Because *Temperature* takes three values, *Hot*, *Mild*, and *Cool*, the fuzzy partitions of *Sunny* with respect to *Temperature* are three fuzzy subsets: *Sunny* ∩ *Hot*, *Sunny* ∩ *Mild*, and *Sunny* ∩ *Cool*. The relative frequencies of the three fuzzy subsets can be, respectively, calculated as follows:

$$p_{Sunny \cap Hot}^{V} = \frac{M(Sunny \cap Hot \cap V)}{M(Sunny \cap Hot)} = \frac{2.1}{3.8} = 0.55$$

$$p_{Sunny \cap Hot}^{S} = \frac{M(Sunny \cap Hot \cap S)}{M(Sunny \cap Hot)} = \frac{3.3}{3.8} = 0.87$$

$$p_{Sunny \cap Hot}^{W} = \frac{M(Sunny \cap Hot \cap W)}{M(Sunny \cap Hot)} = \frac{0.6}{3.8} = 0.16$$

$$p_{Sunny \cap Mild}^{V} = \frac{M(Sunny \cap Mild \cap V)}{M(Sunny \cap Mild)} = \frac{1.2}{2.0} = 0.60$$

$$p_{Sunny \cap Mild}^{S} = \frac{M(Sunny \cap Mild \cap S)}{M(Sunny \cap Mild)} = \frac{1.6}{2.0} = 0.80$$

$$p_{Sunny \cap Mild}^{W} = \frac{M(Sunny \cap Mild \cap W)}{M(Sunny \cap Mild)} = \frac{0.5}{2.0} = 0.25$$

$$p_{Sunny \cap Cool}^{V} = \frac{M(Sunny \cap Cool \cap V)}{M(Sunny \cap Cool)} = \frac{1.4}{1.5} = 0.93$$

$$p_{Sunny \cap Cool}^{S} = \frac{M(Sunny \cap Cool \cap S)}{M(Sunny \cap Cool)} = \frac{0.8}{1.5} = 0.53$$

$$p_{Sunny \cap Cool}^{W} = \frac{M(Sunny \cap Cool \cap W)}{M(Sunny \cap Cool)} = \frac{0.2}{1.5} = 0.33$$

Hence, the fuzzy entropies of the three fuzzy subsets can be obtained:

$$Entr(Sunny \cap Hot) = -\frac{2.1}{3.8}\log_2 \frac{2.1}{3.8} - \frac{3.3}{3.8}\log_2 \frac{3.3}{3.8} - \frac{0.6}{3.8}\log_2 \frac{0.6}{3.8} = 1.07$$

$$Entr(Sunny \cap Mild) = -\frac{1.2}{2.0}\log_2 \frac{1.2}{2.0} - \frac{1.6}{2.0}\log_2 \frac{1.6}{2.0} - \frac{0.5}{2.0}\log_2 \frac{0.5}{2.0} = 1.20$$

$$Entr(Sunny \cap Cool) = -\frac{1.4}{1.5}\log_2 \frac{1.4}{1.5} - \frac{0.8}{1.5}\log_2 \frac{0.8}{1.5} - \frac{0.2}{1.5}\log_2 \frac{0.2}{1.5} = 0.96$$

Finally, the fuzzy classification entropy of *Sunny ∩ Temperature* can be given by

$$Entr(Sunny \cap Temperature) = \frac{3.8}{3.8 + 2.0 + 1.5} \times 1.07 + \frac{2.0}{3.8 + 2.0 + 1.5} \times 1.20$$

$$+ \frac{1.5}{3.8 + 2.0 + 1.5} \times 0.96 = 1.08.$$

Similarly, we have

$$Entr(Sunny \cap Humidity) = \frac{4.0}{4.0 + 3.3} \times 1.00 + \frac{3.3}{4.0 + 3.3} \times 1.17 = 1.08$$

$$Entr(Sunny \cap Windy) = \frac{3.1}{3.1 + 3.9} \times 0.88 + \frac{3.9}{3.1 + 3.9} \times 1.26 = 1.09.$$

It is easy to see that *Entr(Sunny ∩ Humidity)* is the minimum. Therefore, *Humidity* is selected as the extended attribute.

Repeating this process, a fuzzy decision tree is finally generated as shown in Figure 2.6.

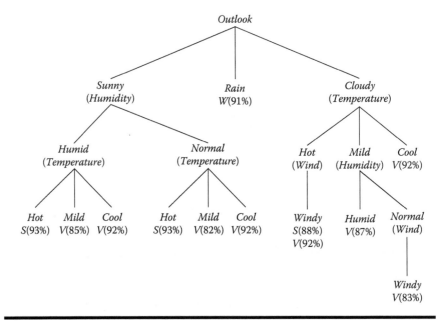

Figure 2.6   The fuzzy decision tree learned from Table 2.5 with fuzzy ID3 algorithm.

The fuzzy decision tree shown in Figure 2.6 can be transformed into 11 fuzzy if-then rules:

>**Rule 1:** If *Outlook* is *Sunny*, *Humidity* is *Humid*, and *Temperature* is *Hot*, then class is *S* (the degree of confidence of rule 1 is 0.93).
>**Rule 2:** If *Outlook* is *Sunny*, *Humidity* is *Humid*, and *Temperature* is *Mild*, then class is *V* (the degree of confidence of rule 2 is 0.85).
>**Rule 3:** If *Outlook* is *Sunny*, *Humidity* is *Humid*, and *Temperature* is *Cool*, then class is *V* (the degree of confidence of rule 3 is 0.92).
>**Rule 4:** If *Outlook* is *Sunny*, *Humidity* is *Normal*, and *Temperature* is *Hot*, then class is *S* (the degree of confidence of rule 4 is 0.94).
>**Rule 5:** If *Outlook* is *Sunny*, *Humidity* is *Humid*, and *Temperature* is *Mild*, then class is *V* (the degree of confidence of rule 5 is 0.82).
>**Rule 6:** If *Outlook* is *Sunny*, *Humidity* is *Humid*, and *Temperature* is *Cool*, then class is *V* (the degree of confidence of rule 6 is 0.92).
>**Rule 7:** If *Outlook* is *Rain*, then class is *W* (the degree of confidence of rule 7 is 0.91).
>**Rule 8:** If *Outlook* is *Cloudy*, *Temperature* is *Hot*, and *Wind* is *Windy*, then class is *S* (the degree of confidence of rule 8 is 0.88).
>**Rule 9:** If *Outlook* is *Cloudy*, *Temperature* is *Mild*, and *Humidity* is *Humid*, then class is *V* (the degree of confidence of rule 9 is 0.873).
>**Rule 10:** If *Outlook* is *Cloudy*, *Temperature* is *Mild*, *Humidity* is *Normal*, and *Wind* is *Windy*, then class is *V* (the degree of confidence of rule 10 is 0.83).
>**Rule 11:** If *Outlook* is *Cloudy* and *Temperature* is *Cool*, then class is *V* (the degree of confidence of rule 11 is 0.92).

2.3 Fuzzy Decision Tree Based on Fuzzy Rough Set Techniques

In this section, we introduce an algorithm of induction of fuzzy decision tree with fuzzy rough set technique [12]. In the presented algorithm, the expanded attributes are selected by using significance of fuzzy conditional attributes with respect to fuzzy decision attributes [13–16]. We first review the basic concepts of fuzzy rough sets and then introduce the algorithm.

2.3.1 Fuzzy Rough Sets

A *DT* [17] refers to a four-tuple $DT = (U, A \cup C, V, f)$, where $U = \{x_1, x_2, \ldots, x_N\}$ is a nonempty finite set of objects and each x_i is usually represented as $x_i = (x_{i1}, x_{i2}, \ldots, x_{in})$, $A = \{a_1, a_2, \ldots, a_n\}$ is a set of conditional attributes, and $C = \{c\}$ is the decision attribute. Without loss of generality we suppose that $c \in \{1, 2, \ldots, p\}$; $V = \bigcup_{j=1}^{n} V_{a_j}$, where $V_{a_j} (1 \leq j \leq n)$ is the domain of value of attribute a_j; $f : U \times A \rightarrow V$ is called an information function, that is, $f(x_i, a_j) = a_{ij}$ $(1 \leq i \leq N; 1 \leq j \leq n)$.

An *FDT* [12] is a fuzzy version of a *DT*, which is also a four-tuple $FDT = (U, A \cup C, V, f)$, where U, V, and f have meanings as same as in the *DT*, where $A = \{A_1, A_2, \ldots, A_n\}$ is a set of fuzzy conditional attributes. As in Section 2.2, A_i $(1 \leq i \leq n)$ consists of a set of fuzzy linguistic terms. C denotes a fuzzy decision attribute with a set of fuzzy linguistic terms $FLT_C = \{C_1, C_2, \ldots, C_m\}$.

There are four fuzzy rough set models that were proposed independently by different authors [13–16]. In this book, we use the fuzzy rough set model developed by Dubois and Prade [13].

Definition 2.10 Let U be a given universe. A partition $P = \{F_1, F_2, \ldots, F_n\}$ of U is a fuzzy partition if and only if the following two requirements hold:

(1) $\forall x_i \in U, \forall F_j \in P, \ \mu_{F_j}(x_i) \leq 1.$
(2) $\forall x_i \in U, \exists F_j \in P, \ \mu_{F_j}(x_i) > 0.$

where $\mu_{F_j}(x_i)$ denotes the membership degree to which x_i belongs F_j.

Definition 2.11 Let U be a given universe. R is a fuzzy equivalence relation over U if the following four requirements hold:

(1) R is a fuzzy relation on U.
(2) R is reflective, that is, $R(x, x) = 1$, $\forall x \in U$.
(3) R is symmetric, that is, $R(x, y) = R(y, x)$, $\forall x, y \in U$.
(4) R is transitive, that is, $R(x, z) \geq \min\{R(x, y), R(y, z)\}$, $\forall x, y, z \in U$.

An equivalence relation can generate a partition of universe U, while a fuzzy equivalence relation can generate a fuzzy partition of universe U.

Definition 2.12 Let U be a given universe and R be a fuzzy equivalence relation over U. The fuzzy equivalence class $[x]_R$ is defined as

$$\mu_{[x]_R}(y) = \mu_R(x, y). \tag{2.13}$$

Definition 2.13 Let U be a given universe and X and P be two fuzzy sets on U. The fuzzy P-lower and P-upper approximations are defined as follows [13]:

$$\mu_{\underline{P}X}(F_i) = \inf_{x \in U} \max\{1 - \mu_{F_i}(x), \mu_X(x)\} \quad (i = 1, 2, \ldots, n) \tag{2.14}$$

$$\mu_{\overline{P}X}(F_i) = \sup_{x \in U} \min\{\mu_{F_i}(x), \mu_X(x)\} \quad (i = 1, 2, \ldots, n), \qquad (2.15)$$

where $F_i \in U/P \, (1 \leq i \leq n)$ denotes a fuzzy equivalence class and U/P denotes the fuzzy partition of U with respect to P.

It is noted that the fuzzy P-lower and P-upper approximations given in (2.14) and (2.15) are defined on fuzzy partition; the equivalent definitions on universe are given as follows.

Definition 2.14 For a given $x \in U$, the fuzzy P-lower approximation and the fuzzy P-upper approximation of X are defined as follows [18]:

$$\mu_{\underline{P}X}(x) = \sup_{F \in U/P} \min\left(\mu_F(x), \inf_{y \in U} \max\{1 - \mu_F(y), \mu_X(y)\}\right) \qquad (2.16)$$

$$\mu_{\overline{P}X}(x) = \sup_{F \in U/P} \min\left(\mu_F(x), \sup_{y \in U} \min\{\mu_F(y), \mu_X(y)\}\right). \qquad (2.17)$$

Definition 2.15 Suppose that P and Q are two fuzzy attributes in a given *FDT*. $\forall x \in U$, regarding x and universe U, the significance of the fuzzy attribute P with respect to the fuzzy attribute Q is defined by

$$\mu_{POS_P(Q)}(x) = \sup_{X \in U/Q} \mu_{\underline{P}X}(x) \qquad (2.18)$$

and

$$\tau_P(Q) = \frac{\sum_{x \in U} \mu_{POS_P(Q)}(x)}{|U|}, \qquad (2.19)$$

where $|U|$ is the cardinality of the universe U.

Definition 2.16 The truth degree of the fuzzy set P with respect to the fuzzy set Q is defined by

$$\beta = T(P, Q) = \frac{\tau_P(Q)}{\sum_{x \in U} \mu_P(x)}. \qquad (2.20)$$

2.3.2 Generating Fuzzy Decision Tree with Fuzzy Rough Set Technique

This section introduces the algorithm for generating fuzzy decision trees based on the significance of fuzzy conditional attribute with respect to fuzzy decision attribute. For the convenience of description, we name the algorithm as FRFDT, which is listed in Algorithm 2.4.

The following (1) or (2) can be defined as the terminal conditions:

(1) If the classification truth degree of a branch with respect to one class exceeds a given threshold β, then the branch is terminated as a leaf node.
(2) At a branch, if no attribute can be selected as the expanded attribute, the branch is terminated as a leaf node or as null node.

During the generation of a fuzzy decision tree, if there is not a threshold to control the growth of the tree, the generated tree will be very complicated and usually the classification accuracy of the rules converted from the tree will be poor. The terminal condition (1), that is, the threshold of classification truth degree β, plays the major role, which controls the growth of the tree. Different β will result in different fuzzy decision trees with different classification accuracies. In general, smaller β may lead to a smaller tree, but the classification accuracy will be lower. Larger β may lead to a larger tree, while the classification accuracy may be higher (on training set). The selection of β depends on the problem to be solved.

Algorithm 2.4: FRFDT

Input: $FDT = (U, A \cup C, V, f)$.
Output: A fuzzy decision tree T.
1 Preprocess the FDT by using formula (2.11);
2 **for** (*Each fuzzy conditional attribute A_i*) **do**
3   **for** (*Each fuzzy linguistic terms A_{ik_i} ($1 \le i \le n$)*) **do**
4   Calculate the significance of A_i with respect to the fuzzy decision attribute C using formula (2.19);
5   **end**
6 **end**
7 Select expanded attribute A_{i_0}, such that $A_{i_0} = \underset{1 \le i \le n}{\mathrm{argmax}} \{\tau_{A_i}(C)\}$;
8 **if** (*The terminal condition is not satisfied*) **then**
9   Partition U;
10   Go to 2;
11 **end**
12 Output a fuzzy decision tree T.

Example 2.3 We will demonstrate the process of generation of fuzzy decision tree by using the small FDT with 16 training instances given in Table 2.5. The universe is $U = \{x_1, x_2, \ldots, x_{16}\}$. The four fuzzy conditional attributes are *Outlook, Temperature, Humidity*, and *Wind*. The fuzzy decision attribute is *Play*.

Let the significant level $\alpha = 0.0$ and the threshold of classification truth degree $\beta = 0.78$. By calculating the significance of each fuzzy conditional attribute A_i $(1 \leq i \leq 4)$ with respect to the fuzzy decision attribute $C = \{Play\}$, we have

$$\tau_{A_1}(C) = \tau_{Outlook}(Play) = \frac{\sum_{x \in U} \mu_{POS_{Outlook}}(Play)^{(x)}}{|U|} = \frac{5.2}{16} = 0.33$$

$$\tau_{A_2}(C) = \tau_{Temperature}(Play) = \frac{\sum_{x \in U} \mu_{POS_{Temperature}}(Play)^{(x)}}{|U|} = \frac{4.8}{16} = 0.30$$

$$\tau_{A_3}(C) = \tau_{Humidity}(Play) = \frac{\sum_{x \in U} \mu_{POS_{Humidity}}(Play)^{(x)}}{|U|} = \frac{3.2}{16} = 0.20$$

$$\tau_{A_4}(C) = \tau_{Wind}(Play) = \frac{\sum_{x \in U} \mu_{POS_{Wind}}(Play)^{(x)}}{|U|} = \frac{3.2}{16} = 0.20.$$

Since the fuzzy conditional attribute *Outlook* has the biggest significance, it is selected as the root node. There are three branches (*Sunny, Cloudy*, and *Rain*) from the root node *Outlook*. At the branch *Rain*, the classification truth degree for W is 0.79 $(0.79 > \beta)$ that meets the terminal condition (1) and becomes a leaf node with label W. At the branch *Cloudy*, $T(Cloudy, W) = 0.19 < \beta$, $T(Cloudy, S) = 0.19 < \beta$, $T(Cloudy, V) = 0.19 < \beta$. None of the classification truth degrees exceeds the threshold $\beta = 0.78$, and further partition based on additional attributes should be considered. We have three fuzzy partitions:

$$Cloudy\text{-}Temperature = \{Cloudy \cap A_{2i}\} \quad (i = 1, 2, 3),$$

where $\{A_{21}, A_{22}, A_{23}\} = \{Hot, Mild, Cool\}$.

$$Cloudy\text{-}Wind = \{Cloudy \cap A_{4i}\} \quad (i = 1, 2),$$

where $\{A_{41}, A_{42}\} = \{Windy, Not\text{-}Windy\}$.
Similarly, we have

$$\tau_{Cloudy\text{-}Temperature}(Play) = \frac{4.0}{16} = 0.25$$

$$\tau_{Cloudy\text{-}Humidity}(Play) = \frac{5.6}{16} = 0.35$$

$$\tau_{Cloudy\text{-}Wind}(Play) = \frac{4.6}{16} = 0.29$$

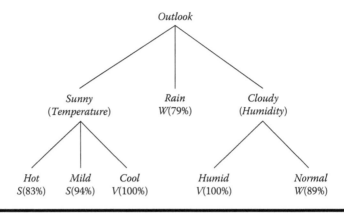

Figure 2.7 Fuzzy decision tree generated by the algorithm FRFDT.

Because the value $\tau_{Cloudy\text{-}Humidity}$ $(Play)$ is the biggest one, the node *Humidity* is added to the branch *Cloudy*. From this node, the branch *Humid* terminates with label V (truth degree is $1 > \beta$) and branch *Normal* terminates with label W (truth degree is $0.89 > \beta$). At the branch *Sunny*, the node *Temperature* is selected as the expended attribute, and from this node, the branch *Hot* terminates with label S (truth degree is $0.83 > \beta$), the branch *Mild* terminates with label S (truth degree is $0.94 > \beta$), and the branch *Cool* terminates with label V (truth degree is $1 > \beta$). Finally, we generate a fuzzy decision tree shown in Figure 2.7.

Now we convert the fuzzy decision tree into a set of fuzzy classification rules. Each path from root node to leaf node can be converted into a fuzzy classification rule that has the highest truth degree for the classification. For the fuzzy decision tree shown in Figure 2.7, we can obtain the following six classification rules:

> **Rule 1:** If *Outlook* is *Sunny* and *Temperature* is *Hot*, then *Play* is S (0.83).
> **Rule 2:** If *Outlook* is *Sunny* and *Temperature* is *Mild*, then *Play* is S (0.94).
> **Rule 3:** If *Outlook* is *Sunny* and *Temperature* is *Cool*, then *Play* is V (1.00).
> **Rule 4:** If *Outlook* is *Rain*, then *Play* is W (0.79).
> **Rule 5:** If *Outlook* is *Cloudy* and *Humidity* is *Humid*, then *Play* is V (1.0).
> **Rule 6:** If *Outlook* is *Cloudy* and *Humidity* is *Normal*, then *Play* is W (0.89).

For each object in the *FDT*, matching it to these fuzzy classification rules, one can acquire a result of classification. Since many rules can be applied to one object at the same time, the object can usually be classified into different classes with different degrees. The method we use to obtain the classification result for a given object is from literature [9].

Upon the same *FDT*, the fuzzy decision tree generated with fuzzy ID3 is shown in Figure 2.6. Comparing Figure 2.7 with Figure 2.6, we find from Figure 2.7 that the subnode of Sunny is Temperature and the subnode of Cloudy is Humidity, while in Figure 2.6, the subnode of Sunny is Humidity and the subnode of Cloudy is Temperature. The expanded attribute selected corresponding to the root node for both trees is the same, but at the subnodes, the expanded attributes selected for both trees are different. The fuzzy decision tree in Figure 2.7 has 6 leaf nodes and 3 inner nodes, while the fuzzy decision tree shown in Figure 2.6 has 11 leaf nodes and 8 inner nodes.

The classification results achieved by fuzzy ID3 and by the algorithm FRFDT on *FDT* 2.5 are, respectively, listed in Table 2.6. Among 16 training instances, 15 instances are correctly classified by the algorithm FRFDT (instance 2 is not correctly classified). The classification accuracy is 94%, which is higher than the classification accuracy (75%) of the fuzzy decision tree generated by the fuzzy ID3 algorithm (instances 2, 8, 13, and 16 are not correctly classified). Obviously with respect to this example, the algorithm FRFDT outperforms the fuzzy ID3 algorithm.

Table 2.6 Comparison between Two Methods

No.	Classification Known in Training Data			Classification with FRFDT			Classification with Fuzzy ID3		
	V	S	W	V	S	W	V	S	W
x_1	0.0	0.6	0.4	0.1	0.7	0.0	0.2	0.7	0.0
x_2	0.7	0.6	0.0	0.4	0.6	0.4	0.2	0.6	0.0
x_3	0.3	0.6	0.1	0.3	0.7	0.2	0.2	0.7	0.0
x_4	0.9	0.1	0.0	0.7	0.3	0.2	0.7	0.2	0.0
x_5	1.0	0.0	0.0	0.7	0.1	0.3	0.5	0.1	0.0
x_6	0.2	0.2	0.6	0.3	0.0	0.7	0.3	0.0	0.7
x_7	0.0	0.0	1.0	0.0	0.0	1.0	0.0	0.0	1.0
x_8	0.3	0.0	0.7	0.1	0.0	0.9	0.9	0.0	0.1
x_9	0.4	0.7	0.0	0.0	1.0	0.0	0.0	0.6	0.0
x_{10}	0.0	0.3	0.7	0.3	0.0	0.7	0.2	0.3	0.7
x_{11}	0.4	0.7	0.0	0.1	0.6	0.0	0.3	0.6	0.1
x_{12}	0.7	0.2	0.1	0.7	0.0	0.3	0.6	0.2	0.0
x_{13}	0.0	0.4	0.6	0.1	0.0	0.9	0.3	0.6	0.1
x_{14}	1.0	0.0	0.0	0.7	0.0	0.3	0.6	0.1	0.1
x_{15}	0.4	0.0	0.6	0.2	0.0	0.7	0.3	0.0	0.7
x_{16}	0.7	0.6	0.0	0.5	0.5	0.0	0.0	0.5	0.0

2.4 Improving Generalization of Fuzzy Decision Tree by Maximizing Fuzzy Entropy

Fuzzy if-then rules extracted from data using fuzzy decision trees and other methods, such as fuzzy neural networks, genetic algorithms, and fuzzy support vector machine, sometimes do not have a satisfying performance. One reason is that uncertainty exists in data or in the approaches to extracting fuzzy if-then rules. Based on fuzzy entropy maximization, in this section, we introduce a refinement framework [19] to improving the generalization capability of fuzzy if-then rules. We first give the idea of the refinement in Section 2.4.1 and then present the globally weighted fuzzy if-then rule reasoning in Section 2.4.2. The refinement approach to updating the parameters is proposed in Section 2.4.3.

2.4.1 Basic Idea of Refinement

The following is the main idea of a refinement approach. Suppose that we have extracted a set of initial fuzzy if-then rules from a training set by using a given training algorithm in which a Boolean vector is considered as the target output, and the set of initial fuzzy if-then rules need to refine. Then, a group of parameters, called global weights, are incorporated into the set of fuzzy if-then rules. The reasoning results of the fuzzy if-then rules will be changing with diverse values of parameters. We attempt to adjust these parameters such that the fuzzy entropy of actual outputs of the fuzzy if-then rules on the training set attains maximum. The adjustment is subject to a number of constraints that indicate that a training object after refinement has a correct output of crisp class if the training object can be classified correctly before refinement. Those constraints imply that the training accuracy will not reduce after refinement. It is worth noting that the fuzzy entropy maximization implies a fuzzification of Boolean vectors, which tries to recover and utilize the inherent classification uncertainty information lost in the training process. The fuzzy entropy maximization application to refining parameters of fuzzy if-then rules, which is realized by solving a quadratic programming problem, is expected to improve the fuzzy if-then rules' generalization capability.

2.4.2 Globally Weighted Fuzzy If-Then Rule Reasoning

According to Zadeh's initial definition of Generalized Modus Ponens [20], the reasoning model of fuzzy IF-THEN rules is described as

A fuzzy if-then rule: IF "x is A" THEN "y is B"
A given fact: "x is A^*"
A conclusion: "y is B^*"

There are many approaches to achieving a fuzzy classification result by matching an object to a set of fuzzy rules. For example, one can achieve the fuzzy classification by using nonlinear regression represented as a Takagi–Sugeno fuzzy model published in [21]. We now focus on a type of globally weighted fuzzy production rules (WFPRs) [22] and its corresponding reasoning mechanism. A WFPR is a parametric fuzzy if-then rule with the conjunctive form

$$\wedge_{j=1}^{n}(V_j = A_j) \Rightarrow (U = C), g,$$

where

V_j $(j = 1, 2, \ldots, n)$ and U are variables
A_j $(j = 1, 2, \ldots, n)$ and C are fuzzy values of these variables (in other words, A_j $(j = 1, 2, \ldots, n)$ are fuzzy sets)
the parameter g is a real number in $[0,1]$ denoting the global weight of the rule R
$\wedge$ denotes the conjunction AND

WFPRs degenerate to fuzzy if-then rules in common sense when the global weight g is ignored.

Consider a set of m WFPRs: $S = \{R_i, \ i = 1, 2, \ldots, m\}$ and a given fact; the reasoning model that slightly modifies the Generalized Modus Ponens is described as

A set of WFPRs:
$R_i : \ \wedge_{j=1}^{n} \left(V_j = A_j^{(i)} \right) \Rightarrow (U = C), \ g_i, \ i = 1, 2, \ldots, m$
A given fact: $V_j = B_j, j = 1, 2, \ldots, n.$
A conclusion: $U = D, \ CF(D)$

where g_i represents the global weight assigned to the ith rule R_i and $CF(D)$ is the certainty factor of the conclusion. It is worth noting that the m rules have the same consequent C. It is possible that the jth proposition of the antecedent of the ith rule (i.e., V_j) is missing. In this case, the membership function of $A_j^{(i)}$ is defined as const 1.

How to draw the conclusion: $U = D, CF(D)$? The following is a scheme to draw the conclusion and to evaluate its certainty factor $CF(D)$. We call the scheme globally weighted reasoning, of which details are given in Algorithm 2.5 [23].

It is easy to see that certainty factor of conclusion is a linear combination of the global weight parameters $g_1, g_2, \ldots, g_m$.

For classification problems, the reasoning result D is exactly equal to C, and the value given in Equation (2.22) denotes the degree of truth of the object belonging to class C. If there are K classes (corresponding to K sets of fuzzy if-then rules) and C_k represents the label of the kth class $(1 \leq k \leq K)$, then the computed result in Equation (2.22) refers to the degree of truth of some class, denoted by x_k $(k = 1, 2, \ldots, K)$. The normalized form of the inferred result is defined as $(d_1, d_2, \ldots, d_k)$ where $d_k = x_k / \max_{1 \leq j \leq K} x_j$ $(k = 1, 2, \ldots, K)$.

We now consider a classification problem with K classes. Let $\Omega = \{x_1, x_2, \ldots, x_N\}$ be a training set from which a set of initial fuzzy if-then rules

---

Algorithm 2.5: Globally Weighted Reasoning Algorithm

    Input: An observed object $B = (B_1, B_2, \ldots, B_n)$ and a group of IF-THEN
          rule $S = \{R_1, R_2, \ldots, R_m\}$.
    Output: $CF(D)$.

1 **for** $(j = 1; j \leq n; j = j + 1)$ **do**
2   **for** $(i = 1; i \leq m; i = i + 1)$ **do**
3   Calculate the membership of the attribute-value B_j belonging to $A_j^{(i)}$ by
          $a_j^{(i)} = A_j^{(i)}(B_j)$;
4   `// where` $A_j^{(i)}(\cdot)$ `denotes its membership`
          `function;`
5   **end**
6 **end**
7 **for** $(i = 1; i \leq m; i = i + 1)$ **do**
8   Calculate parameters a_i by Equation (2.21);
9

$$a_i = \frac{1}{m}\left(\min_{1 \leq j \leq n} a_j^{(i)}\right) \tag{2.21}$$

10   `//` a_i `is the overall degree of matching object` B
          `to rule` R_i`;`
11 **end**
12 Calculate the conclusion's certainty factor $CF(D)$ by Equation (2.22)

$$CF(D) = \sum_{i=1}^{m}(a_i \cdot g_i) \tag{2.22}$$

13 Output $CF(D)$.

$S = \{R_i, \ i = 1, 2, \ldots, m\}$ have been extracted. Suppose that the set of extracted if-then rules have not satisfied performance, and therefore, require a refinement. Considering the global weights of the set of weighted fuzzy if-then rules as a number of parameters to be refined, the following reasoning scheme is diagramed in Figure 2.8. In Figure 2.8, $\{g_i, \ i = 1, 2, \ldots, m\}$ denote the global weights. The value of CF_k, representing the possibility of the object x_i belonging to the kth class $(1 \leq k \leq K)$, is dependent on the global weight $(g_1, g_2, \ldots, g_m)$, that is, $CF_k = CF_k (g_1, g_2, \ldots, g_m)$.

    We now give an example to illustrate how CF_k $(1 \leq k \leq K)$ is dependent on $(g_1, g_2, \ldots, g_m)$.

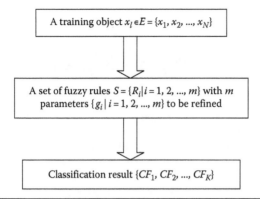

Figure 2.8 The reasoning process for an object.

Table 2.7 Four Fuzzy If-Then Rules

	V_1	V_2	V_3	Class	Global Weight
Rule 1	Big		Small	C_1	g_1
Rule 2	Small		Big	C_1	g_2
Rule 3		Big	Big	C_2	g_3
Rule 4		Small	Small	C_2	g_4

Example 2.4 Consider the four fuzzy if-then rules given in Table 2.7, where V_1, V_2, and V_3 are three variables; the fuzzy sets (Big) and (Small) are defined as

$$Big(x) = \begin{cases} 1 & x \geq 1 \\ x & x \in (0,1) \\ 0 & x \leq 0 \end{cases}$$

$$Small(x) = \begin{cases} 0 & x \geq 1 \\ 1-x & x \in (0,1) \\ 1 & x \leq 0 \end{cases}.$$

Suppose that $A = (0.6, 0.7, 0.2)$ is an object to be classified. Matching object A to rules 1 and 2 according to (2.21) and (2.22), we have

$$CF_1 = \frac{0.6g_1 + 0.2g_2}{2}.$$

Similarity, matching object to rules 3 and 4, we obtain

$$CF_2 = \frac{0.2g_3 + 0.3g_4}{2}.$$

Therefore, the classification result of object A matching to rules 1–4 is

$$\left(\frac{0.6g_1 + 0.2g_2}{2}, \frac{0.2g_3 + 0.3g_4}{2} \right),$$

which is obviously dependent on (g_1, g_2, g_3, g_4). Before weight refinement, the weight vector (g_1, g_2, g_3, g_4) is regarded as $(1, 1, 1, 1)$, which results in a classification result $(0.4, 0.25)$, and therefore, the crisp decision is that object A belongs to class 1. After weight refinement, the weight (g_1, g_2, g_3, g_4) will change. For example, if the refined weight vector (g_1, g_2, g_3, g_4) is $(0.2, 0.3, 0.6, 0.8)$, then the classification result will be $(0.09, 0.18)$ and the crisp decision is that object A belongs to class 2. It shows that the result of crisp classification for an object to be classified is really dependent on the value of global weight.

Example 2.5 illustrates that the change of global weights will have much impact on the classification boundary.

Example 2.5 Consider the four globally weighted fuzzy if-then rules given in Table 2.8.

The membership functions of fuzzy sets Big and Small are defined as Example 2.4. We now use these four rules with different global weights and Equations (2.21) and (2.22) in Algorithm 2.5 to classify each point in $[0, 1] \times [0, 1]$ and then to observe the classification boundary. The classification results for four groups of weights are shown in Figure 2.9a through d where sign $+$ denotes class C_1 and sign $-$ denotes class C_2. From Figure 2.9, one can see that the global weights have a significant impact on the classification boundary of reasoning results.

The key point is what criterion will be used to determine global weights $(g_1, g_2, \ldots, g_m)$ and how to determine them? The maximum fuzzy entropy is used as a criterion in the presented method to refine parameters $g_1, g_2, \ldots, g_m$, and the details are given in the following section.

Table 2.8 Four Globally Weighted Fuzzy If-Then Rules

	V_1	V_2	Class	Global Weight
Rule 1	Big	Big	C_1	g_1
Rule 2	Small	Small	C_1	g_2
Rule 3	Big	Small	C_2	g_3
Rule 4	Small	Big	C_2	g_4

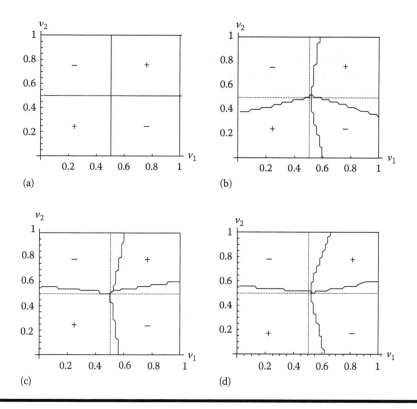

Figure 2.9 The classification results for different (g_1, g_2, g_3, g_4). (a) $(g_1, g_2, g_3, g_4) = (0.5, 0.5, 0.5, 0.5)$, (b) $(g_1, g_2, g_3, g_4) = (0.5, 0.37, 0.24, 0.63)$, (c) $(g_1, g_2, g_3, g_4) = (0.35, 0.65, 0.5, 0.5)$, (d) $(g_1, g_2, g_3, g_4) = (0.32, 0.73, 0.45, 0.57)$.

2.4.3 Refinement Approach to Updating the Parameters

As a type of criterion of information, the fuzzy entropy maximization principle has been widely applied to many fields such as pattern recognition and image processing [24–26] and also applied to the presented method. For convenience, we list here again the Luca–Termini conditions that an entropy function must satisfy the following:

Definition 2.17 Let A be a fuzzy set defined on a space X with the membership function $A(x)$ and $F(X)$ be the set of all fuzzy sets defined on X. A mapping from $F(X)$ to $[0, 1]$, $H(A)$, is called fuzzy entropy of A if $H(A)$ satisfies the following:

(1) $H(A)$ attains its minimum iff $\forall x \in X, A(x) = 0$ or $A(x) = 1$.
(2) $H(A)$ attains its maximum iff $\forall x \in X, A(x) = 1/2$.

(3) When A is more fuzzy than B, that is,
 $\forall x \in X, 1/2 \geq A(x) \geq B(x)$ or
 $1/2 \leq A(x) \leq B(x)$, $H(A) \geq H(B)$.
(4) $H(A) = H(X - A)$ for all $A \in F(X)$.

There are many functions $H(\cdot)$ satisfying (1)–(4). For example, similar to the Shannon's entropy [27], the fuzzy entropy of a finite fuzzy set $A = (\mu_1, \mu_2, \ldots, \mu_T)$ is given in [28] as

$$H_f(A) = -\sum_{j=1}^{T} \left(\mu_j \ln \mu_j + (1 - \mu_j) \ln(1 - \mu_j) \right). \tag{2.23}$$

It is easy to check that the following equation satisfies the four conditions mentioned earlier, and therefore, Equation (2.24) is a quite simple fuzzy entropy function:

$$E_f(A) = \sum_{j=1}^{T} \left(\mu_j \cdot (1 - \mu_j) \right). \tag{2.24}$$

The presented method will use Equation (2.24) as the fuzzy entropy definition. When the membership μ_j of a fuzzy set A is equal to 0.5 for all j, the fuzzy entropy of the fuzzy set attains maximum. In this case, the fuzzy set A has the maximum fuzziness. The fuzzy entropy maximization implies that, for drawing a fuzzy set as the conclusion, we prefer a fuzzy set with bigger fuzziness to other fuzzy sets. In other words, we consider that an event with much uncertainty (fuzzy entropy) will bring us more information when it occurs. The maximum fuzzy entropy principle can be described as follows.

2.4.3.1 Maximum Fuzzy Entropy Principle

Consider a reasoning process that includes a number of parameters to be determined. With respect to a given fact, the reasoning conclusion will be a parametric fuzzy set, which implies that the reasoning conclusion will be changing with diverse parameters. We prefer the parametric fuzzy set with maximum fuzzy entropy (to other fuzzy sets) as the reasoning conclusion, subject to the given constraints. The fuzzy entropy maximization can be realized by parameter adjustment.

Why does the fuzzy entropy maximization improve the classification accuracy for some type of problems? The following is an intuitive explanation.

Suppose that we have a classification problem with n class and A is an object to be classified.

Without any additional information for classification available, a most reasonable classification result for A should be that the possibility of A belonging to each one of the n classes is equal (i.e., $1/n$), which can be achieved by maximizing the entropy of A.

If some additional information for classification is available (i.e., there exists a training set in which each example's class is known), then to get a reasonable and fair classification for A, we should maximize the entropy of A subject to some constraints, each constraint representing that a training example can be classified correctly. These constraints mean that the available information for classification has been utilized and the remaining uncertain information for classification is handled by maximum entropy. The reasonable and fair classification for A is expected to lead a precision increase.

Since A is an object remaining to classify, we have to complete the entropy maximization of A via training set's entropy maximization. Figure 2.10 is an outline of the weight refinement procedure.

Consider Figure 2.8 where the reasoning result for a training object x_i is $\left\{ CF_1^{(i)}, CF_2^{(i)}, \ldots, CF_K^{(i)} \right\}$. Each $CF_j^{(i)}$ denotes the possibility with which the object

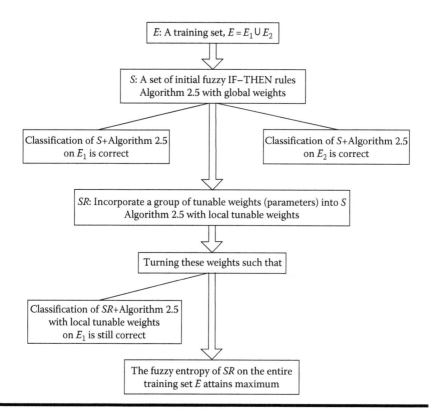

Figure 2.10   Outline of weight refinement procedure.

x_i belongs to the jth class. Noting that each $CF_j^{(i)}$ is a function of parameters $(g_1, g_2, \ldots, g_m)$ that remain to be determined, we denote by

$$CF_j^{(i)} = CF_j^{(i)} \left(g_1, g_2, \ldots, g_m \right) \tag{2.25}$$

Then the fuzzy entropy of the reasoning result with respect to an object can be expressed as

$$E_f \left(x_i;\ g_1, g_2, \ldots, g_m \right) = \sum_{j=1}^{K} \left(CF_j^{(i)} \left(g_1, g_2, \ldots, g_m \right) \left(1 - CF_j^{(i)} \left(g_1, g_2, \ldots, g_m \right) \right) \right) \tag{2.26}$$

The fuzzy entropy on the training set is defined as

$$E_f(g_1, g_2, \ldots, g_m) = \sum_{i=1}^{N} E_f(x_i; g_1, g_2, \ldots, g_m). \tag{2.27}$$

The parameter refinement method attempts to maximize the fuzzy entropy (2.27) subject to a number of constraints that we formulate as follows.

From Figure 2.8 we know that each training object x_i matching to a set of fuzzy if-then rules with m parameters $\{g_i, i = 1, 2, \ldots, m\}$ will lead to a consequent $\{CF_1^{(i)}, CF_2^{(i)}, \ldots, CF_K^{(i)}\}$ dependent on the parameters. We first consider a special case in which all parameters are equal to 1. This case corresponds to the initial (nonrefined) fuzzy if-then rules extracted from the data set. Matching x_i to the set of fuzzy if-then rules with m parameters being equal to 1, we obtain a consequent denoted by $\{d_1^{(i)}, d_2^{(i)}, \ldots, d_K^{(i)}\}$, that is,

$$d_j^{(i)} = CF_j^{(i)} (1, 1, \ldots, 1) \tag{2.28}$$

$j = 1, 2, \ldots, K$. Suppose that x_i belongs to the jth class; we then define an index set I as

$$I = \left\{ i \,\middle|\, 1 \leq i \leq N,\ d_{j_i}^{(i)} > \max_{p \neq j_i} d_p^{(i)} \right\} \tag{2.29}$$

Equation (2.29) represents the indices of training objects that can be classified correctly by the initial fuzzy if-then rules. And then we can mathematically formulate the parameter refinement problem as the following programming problem with constraints:

$$
\left\{
\begin{array}{l}
\max \left(
\begin{array}{l}
E_f\left(g_1, g_2, \ldots, g_m\right) \\
= \displaystyle\sum_{i=1}^{N}\sum_{j=1}^{K}\left(CF_j^{(i)}\left(g_1, g_2, \ldots, g_m\right) \cdot \left(1 - CF_j^{(i)}\left(g_1, g_2, \ldots, g_m\right)\right)\right)
\end{array}
\right), \\
\text{Subject to} \quad CF_{ji}^{(i)} > \max_{p \neq j_i} CF_p^{(i)}, \; i \in I
\end{array}
\right.
$$

$$(2.30)$$

where the index set I is defined as (2.29). It is noted that the number of constraints in (2.30) is equal to the number of objects that can be correctly classified by the initial fuzzy if-then rules extracted from the training set.

From the globally weighted reasoning algorithm given in Section 2.4.2, we know that $CF_j^{(i)}\left(g_1, g_2, \ldots, g_m\right)$ is a linear combination of parameters $\left(g_1, g_2, \ldots, g_m\right)$. Therefore, Equation (2.30) is a quadratic programming problem with linear constraints. We now derive its standard mathematical form.

Suppose m initial if-then rules are classified into K groups (where K is the number of classes) and the kth group has if-then rules with the same consequent. The parameter vector is defined as

$$
\begin{aligned}
G &= \left(g_1, g_2, \ldots, g_m\right)^T \\
&= \left(\underline{g_1, g_2, \ldots, g_{r_1}}; \underline{g_{r_1+1}, g_{r_1+2}, \ldots, g_{r_1+r_2}}; \cdots; \underline{g_{r_1+\cdots+r_{K-1}+1}, \ldots, g_m}\right)^T \\
&= \left(G_1^T; G_2^T; \cdots; G_K^T\right)^T.
\end{aligned}
$$

$$(2.31)$$

According to the globally weighted reasoning algorithm given in Section 2.4.2, we match the ith training object to the K groups of initial if-then rules and then obtain a matching result, denoted by

$$
\begin{aligned}
A_i &= \left(a_{i1}, a_{i2}, \ldots, a_{im}\right)^T \\
&= \left(\underline{a_{i1}, a_{i2}, \ldots, a_{ir_1}}; \underline{a_{i(r_1+1)}, \ldots, a_{i(r_1+r_2)}}; \cdots; \underline{a_{i(r_1+\cdots+r_{K-1}+1)}, \ldots, a_{im}}\right)^T \\
&= \left(A_{i1}^T; A_{i2}^T; \ldots; A_{iK}^T\right)^T
\end{aligned}
$$

$$(2.32)$$

from which the index set I is determined by (2.29). According to the globally weighted reasoning algorithm given in Section 2.4.2, the objective function in (2.30) can be expressed as

$$E_f\left(g_1, g_2, \ldots, g_m\right)$$

$$= \sum_{i=1}^{N} \sum_{k=1}^{K} \left(G_k^T A_{ik}\left(1 - A_{ik}^T G_k\right)\right)$$

$$= \sum_{k=1}^{K} \left(G_k^T \left(\sum_{i=1}^{N} A_{ik}\right) - G_k^T \left(\sum_{i=1}^{N} A_{ik} A_{ik}^T\right) G_k\right)$$

$$= -G^T A G + B^T G, \tag{2.33}$$

where the matrix A and the vector B are defined as

$$A = \begin{pmatrix} \sum_{i=1}^{N} A_{i1} A_{i1}^T & & & \\ & \sum_{i=1}^{N} A_{i2} A_{i2}^T & & \\ & & \ddots & \\ & & & \sum_{i=1}^{N} A_{iK} A_{iK}^T \end{pmatrix}_{m \times m}, \quad B = \begin{pmatrix} \sum_{i=1}^{N} A_{i1} \\ \sum_{i=1}^{N} A_{i2} \\ \vdots \\ \sum_{i=1}^{N} A_{iK} \end{pmatrix}_{m \times 1}.$$

$$\tag{2.34}$$

Noting that the consequent of matching the ith training object to the initial set of fuzzy rules, that is, weighted fuzzy rules with all global weights being 1, is denoted by $\left\{d_1^{(i)}, d_2^{(i)}, \ldots, d_K^{(i)}\right\}$, we suppose $j_i = \text{argmax}_{1 \le j \le K} \, d_j^{(i)}$. Then the constraints given in (2.30) can be expressed as

$$G_{j_i}^T A_{ij_i} > G_k^T A_{ik}, \left(1 \le k \ne j_i \le K; i \in I\right). \tag{2.35}$$

In matrix form, the above constraints can be rewritten as

$$\begin{pmatrix} (C_1)_{(K-1) \times m} \\ (C_2)_{(K-1) \times m} \\ \vdots \\ (C_L)_{(K-1) \times m} \end{pmatrix}_{L(K-1) \times m} \times \begin{pmatrix} G_1 \\ G_2 \\ \vdots \\ G_K \end{pmatrix}_{m \times 1} > \begin{pmatrix} 0 \\ 0 \\ \vdots \\ 0 \end{pmatrix}_{m \times 1}, \tag{2.36}$$

where $L = |I|$, and for each $i \in I$,

$$(C_i)_{(K-1) \times m} = \begin{pmatrix} -A_{i1}^T & 0 & \cdots & A_{ij_i}^T & \cdots & 0 \\ 0 & -A_{i2}^T & \cdots & A_{ij_i}^T & \cdots & 0 \\ \cdots & \cdots & \cdots & \cdots & \cdots & \cdots \\ 0 & 0 & \cdots & A_{ij_i}^T & \cdots & -A_{iK}^T \end{pmatrix}. \tag{2.37}$$

Algorithm 2.6: Parameter Refinement Algorithm

Input: A given training set

Output: A group of weight parameters

1 Extracting a set of fuzzy if-then rules from a given training set according to a given learning algorithm such as fuzzy decision tree.

2 Dividing these rules into K groups (where K is the number of classes) so that rules in one group have the same consequent.

3 For each group, matching training objects to the initial if-then rules to obtain the vector A_i by (2.32).

4 Expressing the parameter vector as (2.31) and determining the index set I by (2.29).

5 Determining the integer j_i for each $i \in I$ according to $j_i = \arg\max_{1 \leq j \leq K} d_j^{(i)}$ which is defined as (2.28).

6 Solving the quadratic programming problem given by the quadratic objective function (2.33) subject to linear constraints (2.36).

7 Output the solution of (2.33), i.e., group of weight parameters.

Summarizing the earlier derivations, we give the following parameter refinement Algorithm 2.6.

Since the maximum fuzzy entropy is attained on the condition that all output components are 0.5, one may argue about how to determine the exact class when we use the maximum fuzzy entropy principle to adjust these weights, which leads to such a case that most class outputs are 0.5. Actually, since the number of training objects is much greater than the number of rules (weights) and many constraints exist, it is almost impossible that the weight adjustment based on maximum entropy brings about such a result that all class outputs are 0.5.

References

1. J. R. Quinlan. Induction of decision trees. *Machine Learning*, 1986, 1(1):81–106.
2. T. M. Tom. *Machine Learning*. China Machine Press, Beijing, China, 1997.
3. U. M. Fayyad, K. B. Irani. On the handling of continuous-valued attributes in decision tree generation. *Machine Learning*, 1992, 8:87–102.
4. L. Breiman, J. Friedman. *Classification and Regression Trees*. Wadsworth International Group, Belmont, CA, 1984.
5. T. Hastie, R. Tibshirani, J. Friedman. *The Elements of Statistical Learning—Data Mining, Inference, and Prediction*, 2nd edn. New York: Springer Science+Business Media, LLC, 2009.
6. M. Umano, H. Okamolo, I. Hatono, H. Tamura. Fuzzy decision trees by fuzzy ID3 algorithm and its application to diagnosis system. In *Proceedings of Third IEEE International Conference on Fuzzy Systems*, June 26–29, 1994, Orlando, Florida, Vol. 3, pp. 2113–2118.

7. Y. Yuan, M. J. Shaw. Induction of fuzzy decision trees. *Fuzzy Sets and Systems*, 1995, 69(2):125–139.
8. J. M. Adamo. Fuzzy decision trees. *Fuzzy Sets and Systems*, 1980, 4(3):207–219.
9. X. Z. Wang, E. C. C. Tsang, D. S. Yeung. A comparative study on heuristic algorithms for generating fuzzy decision trees. *IEEE Transactions on Systems, Man, and Cybernetics—Part B*, April 2001, 31(2):215–226.
10. S. Mitra, K. M. Konwar, S. K. Pal. Fuzzy decision tree, linguistic rules and fuzzy knowledge-based network: Generation and evaluation. *IEEE Transactions on Systems, Man, and Cybernetics—Part C*, 2002, 32(4):328–339.
11. C. Z. Janikow. Fuzzy decision tree: Issues and methods. *IEEE Transactions on System, Man, and Cybernetics—Part B*, 1998, 28(1):1–14.
12. J. H. Zhai. Fuzzy decision tree based on fuzzy-rough technique. *Soft Computing*, 2011, 15(6):1087–1096.
13. D. Dubois, H. Prade. Rough fuzzy sets and fuzzy rough sets. *International Journal of General Systems*, 1990, 17:191–208.
14. L. I. Kuncheva. Fuzzy rough sets: Application to feature selection. *Fuzzy Sets and Systems*, 1992, 51:147–153.
15. S. Nanda. Fuzzy rough sets. *Fuzzy Sets and Systems*, 1992, 45:157–160.
16. Y. Y. Yao. Combination of rough and fuzzy sets based on -level sets. In: *Rough Sets and Data Mining: Analysis for Imprecise Data*, Lin, T.Y. and Cercone, N. (Eds.), Kluwer Academic Publishers, Boston, MA, pp. 301–321, 1997.
17. Z. Pawlak. Rough sets. *International Journal of Information and Computer Sciences*, 1982, 11:341–356.
18. R. Jensen, Q. Shen. Fuzzy-rough data reduction with ant colony optimization. *Fuzzy Sets and Systems*, 2005, 149(1):5–20.
19. X. Z. Wang, C. R. Dong. Improving generalization of fuzzy if-then rules by maximizing fuzzy entropy. *IEEE Transactions on Fuzzy Systems*, 2009, 17(3):556–567.
20. D. Dubois, H. Prade. *Fundamentals of Fuzzy Sets*, Vol. 7, The Handbooks of Fuzzy Sets. Kluwer, Boston, MA, 2000.
21. P. Angelov, X. Zhou, F. Klawonn. Evolving fuzzy rule-based classifiers. In: *First 2007 IEEE International Conference on Computational Intelligence Applications for Signal and Image Processing*, April 1–5, 2007, Honolulu, HI, pp. 220–225.
22. D. S. Yeung, E. C. C. Tsang. Weighted fuzzy production rules. *Fuzzy Sets and Systems*, 1997, 88:299–313.
23. D. S. Yeung, X. Z. Wang, E. C. C. Tsang. Handling interaction in fuzzy production rule reasoning. *IEEE Transactions on Systems, Man and Cybernetics—Part B*, October 2004, 34(5):1979–1987.
24. E. C. C. Tsang, D. S. Yeung, J. W. T. Lee et al. Refinement of generated fuzzy production rules by using a fuzzy neural network. *IEEE Transactions on Systems, Man and Cybernetics—Part B*, February 2004, 34(1):409–418.
25. H. D. Cheng, Y. H. Chen, X. H. Jiang. Thresholding using two-dimensional histogram and fuzzy entropy principle. *IEEE Transactions on Image Processing*, April 2000, 9(4):732–735.

26. W. B. Tao, J. W. Tian, J. Liu. Image segmentation by three-level thresholding based on maximum fuzzy entropy and genetic algorithm. *Pattern Recognition Letters*, December 2003, 24(16):3069–3078.
27. C. E. Shannon. A mathematical theory of communication. *Bell System Technical*, January 1948, 27:379–423; 623–656.
28. A. D. Luca, S. Termin. A definition of a nonprobabilistic entropy in the setting of fuzzy sets theory. *International Journal of Control*, 1972, 20:301–312.

Chapter 3

Clustering under Uncertainty Environment

Clustering is a very old topic on which humans started to study several centuries ago. So far there have been a considerably great number of references regarding the clustering methodologies and algorithms [1,2]. This chapter would like to provide readers with some guidelines about clustering in uncertainty environment.

3.1 Introduction

Given a set of objects, crisp clustering means [3] to find a partition of the set, that is, a group of subsets, such that the intrasimilarity (the similarity within each subset) approaches maximum while the intersimilarity (similarity among the subsets) approaches minimum, where the similarity measure is a function defined on any pair of objects. Unlike supervised learning, objects processed in clustering have no labels. The partition of clustering is obtained based on the similarity between objects, and therefore, clustering is called unsupervised learning. Since clustering generally does not require prior knowledge and can acquire the inherent cluster information, it has been widely applied to many fields such as data mining, pattern recognition, machine learning, and decision-making support systems [1].

Fuzzy clustering [4] means to find a fuzzy partition of the set, that is, a group of fuzzy subsets. Fuzzy clustering has the same evaluation indices as the crisp clustering has, such as the intrasimilarity and intersimilarity. A difference between crisp clustering and fuzzy clustering is that crisp clustering has a clear boundary among the clusters while fuzzy clustering has not. Mathematically fuzzy clustering is an extension of crisp clustering from traditional sets to fuzzy sets. Practically, fuzzy clustering is more useful than crisp clustering since many clustering problems in a variety of domains have not clear boundaries.

Feature weight learning [5], which can be regarded as an extension of feature selection, is an important way to improve clustering performance. Feature weight learning can be modeled as an optimization problem of an evaluation function without constraints, which is usually solved by gradient descent techniques or differential evolution (DE) algorithms. When feature weights are incorporated into the clustering, we call it weighted clustering.

In this chapter, we first briefly introduce two types of clustering, that is, partition-based clustering and hierarchy-based clustering and then review the K-means algorithm and its fuzzy version. After that, a number of validation functions of clustering are discussed. Furthermore, feature weighted fuzzy clustering is introduced, and the feature weight learning techniques are addressed in detail. A new feature weight learning technique based on DE, that is, MEHDE (hybrid differential evolution with multistrategy cooperating evolution), is given for similarity-based fuzzy weighted clustering. And finally a comparison between MEHDE and several commonly used fuzzy clustering methods is conducted.

3.2 Clustering Algorithms Based on Hierarchy or Partition

So far, there have been a lot of clustering algorithms. According to the characteristics of algorithms dividing data, these algorithms are mainly classified into two categories: clustering algorithms based on hierarchy and on partition [1,3,6].

3.2.1 Clustering Algorithms Based on Hierarchy

Clustering algorithms based on hierarchy are top-down or bottom-up clustering algorithms [6]. Top-down clustering is a decomposition process. First, top-down decomposition considers all the data as one category. Second, it selects the most dissimilar two sets of data as two categories, and therefore, the number of clustering categories increases from 1 to 2. Repeat this process until respective categories form for each individual data. Bottom-up clustering is a process of aggregation. Bottom-up aggregation first divides all the individual data into respective categories. Then, it selects the two most similar data and aggregates them together. In this way, one category of clustering is reduced. Repeat this process until all the data are merged into one class. Top-down clustering is an inverse of bottom-up clustering. Crisp clustering algorithm DIANA (Divisive Analysis) [7] and transitive closure–based fuzzy clustering algorithm [8] are two common top-down clustering algorithms, while AGNES (AGglomerative NESting) [9] is a generally used bottom-up clustering algorithm. Overall, the mechanism of clustering algorithms based on hierarchy is simple, but practically it includes two problems. (1) The time complexity is large. (2) Once clustering errors are generated in the previous produced layer, it is almost impossible to correct these errors in the subsequent layers. To solve these problems, some improved algorithms of hierarchical clustering have been proposed, such as BIRCH [10], CURE [11], and ROCK [12].

Clustering algorithms based on partition randomly divide data into K categories according to the predefined number K of clusters. It then calculates the cluster centers for each category of data, and based on the new centers, it recalculates the category membership for each datum. The process mentioned earlier repeats until all categories of the data are not adjusted any more. Finally, the clustering results are obtained. This type of algorithms tries to make similar data into one category and dissimilar data into different categories through iterations. Hard K-means [2] and its fuzzy version [13] are commonly used clustering algorithms based on partition. These algorithms can achieve good results for data with uniform distribution, regular shape, and good dispersion. Otherwise, these algorithms are easy to converge to local optima. The hard K-means algorithm is sensitive to noise data because it uses a point to represent the cluster center. The improved K-central algorithm [14] uses a set of points to represent a clustering center; thereby, the effects of noise data can be reduced.

There is a widespread phenomenon in the real world, namely, one category contains a number of subclasses, and each subclass also contains a number of smaller subcategories. For instance, biology is a general class. It contains several subcategories: animals, plants, and microorganisms. And each subcategory can be divided into many smaller subcategories. For example, animals can be divided into chordate and nonchordate. Hierarchical tree structure can be used to describe this phenomenon, which is shown in Figure 3.1. In Figure 3.1, there are five classes of objects, namely, X_1, X_2, X_3, X_4, and X_5. The longitudinal axis of Figure 3.1 represents the similarity. When the similarity is 1, the five classes of objects have their respective categories. But with the decreasing of similarity, the objects are gradually merged, and eventually they are aggregated into one class. This phenomenon is described by hierarchical clustering algorithms.

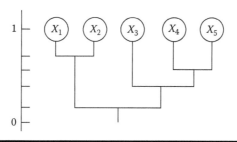

Figure 3.1   Schematic diagram of hierarchical clustering.

The clustering process, shown in Figure 3.1, is a bottom-up clustering algorithm. Initially, each object has its respective category. Then the two most similar classes are merged, and the number of clusters reduces to 1. It gradually aggregates until one category of objects is obtained. This process is called merging clustering. An inverse of the process shown in Figure 3.1 represents the top-down clustering. All the data belong to one class at the beginning. The most dissimilar two subsets of objects are selected to form two categories. This process repeats and repeats, and finally all the objects are divided into respective classes. This process is called decomposing clustering in which the number of clusters is constantly increased. Merging clustering and decomposing clustering are inversed to each other. Merging clustering will be introduced in details as follows.

Merging clustering merges according to the similarity between objects, in which the commonly used similarity measures are defined based on Euclidean distance. They are divided into the following four classes:

$$d_{\min}(C_i, C_j) = \min_{x \in C_i, x' \in C_j} |x - x'| \tag{3.1}$$

$$d_{\max}(C_i, C_j) = \max_{x \in C_i, x' \in C_j} |x - x'| \tag{3.2}$$

$$d_{avg}(C_i, C_j) = \frac{1}{n_i n_j} \sum_{x \in C_i} \sum_{x \in C_j} |x - x'| \tag{3.3}$$

$$d_{mean}(C_i, C_j) = |m_i - m_j| \tag{3.4}$$

where C_i and C_j represent the ith and the jth categories, respectively. Formula (3.1) shows that the minimum distance between the ith and the jth categories for all pairs (i, j) represents the similarity between two categories. As shown in Figure 3.2a, the smaller the minimum distance between two categories is, the more similar the two categories are. Formula (3.2) shows that the maximum distance between the ith and the jth categories for all data represents the similarity between two categories. As shown in Figure 3.2b, the smaller the maximum distance between the two categories is, the more similar the two categories are. A similar explanation can be given for formulae (3.3) and (3.4).

The bottom-up clustering algorithm by merging hierarchy is described as in Algorithm 3.1.

> **Example 3.1** Suppose there are five 2D data: $X = (x_1, x_2, x_3, x_4, x_5)$; each point x_i ($1 \leq i \leq 5$) is described by two attributes a_1 and a_2. The clustering process for the data shown in Table 3.1 is listed as follows:
>
> (1) *Initialization*: Each object forms a respective category at first, which gives five individual clusters in total. The distribution of the initial data is shown in Figure 3.3a. Calculate the pairwise distance to obtain the distance matrix D_1.

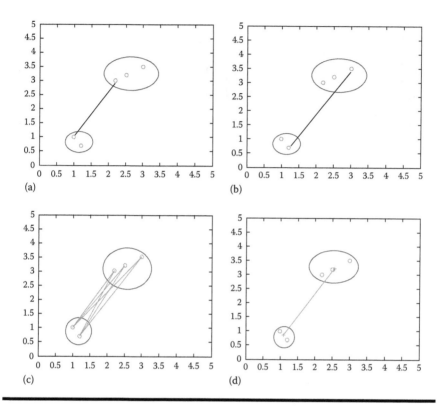

Figure 3.2 Schematic diagram of similarity measure in hierarchical clustering. (a) The minimum distance between classes; (b) the maximum distance between classes; (c) the average distance between classes; (d) the distance between cluster centers.

Algorithm 3.1: Bottom-Up Clustering Algorithm

Input: Continuous value data set without classes
Output: Clusters
1 Initialization: each object forms an individual category;
2 Update Clustering: calculate the distances between any pair of classes, and merge the two classes between which the distance attains the shortest;
3 Iteration: step 2 repeats until all the data are combined together into one category or a specified number of classes is reached.

Table 3.1 Hierarchical Clustering Data Points

	x_1	x_2	x_3	x_4	x_5
a_1	1.0	1.2	2.2	2.5	3.0
a_2	1.0	0.7	3.0	3.2	3.5

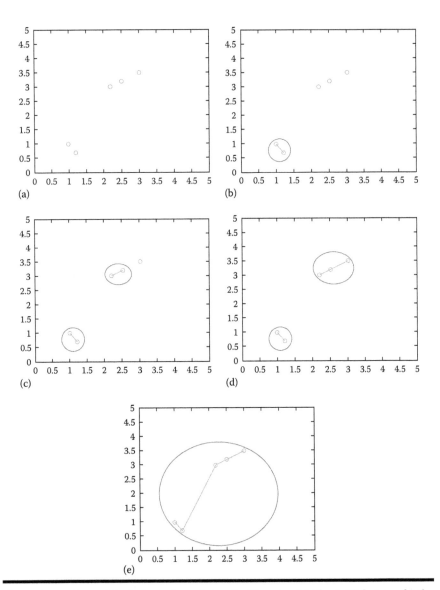

(a)   (b)   (c)   (d)   (e)

Figure 3.3 **Hierarchical clustering schematic diagram. (a) The initial state; (b) the first clustering results; (c) the second clustering results; (d) the third clustering results; (e) the fourth clustering results.**

(2) *The first clustering*: Select the minimum distance $d_{12}^1 = 0.2$ from D_1. Merge x_1 and x_2. The clustering is obtained: $\{x_1, x_2\}, \{x_3\}, \{x_4\}, \{x_5\}$, shown in Figure 3.3b.

(3) *The second clustering*: Calculate the distances between four classes, obtaining the distance matrix D_2. Select the second smallest distance $d_{34}^2 = 0.3$. Merge x_3 and x_4, obtaining the clusters $\{x_1, x_2\}, \{x_3, x_4\}, \{x_5\}$, shown in Figure 3.3c.

(4) *The third clustering*: Calculate the distances between three classes, obtaining the distance matrix D_3. Select the third smallest distance $d_{45}^3 = 0.5$. Merge x_5 and the combination of x_3 and x_4, obtaining the clusters $\{x_1, x_2\}, \{x_3, x_4, x_5\}$. Update $d_{35}^3 = d_{53}^3 = 0.5$ at the same time. It is shown in Figure 3.3d.

(5) *The fourth clustering*: Calculate the distances between two classes, obtaining the distance matrix D_4. Select the forth smallest distance $d_{23}^4 = 1$. Merge all the data into one category, and then obtain the clusters $\{x_1, x_2, x_3, x_4, x_5\}$, shown in Figure 3.3e. Update $d_{13}^4 = d_{14}^4 = d_{15}^4 = d_{24}^4 = d_{25}^4 = 1$ and $d_{31}^4 = d_{41}^4 = d_{55}^4 = d_{42}^4 = d_{52}^4 = 1$ at the same time.

$$D_1 = \begin{bmatrix} 0.0 & 0.2 & 1.2 & 1.5 & 2.0 \\ 0.2 & 0.0 & 1.0 & 1.3 & 1.8 \\ 1.2 & 1.0 & 0.0 & 0.3 & 0.8 \\ 1.5 & 1.3 & 0.3 & 0.0 & 0.5 \\ 2.0 & 1.8 & 0.8 & 0.5 & 0.0 \end{bmatrix} \quad D_2 = \begin{bmatrix} 0.0 & 0.2 & 1.2 & 1.5 & 2.0 \\ 0.2 & 0.0 & 1.0 & 1.3 & 1.8 \\ 1.2 & 1.0 & 0.0 & 0.3 & 0.8 \\ 1.5 & 1.3 & 0.3 & 0.9 & 0.5 \\ 2.0 & 1.8 & 0.8 & 0.5 & 0.0 \end{bmatrix}$$

$$D_3 = \begin{bmatrix} 0.0 & 0.2 & 1.2 & 1.5 & 2.0 \\ 0.2 & 0.0 & 1.0 & 1.3 & 1.8 \\ 1.2 & 1.0 & 0.0 & 0.3 & 0.5 \\ 1.5 & 1.3 & 0.3 & 0.0 & 0.5 \\ 2.0 & 1.8 & 0.5 & 0.5 & 0.0 \end{bmatrix} \quad D_4 = \begin{bmatrix} 0.0 & 0.2 & 1.0 & 1.0 & 1.0 \\ 0.2 & 0.0 & 1.0 & 1.0 & 1.0 \\ 1.0 & 1.0 & 0.0 & 0.3 & 0.5 \\ 1.0 & 1.0 & 0.3 & 0.0 & 0.5 \\ 1.0 & 1.0 & 0.5 & 0.5 & 0.0 \end{bmatrix}$$

The hierarchical clustering results based on the minimum distance are described earlier. Similarly, hierarchical clustering results based on the other distance measures, for example, maximum distance, average distance, and cluster center distance, can be gotten, respectively. We highlight the following points regarding different types of distance measures in hierarchical clustering:

1. Hierarchical clustering based on the minimum distance is susceptible to chain effects. That is, if there are noise points between two classes, the clustering results are usually unclear for the two classes of data. The final clustering results are prone to long-type shape.

2. Hierarchical clustering based on the maximum distance is suitable for handling data that are spherical, evenly distributed, and having roughly same volume. Otherwise, if the data do not follow these properties, the hierarchical clustering based on the maximum distance may produce incorrect results.

3. Hierarchical clustering based on the two measures uses the nearest or farthest distance from one point to another within a class to represent the distance between two classes. Since the shapes of the clustering data are diverse, a point within a class cannot represent the shape or density of the class clearly. Thus, the two types of hierarchical clustering results are sensitive to noise points. Hierarchical clustering based on mean distance and class-center distance is the average of these two clustering algorithms, which is less affected by noise data.

4. Hierarchical clustering can handle data with different shapes based on different similarities. But the time complexity of algorithm is quite large. The large-scale data cannot be dealt effectively.

3.2.2 Clustering Algorithms Based on Partition

The time complexity of hierarchical clustering is large, and therefore, it usually cannot handle large-scale data. In comparison with clustering based on hierarchy, partition clustering algorithm is more effective for large-scale data. In this section, the hard K-means algorithm [3] and fuzzy C-means (FCM) algorithm [4] are used to illustrate the ideological basis of partition clustering.

The basic idea of hard K-means algorithm is explained as follows. It first forms a partition with K clusters according to the cluster number K and then iteratively adjusts the cluster and cluster centers until the categories to which data belong no longer change. Suppose $X = (x_1, x_2, \ldots, x_n)$ is the set of objects to be clustered. Each x_i $(1 \leq i \leq n)$ consists of d attributes $a_1, a_2, \ldots, a_d$. Each x_i is denoted by $x_i = (x_{i1}, x_{i2}, \ldots, x_{id})$, where x_{ij} represents the value of the jth attribute of object x_j. The distance between any two data points is the Euclidean distance. The center of the ith class is defined as v_i, where any component of v_i represents the average of the corresponding attribute values, that is, $v_{ij} = \frac{1}{|v_i|} \sum_{j=1}^{|v_i|} x_{jq}$, $(i = 1, \ldots, K; q = 1, \ldots, d)$. The algorithm termination condition is that the categories of all the data are no longer changed, which corresponds to minimize the objective function $G = \sum_{i=1}^{K} \sum_{x_i \in v_i} d_{ij}$, where d_{ij} is the Euclidean distance between x_i and the center v_j of the jth class. When the objective function G is not changed any longer or attains a required threshold, the algorithm ends. The hard K-means algorithm [3] is described as in Algorithm 3.2.

Algorithm 3.2: Hard K-Means Algorithm

Input: Continuous value data set without classes
Output: Clusters

1 Initialization: The number of clusters is determined as K. Randomly select K points as the cluster center v_i $(1 \leq i \leq K)$;

2 Updating the cluster: Calculate the distances between each data point and each of the K centers v_i; and for each point, select the nearest cluster center to which the datum belongs at the current step;

3 Updating the cluster center: Take the averaged attribute-values of data-points that belong to the same class as the updated cluster center according to the new class of each point;

4 Iteration: Calculate the objective function value $G = \sum_{i=1}^{K} \sum_{x_i \in v_i} d_{ij}$ corresponding to the partition. Repeat Steps 2–4 until G value does not change any longer or attains an expected threshold.

Table 3.2   Hard *K*-Means Clustering Data Points

	x_1	x_2	x_3	x_4	x_5	x_6
a_1	1.0	1.2	1.5	2.2	2.5	3.0
a_2	1.0	0.7	1.2	3.0	3.2	3.5

Example 3.2 Suppose there are six 2D data points as shown in Table 3.2. Clustering the six data points with hard *K*-means algorithm.

The initial state of the data distribution is shown in Figure 3.4a.

(a) *Initialization*: Suppose the six data points are divided into $K = 2$ classes. Randomly select x_2 and x_3 as two cluster centers, which are represented by "+."

(b) *The first clustering*: Calculate the distances between each cluster center and each data point based on the cluster centers shown in Figure 3.4a. Select the nearest cluster center as the category of the current data point. Two clusters x_1, x_2 and x_3, x_4, x_5, x_6 are obtained after the first iteration, which are described as the two circles in Figure 3.4b, $G = 3.935$.

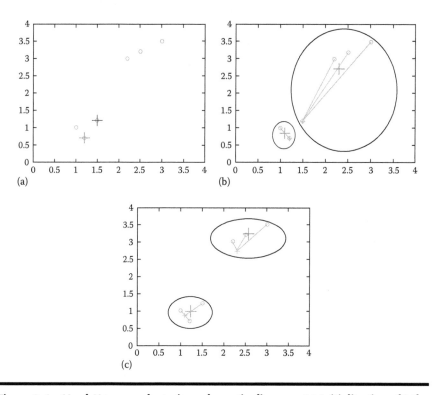

Figure 3.4   Hard *K*-means clustering schematic diagram. (a) Initialization; (b) the first clustering and the updated results of cluster centers; (c) the second clustering and the updated results of cluster centers.

(c) *Updating the cluster center of the first clustering*: Recalculate the cluster centers of the two classes according to the distribution of data shown in Figure 3.4b to obtain two amplified bigger plus signs shown in Figure 3.4c.

Practically there are several problems in hard K-means algorithm. (1) Clustering process is equivalent to iteratively minimize the objective function. This iterative process is sensitive to initial value, and different initial values may guide the function to converge to different solutions. Sometimes it converges to local optima. To avoid falling into local optima, this algorithm can be run multiple times randomly. (2) Hard K-means algorithm uses a center point to represent a whole class, which leads to its sensitivity to noise data. (3) The clustering results of hard K-means algorithm make the data either belong or not belong to a certain category. This kind of results cannot describe the fuzzy phenomenon in the real world.

Considering that hard K-means algorithm cannot handle the fuzzy problems, Bezdek et al. [4] proposed a fuzzy version of hard K-means in 1973. It is the FCM algorithm that uses membership to determine the degree of each data point belonging to a cluster. FCM algorithm divides n objects $X = \{x_1, x_2, \ldots, x_n\}$ into K fuzzy groups, and calculates the cluster center v_i ($i = 1, 2, \ldots, K$) of each group so that the nonsimilarity index value function reaches the minimum. The main difference between FCM algorithm and hard K-means algorithm is that a membership value in the interval [0, 1] for each given data point is used to determine its degree of belonging to every group. It introduces a fuzzy partition, and the elements of membership matrix U take values in [0, 1]. After a normalization, the sum of memberships of a data set always equals to 1, that is, we have

$$\sum_{i=1,\ldots,K} u_{ij} = 1, \quad \forall j = 1, 2, \ldots, n. \tag{3.5}$$

The objective function of FCM is described as follows:

$$J(U, v_1, v_2, \ldots, v_K; X) = \sum_{i=1}^{K} \sum_{j=1}^{n} u_{ij}^m d_{ij}^2, \tag{3.6}$$

where
$X = x_i | i = 1, 2, \ldots, n$
$x_i = (x_{i1}, x_{i2}, \ldots, x_{id})$
u_{ij} denoting the membership degree of the jth object belonging to the ith cluster takes value between 0 and 1
v_i is the cluster center of the fuzzy group
$d_{ij} = \sqrt{\sum_{k=1}^{d}(v_{ik} - x_{jk})^2}$ is the Euclidean distance between the ith cluster center and the jth data point
$m \in [1, \infty)$ is a weighted index, and we generally suppose $m = 2$

A new objective function is constructed as (3.7) that can be used to obtain the necessary condition that makes (3.6) reach its minimum:

$$J(U, v_1, \ldots, c_K, \lambda_1, \ldots, \lambda_n) = J(U, v_1, \ldots, c_K) + \sum_{j=1}^{n} \lambda_j \left(\sum_{i=1}^{K} u_{ij} - 1 \right)$$

$$= \sum_{i=1}^{K} \sum_{j=1}^{n} u_{ij}^m d_{ij}^2 + \sum_{j=1}^{n} \lambda_j \left(\sum_{i=1}^{K} u_{ij} - 1 \right), \quad (3.7)$$

where λ_j, $j = 1, \ldots, n$ are Lagrange multipliers of the n constraints. Derivating all the input parameters, we obtain the necessary condition that makes expression (3.7) attains its minimum. That is,

$$v_i = \frac{\sum_{j=1}^{n} u_{ij}^m x_j}{\sum_{j=1}^{n} u_{ij}^m} \quad (3.8)$$

$$u_{ij} = \frac{1}{\sum_{k=1}^{K} (d_{ij}/d_{kj})^{2/(m-1)}}. \quad (3.9)$$

The FCM [4] is described as in Algorithm 3.3.

The clustering process of FCM algorithm is similar to hard K-means algorithm. The difference is the calculation formulae used to update the clustering and cluster center. FCM algorithm introduces fuzzy membership to hard K-means algorithm, which extends the application area of hard K-means algorithm to fuzzy environment. In most real applications, FCM algorithm performs better than hard K-means algorithm.

Algorithm 3.3: Fuzzy C-Means Algorithm

Input: Continuous value data set without classes
Output: Fuzzy clusters
1 Initialize the membership matrix U with the random numbers in [0, 1], such that the matrix satisfies the constraint (3.5);
2 Calculate K cluster centers v_i, $i = 1, \ldots, K$ based on formula (3.8);
3 Calculate the value function based on formula (3.6). If it is less than a given threshold or the variation in comparison with the result of the former value function is less than a threshold, the algorithm ends;
4 Calculate a new matrix U based on formula (3.9); back to 2.

3.3 Validation Functions of Clustering

Data processed by clustering algorithms are without category tags, but the clustering results are used to mark the categories of the data. Under the premise of no any prior knowledge, how to evaluate the clustering results is a problem worthy of study. In order to evaluate the clustering algorithms, the researchers introduced a clustering criterion function that can be used not only to evaluate the quality of clustering but also to select the optimal parameter values for the clustering algorithms (e.g., to select the cluster number of hard K-means algorithm). Commonly used clustering criterion functions include error square sum and dispersion [15–18].

Suppose there are n objects $X = \{x_1, \ldots, x_n\}$. They are partitioned into K categories by the clustering algorithm. The cluster center of every category is v_i ($i = 1, \ldots, K$). There are n_i data for each category. The cluster center v_i of each category is defined as

$$v_i = \frac{1}{n_i} \sum_{x_j \in v_i} x_j. \tag{3.10}$$

The error square sum criterion is defined as

$$J_e = \sum_{i=1}^{K} \sum_{x_j \in v_i} \|x_j - v_i\|, \tag{3.11}$$

where $\|x_j - v_i\|$ is the difference between the data of the ith class and their cluster center v_i. Equation (3.11) represents the sum of distance between every data point and its center, that is, the error square sum. The smaller the error square sum criterion value J_e is, the closer the data and their cluster centers are. In other words, the obtained cluster is very compact, which indicates a good clustering result. The minimum value of error square sum criterion J_e usually corresponds to a good clustering result.

When the cluster center of each class is not defined, the error square sum criterion J_e can be described as

$$J_e = \frac{1}{2n^2} \sum_{i=1}^{K} \sum_{x_k, x_k' \in v_i} \|x_k - x_k'\|, \tag{3.12}$$

where $\|x_k - x_k'\|$ still is the difference between any two data of the ith category. Formula (3.12) represents the average of the difference between any two data within a class. Similarly, the smaller the value of formula (3.12) is, the better the clustering is.

Good clustering results not only require the same class of data "holding together," but also require different classes of data keep away from each other, which lead to the dispersion criterion.

The cluster center v_i is defined as the average of vectors in the ith class. The amount of data in the ith category is n_i. The weighted average of class mean vectors is marked as the general mean vector:

$$v = \frac{1}{n} \sum_{i=1}^{K} n_i v_i. \tag{3.13}$$

The scatter matrix of the ith class, which describes the dispersion degree of the data within the ith class, is defined as

$$S_i = \sum_{x \in v_i} (x - v_i)(x - v_i)^T. \tag{3.14}$$

The sum of all the within class scatter matrices is $S_W = \sum_{i=1}^{K} S_i$. The scatter matrix among the classes describes the dispersion degree among different classes. It is defined as follows:

$$S_B = \sum_{i=1}^{K} n_i (v_i - v)(v_i - v)^T. \tag{3.15}$$

The clustering quality can be measured based on the determinant values of the scatter matrices within class S_W and scatter matrix S_B among classes. The smaller the determinant value within class scatter matrix S_W, the more compact the data within a class are. The larger the determinant value between class scatter matrix S_B is, the more separate the data with different classes are. The determinant within class scatter matrix S_W can be denoted as $tr(S_W) = \sum_{i=1}^{K} tr(S_i) = \sum_{i=1}^{K} \sum_{x_j \in v_i} \| x_j - v_i \|$, while the determinant between class scatter matrix S_B can be denoted as $tr(S_B) = \sum_{i=1}^{K} n_i \| v_i - v \|$. It is easy to see that minimizing the determinant value within class scatter matrix S_W or maximizing the determinant value between class scatter matrix S_B is equivalent to minimizing the error square sum functions.

3.4 Feature Weighted Fuzzy Clustering

Let $X = \{x_1, x_2, \ldots, x_n\}$ represent n given samples, where x_i is a d-dimensional real vector, that is, $x_i = (x_{i1}, x_{i2}, \ldots, x_{id}) \in R^d$. Let $w = (w_1, w_2, \ldots, w_d)$ represent feature weighted vector, where w_i $(1 \leq i \leq d)$ is the significance degree of the ith feature.

In similarity-based fuzzy weighted clustering [5], the samples are split to several subsets (clusters) based on the similarity matrix S. The concept of similarity matrix is defined as

$$S = \left(\delta_{pq}^{(w)} \right)_{n \times n}, \tag{3.16}$$

where $\delta_{pq}^{(w)}$ $(1 \leq p, q \leq n)$ represents the weighted similarity degree between the sample x_p and x_q, and

$$\delta_{pq}^{(w)} = \delta^{(w)}(x_p, x_q) = \frac{1}{1 + \beta d_{pq}^{(w)}}. \tag{3.17}$$

In formula (3.17), parameter β is a positive real value that can be determined by the following formula:

$$\frac{2}{n(n-1)} \sum_{q>p} \delta_{pq}^{(1)} = 0.5, \tag{3.18}$$

where $\delta_{pq}^{(1)}$ represents the similarity degree when every weight is set to 1 (that is the case of no weight). Formula (3.18) implies that an assumption to determine β, that is, the similarities degree of samples uniformly distribute around 0.5 when no other information about sample similarity is given. The $\delta_{pq}^{(w)}$ in formula (3.17) denotes the weighted Euclidean distance between samples x_p and x_q:

$$d_{pq}^{(w)} = d_{pq}^{(w)}(x_p, x_q) = \left(\sum_{j=1}^{d} w_j^2 (x_{pj} - x_{qj})^2 \right)^{1/2}. \tag{3.19}$$

From Equations (3.16) and (3.17), we know that the similarity matrix S is a fuzzy matrix. The fuzziness of a similarity matrix S is defined as follows [19]:

$$E(w) = \frac{2}{n(n-1)} \sum_{q>p} \frac{1}{2} \left(\delta_{pq}^{(w)} \left(1 - \delta_{pq}^{(1)} \right) + \delta_{pq}^{(1)} \left(1 - \delta_{pq}^{(w)} \right) \right), \tag{3.20}$$

where n represents the number of samples. By (3.20), it is easy to see that the degree of fuzziness reaches its maximum when the similarity degree between any two of the samples is 0.5, whereas it reaches its minimum when those similarity degrees are 1 or 0. What is more, the smaller the fuzziness degree is, the clearer the clustering result is. Otherwise, it is hard to obtain the clear clustering result since many uncertainties exist. Moreover, from (3.17), (3.19), and (3.20), it is easy to know that the fuzziness degree is changing with the adjustment of feature weights. Based on the analysis mentioned earlier, the model of weight learning is designed as follows:

$$\min_{w} E(w). \tag{3.21}$$

In (3.20), the definition of fuzziness comes from the following simple function:

$$f(x, y) = x(1 - y) + y(1 - x), \quad 0 \leq x, y \leq 1. \tag{3.22}$$

We have the following properties [20]:

$$\begin{cases} \frac{\partial f}{\partial x} > 0, & \text{if } y < 0.5; \\ \frac{\partial f}{\partial x} < 0, & \text{if } y > 0.5. \end{cases} \tag{3.23}$$

That is to say, by minimizing the fuzziness of similarity matrix, the following results can be obtained: (1) it may make $\delta_{pq}^{(w)}$ more closely approximate 0 by adjusting the weights if the similarity degree between x_p and x_q is smaller than 0.5 in the case of weight being 1 (i.e., $\delta_{pq}^{(1)} < 0.5$); (2) it may make $\delta_{pq}^{(w)}$ more closely approximate 1 by adjusting the weights if the similarity degree between x_p and x_q is larger than 0.5 in the case of weight being 1 (i.e., $\delta_{pq}^{(1)} > 0.5$). As a result, the fuzziness of similarity may be decreased after the model is weighted according to (3.21), and then the hardness of obtaining clear clustering is reduced. At the same time, it makes the similarity degrees of the samples among the same cluster larger, and the similarity degrees among the different clusters smaller. Thus, a better clustering result is obtained [5].

Once the weights are determined, the clustering is then determined by using similarity-based fuzzy clustering algorithms. The most common algorithms include similarity matrix's transitive closure clustering, SMTC-C [21], W-SMTC-C [22], and fuzzy C-means (FCM) [4].

Gradient descent techniques can be used to solve the optimization model given in formula (3.21). To overcome some defects of the search algorithm based on gradient descent, an improved DE algorithm [20] will be given in the next section, which is proposed to solve the model given in (3.21), to find the optimal feature weights, and finally to improve the performance of fuzzy clustering based on similarity.

3.5 Weighted Fuzzy Clustering Based on Differential Evolution

In this section, we first discuss the basic procedure of DE and a variety of common DE strategies. And then a new DE algorithm based on multi-evolutionary strategy is proposed [20]. Finally, we introduce a kind of weighted fuzzy clustering algorithm based on an improved DE mechanism [20].

3.5.1 Differential Evolution and Dynamic Differential Evolution

3.5.1.1 Basic Differential Evolution Algorithm

The basic DE algorithm [20,23–25] is a kind of swarm optimization algorithm based on real number encoding. Let the objective function $f(x) : R^d \rightarrow R(LB \leq x \leq UB)$ be a real number function, where $LB = \left(x_1^{\min}, \ldots, x_d^{\min}\right)$ and

$UB = \left(x_1^{\max}, \ldots, x_d^{\max}\right)$ represent lower bound and upper bound vectors of d-dimensional independent variables, namely, $x_j^{\min} \leq x_j \leq x_j^{\max}$ $(j = 1, \ldots, d)$.

The goal of this algorithm is to find $f(x^*)$ that is the minimum or almost approximate minimum of objective function $f(x)$. Similar to other swarm optimization algorithms, DE obtains the optimal solution or approximate optimal solution of the objective function based on iteratively performing a series of evolution operations on a set of candidate solutions.

In the basic DE algorithm, it is necessary to assign four parameters: the population size NP, the maximum number of iterations MI, differential zoom factor F, and crossover probability CR before performing the algorithm. And then the algorithm performs the following steps iteratively to acquire the solution [24,25]:

1. The population initialization: Let the number of generations $G = 0$ complete the initialization of population according to the determined population size. The initialization equation is listed as follows:

$$x_{ij}(0) = x_j^{\min} + \text{rand}(0, 1)$$
$$\times \left(x_j^{\max} - x_j^{\min}\right), \quad (i = 1, \ldots, NP;\ j = 1, \ldots, d), \quad (3.24)$$

   where $x_{ij}(0)$ represents the jth element of the ith candidate solution in the 0th generation and $\text{rand}(0, 1)$ represents a random number that follows the uniform distribution on interval $[0, 1]$.

2. Calculating the individual fitness of the initial population: Calculate the fitness $f(x_i)$ of every individual x_i in a population according to the objective function $f(x)$.

3. For every individual $x_{i,G}$ in the current generation, perform the following evolution operations in turn:

   a. *Variation*: Based on several different individuals that are randomly selected from current generation (i.e., the Gth generation), generate a variation $v_{i,G}$ according to the selected mutation strategy. Several common variation strategies are shown in the following formulae (3.25) through (3.29)

$$\text{DE/rand/1: } v_{i,G} = x_{p1,G} + F\left(x_{p2,G} - x_{p3,G}\right) \qquad (3.25)$$

$$\text{DE/rand/2: } v_{i,G} = x_{p1,G} + F\left(x_{p2,G} - x_{p3,G}\right) + F\left(x_{p4,G} - x_{p5,G}\right) \quad (3.26)$$

$$\text{DE/best/1: } v_{i,G} = x_{best,G} + F\left(x_{p1,G} - x_{p2,G}\right) \qquad (3.27)$$

$$\text{DE/best/2: } v_{i,G} = x_{best,G} + F\left(x_{p1,G} - x_{p2,G}\right) + F\left(x_{p3,G} - x_{p4,G}\right) \quad (3.28)$$

$$\text{DE/rand-to-best/1: } v_{i,G} = x_{i,G} + F\left(x_{best,G} - x_{i,G}\right) + F\left(x_{p1,G} - x_{p2,G}\right)$$
$$(3.29)$$

where p_1, p_2, p_3, p_4 are four different integers that are randomly selected from the set of subscripts $1, 2, \ldots, i - 1, i + 1, \ldots, NP$. And $x_{best,G}$ is an individual with the smallest fitness in the Gth generation, that is, the best individual.

b. *Cross:* By using crossover probability CR, the individual $x_{i,G}$ and its corresponding variation $v_{i,G}$ generate a middle individual $t_{i,G}$. Common crossover strategy includes the binomial crossover and the exponential crossover. Basic binomial crossover strategy is listed in the following equation:

$$
t_{i,G}^{j} = \begin{cases} v_{i,G}^{j}, & \text{if } (\text{rand}_j[0, 1) < CR) \text{ or } j = j_{\text{rand}} \\ x_{i,G}^{j}, & \text{otherwise} \end{cases}, \tag{3.30}
$$

where

$t_{i,G}^{j}$ represents the jth element of the middle individual corresponding to the individuals $x_{i,G}^{j}$

j_{rand} represents an integer that is randomly selected from the set of integers $\{1, 2, \ldots, d\}$

Its purpose is to ensure that there exists at least one element in the middle individual $t_{i,G}$, which is selected from variation $v_{i,G}$, in the procedure of crossover.

c. *Selection:* Check whether the values of the new generated middle variable $t_{i,G}$ are beyond the bound or not. For those elements beyond the bound, change their values according to a certain strategy until all elements are within the range determined by the upper bound vector UB and the lower bound vector LB of the variable. Then, calculate the fitness $f(t_{i,G})$ of the middle individual $t_{i,G}$. Finally, conduct selection operation according to the following equation:

$$
x_{i,G+1} = \begin{cases} t_{i,G}, & \text{if } f(t_{i,G}) < f(x_{i,G}) \\ x_{i,G}, & \text{otherwise} \end{cases}. \tag{3.31}
$$

4. Check whether the termination condition of the algorithm is satisfied or not. If not, let $G = G + 1$, go to step 3; otherwise, go to step 5.
5. Output the best individual vector of the current generation as the final solution of algorithm.

In the basic DE algorithms [23–25], the commonly used algorithm termination conditions include the following: (1) the evolution generation number reaches the maximum number of iterations MI, (2) the optimal solution of the objective function value is smaller than a given threshold (commonly used one is the minimum of objective function $f(x^*) = 0$), and (3) other termination conditions specified by the user.

In addition, it is easy to know by the previous algorithm steps, in the G generation mutation of the basic DE algorithm, variation and other operations are based on the individuals in the population of Gth generation. And the best individual $x_{best,G}$ in the Gth iteration keeps invariant. It increases the stability and robustness of the algorithm, but it is not helpful for the algorithm's convergence speed [26]. As a result, some scholars proposed the dynamic DE algorithm (dynamic differential evolution [DDE]) [27]. We will discuss the main ideas of DDE in the next section.

To clearly state, we abbreviate mutation strategy DE/rand/1 and binomial crossover strategy of DE algorithm as "DE/rand /1/ bin." Similarly, the other mutation strategy of DE can be respectively abbreviated as "DE/rand /2/ bin," "DE/best/ 1/ bin," "DE/best /2/bin," "DE/rand-to-best/1/bin," etc. The pseudocode and the flowchart of the basic DE algorithm "DE/rand/1/bin" are, respectively, shown in Algorithm 3.4 and Figure 3.5.

In Algorithm 3.4, $f(x) : R^d \rightarrow R$ is the objective function, $LB \leq x \leq UB$, and $LB = \left(x_1^{\min}, \ldots, x_d^{\min}\right)$, $UB = \left(x_1^{\max}, \ldots, x_d^{\max}\right)$; NP is the population size; MI is the maximum number of iterations; CR is crossover probability; F is the differential zoom factor. $f(x_{best,G})$ is the returned value representing the minimum

---

Algorithm 3.4: Basic Differential Evolution Algorithm

    Input: $f(x), LB, UB, NP, MI, CR$ and F.

    Output: $f(x_{best,G})$ and $x_{best,G}$.

1 Let $G = 0$, according to (3.24) initialize the population $P(0)$;

2 Compute the finesses of all individuals in $P(0)$, and find the initial optimal individual $x_{best,0}$;

3 Check whether the termination condition is satisfied. If yes, go to step 13; otherwise, go to step 4;

4 **for** *(each individual $x_{i,G}$ in the Gth generation)* **do**

5   Generate the variation $v_{i,G}$ according to (3.25) through (3.29);

6   Generate the middle individual $t_{i,G}$ according to the binomial crossover strategy given in (3.30), and compute $f(t_{i,G})$;

7   Generate the ith individual $x_{i,G+1}$ in the $(G + 1)$th generation population according to the selection strategy given in (3.31);

8   **if** $(f(x_{i,G+1}) < f(x_{best,G+1}))$ **then**

9 | $x_{best,G+1} = x_{i,G}$;

10   **end**

11 **end**

12 Let $G = G + 1$, go to step 3;

13 Return $f(x_{best,G})$ and $x_{best,G}$.

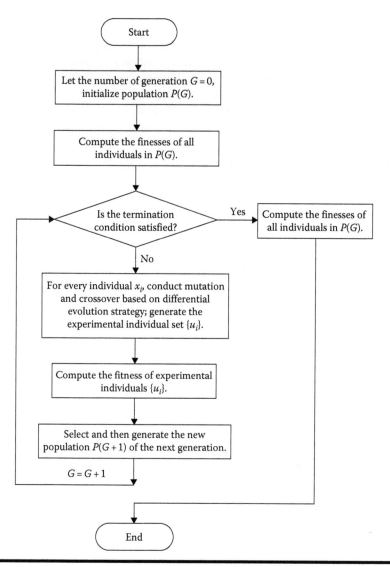

Figure 3.5   The flowchart of the basic differential evolution algorithm.

of the objective on function f on the given input space, and $x_{best,G}$ is corresponding optimal solution.

3.5.1.2 Dynamic Differential Evolution Algorithm

To improve the convergence speed of traditional DE algorithm, Qing [27], proposed a DDE algorithm. The main idea of the DDE is that, in the process of evolution of every generation of DE, a new individual with better fitness selected in the current population immediately replace the corresponding old individuals, and the best individual is then dynamically updated according to the new added individual. Thus, when we conduct searching according to certain evolutionary strategy given in (3.25) through (3.29), the individual randomly selected to conduct mutation and the current optimal individual $x_{best,G}$ are always based on the latest population. As a result, the algorithm has stronger performance of local search and quicker convergence speed. Furthermore, the algorithm has the less space complexity since the dynamically updating population does not need additional space to store the next generation.

Similar to those DE algorithms with the different mutation strategies, we, respectively, adopt the evolutionary strategy (3.25) through (3.29) and binomial crossover strategy of DDE algorithm and so on, denoted by "DDE/rand/1/bin," "DDE/rand/2/bin," "DDE/best/1/bin," "DDE/best/2/bin," "DDE/rand-to-best/1/bin," and so on.

Generally speaking, in comparison with the traditional DE algorithms, DDE has greedier search bias, stronger global search ability, and quicker search speed. However, the traditional DE has better stability and stronger global searching ability. Considering optimization problems with various complexities, to obtain a good result and acceptable search efficiency, we should balance three aspects of the algorithms, that is, the local search ability, the global search ability, and the algorithm convergence speed. In the next section, we will introduce how to balance two types of search strategies in the algorithm so that the algorithm can reserve as much advantages of DE and DDE as possible.

3.5.2 Hybrid Differential Evolution Algorithm Based on Coevolution with Multi-Differential Evolution Strategy

A lot of existing research works have shown that the DE algorithms using different DE strategies have different performance in solving a variety of optimization problems [28–31]. That is to say, one DE strategy is only suitable for solving some or certain kinds of the optimization problems. This result is consistent with the famous "no free lunch theorem." That is, if there is no prior assumption, there is not such a learning algorithm or classifier that is always superior to another learning algorithm or classifier. Here a question is, in the lack of prior knowledge of optimization problems (it is the fact in the majority applications), what evolution strategy should be selected to perform the DE algorithm for solving the specific problem? To answer this question, generally speaking, we have two solutions: (1) to solve the problem by using the traditional single evolution strategy DE algorithms and find the optimal result by simultaneously using different evolutionary strategies and (2) to solve the problem without considering the problem itself by using DE algorithm based on multievolutionary strategy, which usually has an improved stability and accuracy. Obviously, the first plan needs a large computational cost, and the cost will become larger especially when the problem is more complex. Moreover, the stability of this kind of algorithms is poor. The second plan, which ignores the problem itself and provides a solution to a wide range of problems, boosts the adaptability of problems. In comparison with the single differential evolution strategy DE, multiple difference strategy usually improves search efficiency, stability, and accuracy of DE algorithm.

1. We chose five kinds of mutation strategies to build the DE process in MEHDE [20,31], which is a multiple DES method with hybrid DE. They are rand/1, rand/2, best/1, best/2, rand-to-best/1. In these mutation strategies, some have a stronger global searching ability (such as rand/1, rand/2) in boosting the diversity of population, some have a stronger local search ability of strategy (such as best/1, best/2) in improving the convergence speed.

2. The improved algorithm includes evolution strategies based both on DE and on DDE. Just as mentioned in the previous section, evolution strategies based on DE and on DDE have their respective advantages and disadvantages. Merging both strategies into MEHDE expects to reserve their advantages and to avoid its disadvantages.

3. To save the computation time, in each generation of MEHDE evolution, only an evolution strategy is orderly selected to complete mutation and crossover of the current individual $x_{i,G}$ and to get its corresponding middle individual $v_{i,G}$, and then an evolution is finished by the selection. For the next individual $x_{i+1,G}$, another DE strategy in the strategy pool is used to complete the evolution. This process repeats until a termination condition is met. It is easy to see that MEHDE does not need extra computational amount in comparison with the single differential evolution strategy DE/DDE.

4. Many studies have shown that DE based on binomial crossover strategy is often superior to DE based on the index cross strategy [26]. This is why MEHDE adopts the binomial crossover strategy to complete the crossover.

In the candidate pool of DE strategies of MEHDE, we place 10 strategies that are abbreviated and listed in Algorithm 3.5. In addition, MEHDE introduces an indicator variable IV that is used to select DE strategy for the current individual $x_{i,G}$. In the beginning of algorithm, IV is initialized to 0. Then during the iteration of the Gth generation, IV is updated based on the following formula (3.32):

$$IV_{new} = \begin{cases} IV + 1, & \text{if } (IV + 1) < 10; \\ IV + 1 - 10, & \text{else} \end{cases} \tag{3.32}$$

and then IV_{new} DE strategies are selected from the candidate pool of DE strategy to complete an evolution of the current individual $x_{i,G}$, and let $IV = IV_{new}$. The algorithm stops when the evolution for every individual finishes.

Algorithm 3.5: Hybrid Differential Evolution Algorithm

 Input: $f(x), LB, UB, NP, MI, CR, F$ and DES.
 Output: $f(x_{best,G})$ and $x_{best,G}$.
 1 Let $G = 0, IV = 0$, according to (3.24) initialize the population $P(0)$;
 2 Compute the finesses of all individuals in $P(0)$, and find the initial optimal individual $x_{best,0}$;
 3 Check whether a termination condition is satisfied. If yes, go to step 13; otherwise, let $P(G+1) = P(G)$ and go to step 4;
 4 **for** (*each individual $x_{i,G}$ in the Gth generation*) **do**
 5   Calculate IV_{new} according to (3.32);
 6   Based on the IV_{new} evolution strategy in the candidate pool of differential evolution strategies DES, complete the mutation and crossover. If it is based on the DE evolutionary strategy, then complete variation based on $P(G)$ and $x_{best,G}$; otherwise, complete variation based on $P(G+1)$ and x_{best}. And then obtain the middle individuals $t_{i,G}$, and compute $f(t_{i,G})$;
 7   Update the ith individual $x_{x,G+1}$ in the Gth generation population $P(G+1)$ according to the selection strategy given in (3.31);
 8   **if** $(f(x_{i,G+1}) < f(x_{best}))$ **then**
 9 | $x_{best} = x_{i,G}$;
 10   **end**
 11 **end**
 12 Let $IV = IV_{new}, G = G+1, x_{best,G} = x_{best}$, go to step 2;
 13 Return $f(x_{best,G})$ and $x_{best,G}$.

The termination conditions in MEHDE mainly include three: (1) the algorithm reaches the maximum number of iterations MI, (2) the objective function is less than a given threshold, and (3) the algorithm is convergent or approximately convergent. The pseudocode of MEHDE is presented in Algorithm 3.5 [20,31].

In Algorithm 3.5, $f(x), LB, UB, NP, MI, CR, F$ are the same as in Algorithm 3.4. DES is the candidate set of DE strategies, and the strategy pool. $DES = \{DE/rand/1/bin, DE/rand/2/bin, DE/best/1/bin, DE/best/2/bin, DE/rand - to - best/1/bin, DDE/rand/1/bin, DDE/rand/2/bin, DDE/best/1/bin, DDE/best/2/bin, DDE/rand - to - best/1/bin\}$.

3.6 Feature Weight Fuzzy Clustering Learning Model Based on MEHDE

This section will introduce the feature weighted fuzzy clustering learning model based on MEHDE [20].

3.6.1 MEHDE-Based Feature Weight Learning: MEHDE-FWL

As described in Section 3.3, similarity between samples plays an important role in the weighted fuzzy clustering. Similarity between the samples depends on the weighted Euclidean distance; it is a function of weights. As a result, by adjusting the feature weight such that the fuzziness of similarity matrix attains its minimum, it makes two samples, whose similarity degree is less than 0.5 in the original space (where all weights are 1), less similar (i.e., their weighted similarity degree δ_{pq}^w is close to 0); otherwise, it makes two samples, whose similarity degree is greater than 0.5 in the original space (where all weights are 1), more similar (i.e., their weighted similarity degree δ_{pq}^w is close to 1). In other words, the feature weight determined by (3.21) may make the similarity of similar samples larger, but it may make the similarity of nonsimilar samples smaller. It explicitly increases the degree of being clear and then makes the decision related to clustering easy.

Based on the earlier discussions, we assume that the scope of feature weight value is $[w_{low}, w_{up}]$ and model the feature weight learning problems based on similarity as follows [20]:

$$\min E(w)$$

$$s.t. \ w \in R^d, \ w_{low} \leq w \leq w_{up} \tag{3.33}$$

where
 d is the number of the sample features and
 w is the feature vector

According to Equations (3.20) and (3.17), (3.33) can be modified as (3.34)

$$\min \sum_{q<p} \left(\frac{1}{1 + \beta d_{pq}^{(w)}} \left(1 - \frac{1}{1 + \beta d_{pq}^{(1)}} \right) + \frac{1}{1 + \beta d_{pq}^{(1)}} \left(1 - \frac{1}{1 + \beta d_{pq}^{(w)}} \right) \right)$$

$$s.t. \ w \in R^d, \ w_{low} \leq w \leq w_{up}, \tag{3.34}$$

where
 $d_{pq}^{(1)}$ represents a traditional Euclidean distance
 $d_{pq}^{(w)}$ represents a weighted Euclidean distance that can be calculated according to (3.19)

β is a nonnegative constant that is solved from Equation (3.18). The Euclidean distance $d_{pq}^{(1)}$ between the samples and the parameter β for a given data set are fixed, and the feature weight w is expected to be solved by the optimization model (3.34).

It is necessary to point out that since the feature weight w represents the significance degree of each feature, we might assume that the lower bound vector w_{low} is zero vector, and the upper bound vector w_{up} is d-dimensional vector near the origin and staying in the space of positive axis in d-dimensional Euclidean space. Experimental results show that the optimal solution of model (3.34) is always near the origin and staying in the space in the direction of positive axis, especially all the features are normalized to the interval [0, 1]. It is also necessary to point out that, to make *DE* algorithm more accurate and efficient in solving the model (3.34), the smaller scope to optimize variable is better. We assume that the upper bound of feature weight is 10, that is, the upper bound of feature weight vector $w_{up} = 10 \cdot I_d$, where I_d is a d-dimensional vector with each component being 1. As a result, for any given data set, feature weighted model determined by (3.34) becomes a d-dimensional real function optimization problem, which can be solved by any real value optimization methodology. Once the optimal feature weights are determined, fuzzy partition may be conducted based on these feature weights and then the clustering is achieved.

However, for most of the data sets, the optimization problem determined by (3.34) is a complex multidimensional optimization problem, whose objective function with respect to feature weight vector often has multiple peaks. It shows that the objective function usually has many local extremes, which inevitably increases the difficulty of solving the problem. Due to the inherent disadvantages of the gradient descent algorithm, the existing feature weight learning methods based on gradient descent have many defects, such as convergence to local optimum, depending on the learning rate and initial solution, low convergence rate. The MEHDE algorithm for solving (3.34) overcomes these defects to a great extent, which significantly improves the performance of weighted clustering based on similarity. For convenience, we abbreviate the method as MEHDE-FWL (MEHDE-based feature weight learning) [20], and we abbreviate the feature weight learning based on gradient descent method as GD-FWL (gradient descent–based feature weight learning).

3.6.2 Experimental Analysis

In order to evaluate the performance of MEHDE-FWL method [20], we experimentally compare it with the GD-FWL method and the classical similarity-based clustering method that does not incorporate feature weights. In the experiments, 11 benchmark data sets are used, among which one data set called rice taste data is from [32] and the remaining data sets are from UCI machine learning data repository [33]. Since these data sets are originally for classification, we ignore the class label feature and regard them as clustering problems. A summary of these data sets is given in Table 3.3.

To avoid an influence from different ranges of features, for each data set, all features will be normalized to the interval [0, 1]. Meanwhile, the β, one constant used in calculation of weighted similarity, will be individually determined for each data set by solving Equation (3.18). Moreover, based on the experiences and recommendations from [26,28,34,35], the differential scale factor F and crossover probability CR of MEHDE-FWL are required to lie in the intervals [0.3, 0.9] and [0.1, 1],

Table 3.3 Summary of Selected Data Sets in the Experiments

Data Set	#Samples	#Features
Rice	105	5
Iris	150	4
Servo	167	4
Thyroid	215	5
BUP	345	6
MPG	398	8
Boston	506	13
Pima	768	8
Image	2310	19
Libras	360	90
Gas	445	128

Table 3.4 Parameters of the MEHDE-FWL

Population size NP	$10 \times$#feature
Maximal iteration MI	1000
The interval of feature weight w	$0 \leq w \leq 10$

respectively. The values of F and CR for each data set are given by the trial-and-error method. Tables 3.4 and 3.5 list the final values of these parameters used in the experiments.

For the GD-FWL, we set the maximal number of iteration as 6000 and define a range for the learning ratio η. In each loop of GD, the learning ratio can be dynamically updated by the Fibonacci searching algorithm [5].

Two most popular similarity-based fuzzy clustering methods, that is, the clustering based on similarity matrix's transitive closure (SMTC-C) [21] and the FCM clustering [4], are selected for the experimental comparison. In the experiments, the MEHDE-FWL algorithm will be compared with the SMTC-C, FCM, and their weighted versions, that is, weighted SMTC-C (WSMTC-C) and weighted FCM (WFCM), in terms of some selected clustering evaluation indices.

Table 3.5   Values of CR and F for Each Data Set

Data Sets	CR	F
Rice	0.8	0.6
Iris	1.0	0.4
Servo	0.4	0.4
Thyroid	1.0	0.4
BUPA	1.0	0.4
MPG	0.4	0.4
Boston	0.6	0.4
Pima	0.8	0.4
Image	0.8	0.4
Libras	0.6	0.8
Gas	0.6	1.0

3.6.2.1 Comparison between MEHDE-FWL and GD-FWL Based on FCM

The authors of paper in [36] proposed one gradient descent-based WFCM algorithm (WFCM-GD), and in their work, four indices were adopted to evaluate the performance of fuzzy clustering. In order to conveniently conduct the comparison between MEHDE-FWL and their method, we also use the same four indices to quantify the clustering performance of classical FCM, WFCM-GD, and WFCM-MEHDE.

Table 3.6 gives a brief summary of definitions and characteristics of the four selected evaluation indices for clustering, which are named as the partition coefficient V_{pc} [37], the partition entropy V_{pe} [38], the Fukuyama–Sugeno function V_{fs} [39], and the Xie–Beni function V_{xb} [40], respectively. One can easily see that, the former two indices are based on the fuzzy partition of sample set, while the latter two are based on the geometric distribution structure of samples. Moreover, empirical studies in [41] have shown that a good interpretation of the partition over the samples may be obtained by maximizing V_{pc} or minimizing V_{pe}. Meanwhile, Xie and Wang have found that a good partition, in which the samples of one cluster are compact and the samples among different clusters are separate, usually has minimal V_{fs} or V_{xb} [36,40].

To illustrate the validity of the optimization model for feature weight learning, the clustering result of the famous Iris data by WFCM is given in Figure 3.6. It is noted that since the feature weight vector $w^* = (0.0001, 0.0005, 3.5292, 0.0011)$,

Table 3.6   Brief Summary of the Four Evaluation Indices for Fuzzy-C Means

Name of Index	Definition	Optimal Value
Partition coefficient	$V_{pc}(U) = \frac{1}{n}\left(\sum_{j=1}^{n}\sum_{i=1}^{k} u_{ij}^2\right)$	$\max\left(V_{pc}\right)$
Partition entropy	$V_{pe}(U) = -\frac{1}{n}\left(\sum_{j=1}^{n}\sum_{i=1}^{k}\left(u_{ij}\log_2 u_{ij}\right)\right)$	$\min\left(V_{pe}\right)$
Fukuyama–Sugeno function	$V_{fs}(U, v_1, L, v_c; X)$ $= \sum_{j=1}^{n}\sum_{i=1}^{k} u_{ij}^2\left(\| X_j - v_i \|^2 - \| v_i - \bar{v} \|^2\right)$	$\min\left(V_{fs}\right)$
Xie–Beni function	$V_{xb}(U, v_1, L, v_c; X) = \dfrac{\sum_{j=1}^{n}\sum_{i=1}^{k} u_{ij}^2\|X_j - v_i\|^2}{n\cdot(\min_{i\neq k}\{\|v_i - v_k\|^2\})}$	$\min\left(V_{xb}\right)$

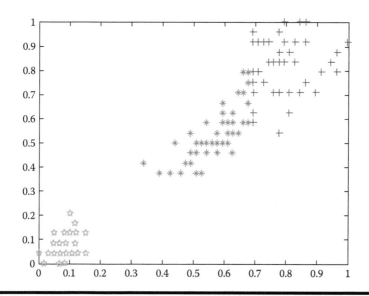

Figure 3.6   Clustering of IRIS by fuzzy C-means based on feature weight vector w*.

which is determined by MEHDE-FWL, has very small weights for the first and second features, so we omit these two features in Figure 3.6. From this figure one can clearly see that the MEHDE-FWL method obtains a satisfying clustering result, and the learned feature weights reflect the importance of corresponding features accurately.

Table 3.7 gives the clustering results of FCM, WFCM-GD, and WFCM-MEHDE in terms of the 4 evaluation indices on 11 selected data sets. In the

Table 3.7 Comparisons between FCM, WFCM-GD, and WFCM-MEHDE

Data Sets	Clustering Method	V_{pc}	V_{pe}	V_{fs}	V_{xb}
Iris	FCM	0.86	0.25	−17.59	**0.08**
	WFCM-GD	**0.93(0.000)**	**0.14(0.001)**	**−19.85(0.130)**	**0.08(0.000)**
	WFCM-MEHDE	**0.93(0.000)**	**0.13(0.000)**	**−20.01(0.000)**	**0.08(0.000)**
Pima	FCM	0.57	0.62	68.75	1.17
	WFCM-GD	0.60(0.050)	0.59(0.050)	67.72(6.960)	1.57(1.390)
	WFCM-MEHDE	**0.81(0.004)**	**0.31(0.007)**	**64.19(0.320)**	**0.62(0.004)**
Rice	FCM	0.75	0.41	0.09	0.19
	WFCM-GD	0.77(0.027)	0.38(0.041)	0.21(0.317)	**0.19(0.013)**
	WFCM-MEHDE	**0.82(0.000)**	**0.30(0.005)**	**−0.14(0.035)**	0.20(0.009)
Servo	FCM	0.62	0.56	26.41	0.50
	WFCM-GD	0.68(0.107)	0.48(0.144)	25.54(7.577)	**0.69(0.232)**
	WFCM-MEHDE	**0.99(0.035)**	**0.03(0.082)**	**10.21(1.026)**	2.10(0.095)
Thyroid	FCM	0.70	0.47	8.34	0.56
	WFCM-GD	0.82(0.019)	0.32(0.055)	**1.43(3.800)**	**0.25(0.124)**
	WFCM-MEHDE	**0.87(0.022)**	**0.24(0.053)**	1.73(3.172)	**0.25(0.092)**

(Continued)

Table 3.7 (Continued) Comparisons between FCM, WFCM-GD, and WFCM-MEHDE

Data Sets	Clustering Method	V_{pc}	V_{pe}	V_{fs}	V_{xb}
Bupa	FCM	0.60	0.58	16.81	0.93
	WFCM-GD	0.64(0.055)	0.54(0.067)	16.00(1.881)	0.84(0.277)
	WFCM-MEHDE	**0.77(0.004)**	**0.38(0.005)**	**13.21(0.042)**	**0.47(0.000)**
MPG	FCM	0.73	0.43	2.53	0.19
	WFCM-GD	0.83(0.135)	0.28(0.210)	−50.59(80.10)	**0.31(0.151)**
	WFCM-MEHDE	**0.96(0.008)**	**0.09(0.019)**	**−103.21(41.38)**	0.46(0.011)
Boston	FCM	0.74	0.42	33.46	0.23
	WFCM-GD	0.73(0.030)	0.40(0.390)	47.72(17.409)	**0.25(0.019)**
	WFCM-MEHDE	**0.97(0.009)**	**0.09(0.179)**	**−54.24(1.2298)**	0.33(0.004)
Image	FCM	0.40	1.25	−464	0.58
	WFCM-GD	0.39(0.016)	1.27(0.029)	−417.88(25.016)	0.90(0.133)
	WFCM-MEHDE	**0.64(0.014)**	**0.75(0.027)**	**−787(18.213)**	**0.65(0.043)**
Libras	FCM	**0.07**	2.71	103.61	2.74E+08
	WFCM-GD	0.07(0.125)	2.70(0.024)	103.61(25.016)	4.59E+07(1.02E+07)
	WFCM-MEHDE	0.07(0.012)	**2.69(0.0001)**	**101.52(3.176)**	**2.42E+05(1.03E+04)**
Gas	FCM	0.41	1.52	−703.20	0.36
	WFCM-GD	**0.42(0.086)**	1.50(0.180)	−717.05(121.70)	**0.34(0.073)**
	WFCM-MEHDE	**0.42(0.001)**	**1.49(0.012)**	**−726.15(27.61)**	0.39(0.002)

Note: Values in brackets denote the standard deviation of the corresponding indices. Values in bold denote emphasize that they are maximum or minimum among three values.

experiments, to get more accurate and reasonable results, both WFCM-GD and WFCM-MEHDE repeat 20 times, and then the averaged values are taken. The standard deviations of these indices are also given in Table 3.7 from which several conclusions can be drawn as follows:

1. Among the three clustering methods, WFCM-MEHDE obtained the best results, WFCM-GD is the second, and FCM is the last one. This conclusion is consistent with intuitive knowledge. It confirms that the feature weighting technique can generally improve the performance of fuzzy clustering algorithms, and meanwhile the MEHDE optimization approach usually has the searching ability better than gradient descent-based optimization methods have.

2. Compared to WFCM-GD, the results of WFCM-MEHDE have smaller standard deviations, which denotes that by incorporating various evolution strategies and combining the DE and DDE techniques, the MEHDE algorithm has more stable searching ability and better adaptability.

3. The data in Table 3.7 show that the superiority of WFCM-MEHDE over WFCM-GD is more obvious in these complex data sets, which reflects that in more complex multidimensional programming problems, the MEHDE has more superiority over GD in terms of searching efficiency and accuracy.

4. Given a data set, the four indices generally may not achieve their optimal values simultaneously. For example, when we maximize the partition coefficient, the remaining three indices do not always achieve their minimal values (because for the remaining three indices, their smaller values are preferred for us). Therefore, if we need to determine an optimal number of clusters, we may take the cluster number for which the majority of indices attain the optimal.

3.6.2.2 Comparisons Based on SMTC Clustering

In this section, we will use the SMTC-C to conduct the clustering and compare the clustering performance among the classical SMTC-C without feature weights: weighted SMTC-C based on gradient descent (SMTC-C-GD) and weighted SMTC-C based on MEHDE. The basic idea of SMTC-C can be briefly summarized as follows. Assume that the transitive closure of similarity matrix $S_{n \times n}$ is $TC(S) = (t_{ij})_{n \times n}$, the n objects $\{x_1, x_2, \ldots, x_n\}$ can be categorized into several clusters in terms of the criterion "x_i and x_j belong to the same cluster if $t_{ij} \geq \alpha$," where α is a given threshold.

It the MEHDE algorithm, we use the same parameter setting as these are adopted in the previous subsection. Meanwhile, in order to conveniently conduct the comparison between the method and the SMTC-C-GD proposed by Yeung et al. in [5], we choose the five indices used in [5] to evaluate the performance of clustering.

One can find their detailed definitions in Reference [5]. Here we only give a brief introduction:

1. *Fuzziness of the similarity matrix (fuzziness)*: It is obvious that the similarity matrix with a smaller fuzziness will generate a partition with clearer clustering boundary.
2. *Intraclass similarity (intrasimilarity)*: It is defined as the average similarity of all pairs of objects in one cluster. And for a partition with C clusters, the average of all intraclass similarities is adopted. Obviously, the bigger value of this index is preferred.
3. *Interclass similarity (intersimilarity)*: This index is defined as the average similarity of all pairs of objects coming from different clusters. One can easily see that smaller interclass similarity is preferred for obtaining satisfying clustering results.
4. *Ratio of intraclass similarity to interclass similarity*: It is defined to evaluate the overall quality of a partition and to achieve a trade-off between intraclass similarity and interclass similarity. One can see that in the SMTC-C, different values of threshold α will usually generate different partitions on the same data set. Therefore, if one crisp decision is needed, the partition with the maximal ratio will be returned.
5. *Nonspecificity*: This index evaluates the difficulty of determining a crisp partition from multiple partitions generated by SMTC-C algorithm with different threshold α. Its value is calculated based on the list of ratio of intraclass similarity to interclass similarity, and obviously, smaller nonspecificity is preferred. Suppose that $\alpha_1, \alpha_2, \ldots, \alpha_m$ are the m values of threshold α and each threshold value will generate a partition with more than one cluster. It is obvious that the nonspecificity does exist in this situation. Furthermore, let R_i be the normalized ratio of intraclass similarity to interclass similarity corresponding to α_i, and then a similarity ratio vector $V = (R_1, R_2, \ldots, R_m)$ is obtained, in which R_i is calculated by the following formula:

$$R_i = \frac{R(\alpha_i)}{\max_{1 \leq i \leq m}\{R(\alpha_i)\}}. \tag{3.35}$$

According to the definition of similarity ratio, the R_i can be regarded as the possibility of selecting the ith partition from all candidate partitions, and therefore, the vector V is a possibility distribution. Then, according to Reference [42], the nonspecificity can be defined as:

$$Nonspecificity(V) = \sum_{i=1}^{m}(\pi_i - \pi_{i+1})\ln i. \tag{3.36}$$

The detailed experimental process of this subsection can be summarized as follows. First, the feature weights of each data set will be determined by GD-FWL and

MEHDE-FWL, respectively. Second, the classical SMTC-C and weighted SMTC-C algorithm are used to conduct the clustering based on learned feature weights (if any). Meanwhile, based on different threshold α, each method will generate a clustering graph on each data set. Finally, based on these clustering graphs, the five indices mentioned earlier for each method can be calculated. It is noted that, similar to the previous section, the indices for GD-FWL and MEHDE-FWL are also the averaged values over 20 iterations and their standard deviations are also given in corresponding brackets. The experimental results are listed in Table 3.8.

To intuitively compare the values of these indices, Figures 3.7 through 3.11 give the histogram of each index determined by three methods on 11 data sets, respectively.

From Table 3.8 and Figures 3.7 through 3.11, one can see that among the three clustering methods, the clustering performance of WSMTC-C-MEHDE is optimal, and the second is WSMTC-C-GD, while the results of classical SMTC-C without feature weights are worst. It again confirms that the incorporating of feature weights into fuzzy clustering can improve the clustering performance. Noting that the MEHDE algorithm has better optimization capability and more robust outputs than GD-based approaches have, better feature weights are usually expected to be obtained by using MEHDE-FWL to further improve the performance of SMTC clustering.

From the experimental results, one can see that in comparison with the other two clustering algorithms, the WSMTC-C-MEHDE has more obvious superiorities in terms of the following three indices, that is, nonspecificity, fuzziness, and the ratio of intraclass similarity to interclass similarity. For SMTC-C-based clustering algorithms, it is obvious that the nonspecificity directly affects determining a final crisp partition. Meanwhile, being a dimensionless evaluation index, the similarity ratio is more valuable than the intraclass similarity and interclass similarity (since the values of the latter two indices are affected by the range of values of feature weights).

Similar to Section 3.6.2.1, the standard derivations of most indices obtained by WSMTC-C-MEHDE are smaller than those obtained by WSMTC-C-GD, which indicates that the former method has better robustness and adaptability, and the superiority is increasing with the increase of complexity of clustering problems. The reasons may be that the MEHDE adopts multiple DE-based or DDE-based differential evolution strategies and uses these multiple strategies sequentially during its iteration process.

3.6.2.3 Efficiency Analysis of GD-, DE-, DDE-, and MEHDE-Based Searching Techniques

GD-based methods' efficiency usually depends strongly on the initialization of solution and the value of learning ratio. If improper initialized solutions or learning ratios are given, the GDs may have very slower convergence speed, and some may

Table 3.8 Comparisons between SMTC-C, WSMTC-C-GD, and WSMTC-C-MEHDE

Data Sets	Clustering Method	Intra-S	Inter-S	Ratio	M-Ratio	Fuzziness	Non-S
Iris	SMTC-C	**0.88**	0.44	1.99	2.16	0.32	1.78
	WSMTC-C-GD	0.85(0.00)	0.32(0.00)	2.75(0.03)	3.28(0.04)	**0.27(0.00)**	1.25(0.04)
	WSMTC-C-MEHDE	0.85(0.00)	**0.31(0.00)**	**2.78(0.00)**	**3.30(0.00)**	**0.27(0.00)**	**1.17(0.00)**
Pima	SMTC-C	0.94	0.42	2.25	2.7	0.34	1.83
	WSMTC-C-GD	**0.96(0.00)**	0.24(0.00)	4.78(0.62)	**6.42(0.74)**	**0.21(0.00)**	1.74(0.02)
	WSMTC-C-MEHDE	0.93(0.00)	**0.22(0.00)**	**4.79(0.00)**	6.13(0.01)	0.31(0.00)	**1.25(0.00)**
Rice	SMTC-C	**0.92**	0.40	2.38	2.79	0.33	1.85
	WSMTC-C-GD	0.91(0.00)	**0.17(0.00)**	**4.00(2.13)**	**6.40(3.56)**	**0.22(0.00)**	1.72(0.03)
	WSMTC-C-MEHDE	0.89(0.00)	0.30(0.00)	3.48(0.07)	5.68(0.22)	0.30(0.00)	**1.54(0.00)**
Servo	SMTC-C	0.73	0.47	1.54	1.99	0.34	0.87
	WSMTC-C-GD	0.72(0.02)	0.18(0.00)	4.28(1.21)	5.80(2.25)	0.22(0.00)	0.93(0.15)
	WSMTC-C-MEHDE	**0.99(0.00)**	**0.17(0.00)**	**6.15(0.70)**	**6.25(0.29)**	**0.16(0.00)**	**0.07(0.05)**
Thyroid	SMTC-C	**0.92**	0.34	2.83	3.49	0.32	1.75
	WSMTC-C-GD	0.91(0.00)	0.26(0.00)	4.18(0.47)	7.44(2.93)	0.29(0.00)	1.57(0.05)
	WSMTC-C-MEHDE	0.91(0.00)	**0.24(0.00)**	**4.57(0.00)**	**7.65(0.00)**	**0.28(0.00)**	**1.19(0.00)**
Bupa	SMTC-C	0.94	0.39	2.47	2.91	0.33	1.90
	WSMTC-C-GD	**0.97(0.00)**	**0.14(0.00)**	**4.22(0.58)**	**7.49(0.95)**	0.31(0.00)	1.69(0.01)
	WSMTC-C-MEHDE	0.95(0.00)	0.30(0.00)	3.39(0.00)	6.55(0.01)	**0.30(0.00)**	**1.37(0.00)**

(Continued)

Table 3.8 (*Continued*) Comparisons between SMTC-C, WSMTC-C-GD, and WSMTC-C-MEHDE

Data Sets	Clustering Method	Intra-S	Inter-S	Ratio	M-Ratio	Fuzziness	Non-S
MPG	SMTC-C	0.85	0.48	1.76	2.00	0.33	1.69
	WSMTC-C-GD	0.89(0.00)	0.17(0.00)	5.26(0.55)	6.03(0.37)	0.20(0.00)	1.65(0.58)
	WSMTC-C-MEHDE	**0.94(0.00)**	**0.19(0.00)**	**5.46(0.78)**	**6.56(0.15)**	**0.17(0.00)**	**0.92(0.02)**
Boston	SMTC-C	0.86	0.45	1.92	2.14	0.33	1.97
	WSMTC-C-GD	0.88(0.00)	0.16(0.00)	**5.64(0.93)**	6.32(1.19)	0.22(0.00)	**2.29(0.01)**
	WSMTC-C-MEHDE	**0.94(0.00)**	**0.26(0.00)**	4.14(0.02)	**6.73(0.02)**	**0.23(0.00)**	1.03(0.00)
Image	SMTC-C	**0.91**	0.44	2.08	2.32	0.33	1.95
	WSMTC-C-GD	0.89(0.00)	0.23(0.00)	4.03(0.40)	4.93(0.23)	0.27(0.00)	2.02(0.05)
	WSMTC-C-MEHDE	**0.91(0.00)**	**0.16(0.00)**	**5.70(0.01)**	**6.15(0.09)**	**0.22(0.00)**	**2.39(0.01)**
Libras	SMTC-C	0.90	0.48	1.91	1.97	0.34	2.00
	WSMTC-C-GD	0.91(0.00)	0.20(0.00)	4.64(0.18)	4.87(0.21)	0.25(0.01)	1.95(0.02)
	WSMTC-C-MEHDE	**0.93(0.00)**	**0.15(0.00)**	**6.10(0.07)**	**6.39(0.05)**	**0.21(0.00)**	**1.88(0.00)**
Gas	SMTC-C	**0.94**	0.39	2.45	2.68	0.32	2.06
	WSMTC-C-GD	**0.94(0.00)**	0.16(0.02)	6.13(0.63)	8.43(0.42)	0.24(0.06)	1.73(0.02)
	WSMTC-C-MEHDE	**0.94(0.00)**	**0.13(0.00)**	**7.25(0.15)**	**10.3(0.02)**	**0.20(0.00)**	**1.70(0.00)**

Note: Values in brackets denote the standard deviation of corresponding indices. Values in bold denote emphasize that they are maximum or minimum among three values.

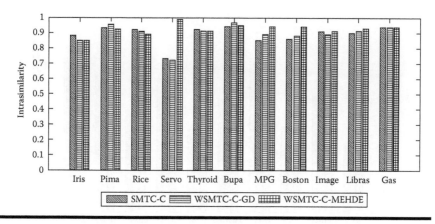

Figure 3.7 **The intraclass similarity of SMTC-C, WSMTC-C-GD, and WSMTC-C-MEHDE.**

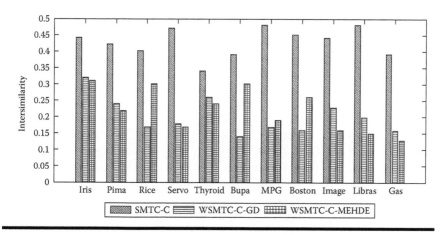

Figure 3.8 **The interclass similarity of SMTC-C, WSMTC-C-GD, and WSMTC-C-MEHDE.**

not convergent within an acceptable time. In comparison with GD-based methods, DE-based methods demonstrate their stronger searching ability and more robust performance.

Compared with DEs and DDEs, the MEHDE usually has better searching ability and more robust performance without increasing additional cost of computation. MEHDE achieves these improvements through two techniques. (1) It integrates multiple DE strategies that are efficient either in local searching or in global searching. (2) It sequentially selects different evolution strategies to update the current individuals in population, and its computational complexity of MEHDE is basically identical to that of "DE/rand/1/bin." As pointed in [43], since the mutation

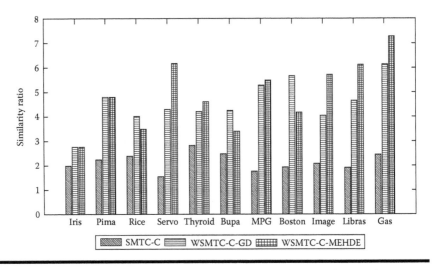

Figure 3.9 **The ratio of intraclass similarity to interclass similarity of SMTC-C, WSMTC-C-GD, and WSMTC-C-MEHDE.**

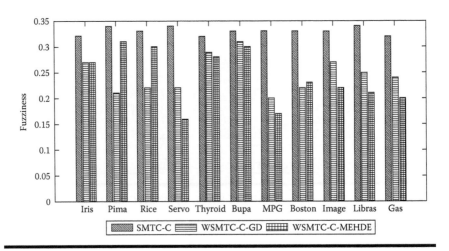

Figure 3.10 **The fuzziness of SMTC-C, WSMTC-C-GD, and WSMTC-C-MEHDE.**

and crossover operations are performed at the component level for each DE vector, the amount of fundamental operations in "DE/rand/1/bin" is proportional to the total number of loops conducted before the termination of the algorithm.

Finally, it should be indicated that MEHDE optimization technique uses trial-and-error method to tune the scaling factor F and the crossover probability CR, which has a big computational cost for large scale of clustering problems.

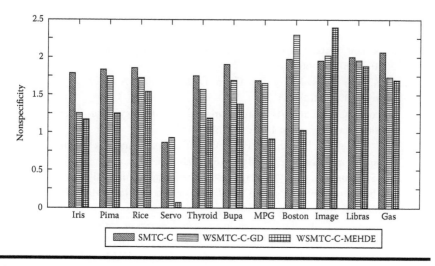

Figure 3.11 The nonspecificity of SMTC-C, WSMTC-C-GD, and WSMTC-C-MEHDE.

3.7 Summary

Two types of clustering, that is, partition-based clustering and hierarchy-based clustering, are introduced, and the K-means algorithm and its fuzzy version are reviewed. A new feature weight learning technique based on DE, that is, MEHDE, is given for similarity-based fuzzy weighted clustering.

Aiming at the feature weight learning problem in similarity-based weighted fuzzy clustering, we develop a feature weight learning model by minimizing the fuzziness of fuzzy similarity matrix. Then the MEHDE algorithm that adopts multiple DE strategies is proposed and applied to search the optimal feature weights of the learning model. To validate the performance of MEHDE, we conduct an experimental comparison between MEHDE-based fuzzy clustering and two popular fuzzy clustering algorithms, that is, the FCM and SMTC-C, on 11 selected benchmark data sets. In the experiment, the clustering results of traditional fuzzy clustering, GD-based fuzzy clustering, and MEHDE-based fuzzy clustering are determined and compared, respectively. Five evaluation indices, that is, fuzziness of fuzzy similarity matrix, intraclass similarity, interclass similarity, ratio of intraclass similarity to interclass similarity, and nonspecificity, are used for SMTC-C-based clustering. The experimental results show that the appropriate incorporation of feature weights can significantly improve the performance of fuzzy clustering, and the MEHDE-based fuzzy clustering scheme has better performance and stronger robustness than the GD-based fuzzy clustering approach has.

References

1. A. K. Jain. Data clustering: 50 years beyond K-means. *Pattern Recognition Letters*, 2010, 31(8):651–666.
2. A. K. Jain, M. N. Murty, P. J. Flynn. Data clustering: A review. *ACM Computing Surveys*, 1999, 31(2):264–323.
3. E. Forgy. Cluster analysis of multivariate data: Efficiency versus interpretability of classification. *Biometrics*, 1965, 21(3):768–769.
4. J. C. Bezdek, R. Ehrlich, W. Full. FCM: The fuzzy c-means clustering algorithm. *Computers and Geosciences*, 1984, 10(84):191–203.
5. D. S. Yeung, X. Z. Wang. Improving performance of similarity-based clustering by feature weight learning. *IEEE Transactions on Pattern Analysis and Machine Intelligence*, 2002, 24(4):556–561.
6. T. Hastie, R. Tibshirani, J. Friedman. *The Elements of Statistical Learning: Data Mining, Inference, and Prediction*, 2nd edn. Springer-Verlag, New York, 2009.
7. L. Kaufman, P. J. Rousseeuw. Divisive analysis (Program DIANA). In: *Finding Groups in Data: An Introduction to Cluster Analysis*. New Jersey: John Wiley & Sons, Inc., pp. 253–279, 2008.
8. S. Zeng, X. Tong, N. Sang. Study on multi-center fuzzy C-means algorithm based on transitive closure and spectral clustering. *Applied Soft Computing*, 2014, 16(3): 89–101.
9. J. J. Zeng. Implementation and application of improved AGNES algorithm on technical-tactics analysis of badminton match. *Computer Knowledge and Technology*, 2009, 5(33):9343–9345.
10. T. Zhang, R. Ramakrishnan, M. Livny. BIRCH: An efficient data clustering method for very large databases. In: *Proceedings of 1996 ACM SIGMOD International Conference on Management of Data*, Montreal, Quebec, Canada. June 4–6, 1996, Vol. 25, pp. 103–114.
11. S. Guha, R. Rastogi, K. Shim. CURE : An efficient clustering algorithm for large databases. In: *Proceedings of the ACM SIGMOD International Conference on Management of Data*, Seattle, WA. June 2–4, 1998, pp. 73–84.
12. S. Guha, R. Rastogi, K. Shim. Rock: A robust clustering algorithm for categorical attributes. *Information Systems*, 2000, 25(5):345–366.
13. J. C. Dunn. A fuzzy relative of the ISODATA process and its use in detecting compact well-separated clusters. *Journal of Cybernetics*, 1973, 3(3):32–57.
14. J. Han, M. Kamber, J. Pei. *Data Mining: Concepts and Techniques*, 3rd edn. Morgan Kaufmann Publishers, San Francisco, CA, 2012.
15. O. Arbelaitz, I. Gurrutxaga, J. Muguerza. An extensive comparative study of cluster validity indices. *Pattern Recognition*, 2013, 46(1):243–256.
16. S. Saha, S. Bandyopadhyay. Some connectivity based cluster validity indices. *Applied Soft Computing*, 2012, 12(5):1555–1565.
17. U. Maulik, S. Bandyopadhyay. Performance evaluation of some clustering algorithms and validity indices. *IEEE Transactions on Pattern Analysis and Machine Intelligence*, 2002, 24(12):1650–1654.

18. J. C. Bezdek, N. R. Pal. Some new indexes of cluster validity. *IEEE Transactions on Systems, Man, and Cybernetics, Part B: Cybernetics*, 1998, 28(3):301–315.

19. J. Basak, R. K. De, S. K. Pal. Unsupervised feature selection using a neuro-fuzzy approach. *Pattern Recognition Letters*, 1998, 19(11):997–1006.

20. C. R. Dong, W. W. Y. Ng, X. Z. Wang et al. An improved differential evolution and its application to determining feature weights in similarity-based clustering. *Neurocomputing*, 2014, 146(1):95–103.

21. D. Dubois. *Fuzzy Sets and Systems: Theory and Applications.* Academic Press, New York, 1980.

22. J. C. Dunn. Some recent investigations of a new fuzzy partition algorithm and its application to pattern classification problems. *Journal of Cybernetics*, 1974, 4(2): 1–15.

23. R. Storn, K. V. Price. Differential evolution: A simple and efficient adaptive scheme for global optimization over continuous spaces. ICSI, Berkeley, CA, Technical Report TR-95-012, 1995.

24. R. Storn. On the usage of differential evolution for function optimization. In: *Proceedings of the Biennial Conference of the North American Fuzzy Information Processing Society (NAFIPS)*, Berkeley, CA. June 19–22, 1996, pp. 519–523.

25. R. Storn, K. Price. Differential evolution—A simple and efficient heuristic for global optimization over continuous spaces. *Journal of Global Optimization*, 1997, 11(4): 341–359.

26. G. Jeyakumar, C. S. Velayutham. A comparative performance analysis of differential evolution and dynamic differential evolution variant. In: *World Congress on Nature and Biologically Inspired Computing.* IEEE, Coimbatore, India. December 9–11, 2009, pp. 463–468.

27. A. Qing. Dynamic differential evolution strategy and applications in electromagnetic inverse scattering problems. *IEEE Transactions on Geoscience and Remote Sensing*, 2006, 44(1):116–125.

28. A. K. Qin, V. L. Huang, P. N. Suganthan. Differential evolution algorithm with strategy adaptation for global numerical optimization. *IEEE Transactions on Evolutionary Computation*, 2009, 13(2):398–417.

29. S. Das, A. Abraham, U. K. Chakraborty et al. Differential evolution using a neighborhood based mutation operator. *IEEE Transactions on Evolutionary Computation*, 2009, 13(3):526–553.

30. J. Zhang, A. C. Sanderson. JADE: Adaptive differential evolution with optional external archive. *IEEE Transactions on Evolutionary Computation*, 2009, 13(5): 945–958.

31. Y. C. He, X. Z. Wang, K. Q. Liu et al. Convergent analysis and algorithmic improvement of differential evolution. *Journal of Software*, 2010, 21(5):875–885.

32. K. Nozaki, H. Ishibuchi, H. Tanaka. A simple but powerful heuristic method for generating fuzzy rules from numerical data. *Fuzzy Sets and Systems*, 1997, 86(3): 251–270.

33. A. Frank, A. Asuncion. UCI machine learning repository, http://archive.ics.uci.edu/ml, November 10, 2012.

34. J. Vesterstrom, R. Thomsen. A comparative study of differential evolution, particle swarm optimization, and evolutionary algorithms on numerical benchmark problems. In: *Congress on Evolutionary Computation*, Portland, OR, 2004, pp. 1980–1987.

35. M. M. Efren, V. R. Jesus, A. C. C. Carios. A comparative study on differential evolution variants for global optimization. In: *Genetic and Evolutionary Computation Conference, GECCO'06*, ACM, Seattle, WA. July 8–12, 2006, pp. 485–492.

36. X. Z. Wang, Y. D. Wang, L. J. Wang. Improving fuzzy C-means clustering based on feature-weight learning. *Pattern Recognition Letters*, 2004, 25(10):1123–1132.

37. J. C. Bezdek. Cluster validity with fuzzy sets. *Journal of Cybernetics*, 1974, 3(3):58–73.

38. J. C. Bezdek. Mathematical models for systematic and taxonomy. In: *Proceedings of Eighth International Conference on Numerical Taxonomy*, San Francisco, CA, 1975, pp. 143–166.

39. Y. Fukuyama, M. Sugeno. A new method of choosing the number of clusters for the fuzzy C-means method. In: *Proceedings of Fifth Fuzzy System Symposium*, Kobe, Japan. June 2–3, 1989, pp. 247–250.

40. X. L. Xie, G. Beni. A validity measure for fuzzy clustering. *IEEE Transactions on Pattern Analysis and Machine Intelligence*, 1991, 13(8):841–847.

41. J. C. Dunn. Indices of partition fuzziness and the detection of clusters in large data sets. In: *Fuzzy Automata and Decision Process*, Gupta, M.M. (Ed.), Elsevier, New York, 1976.

42. M. Higashi, G. J. Klir. Measures on uncertainty and information based on possibility distribution. *International Journal on General Systems*, 1983, 9:43–58.

43. K. Zielinski, R. Laur. Constrained single-objective optimization using differential evolution. In: *Proceedings of IEEE Congress Evolution Computing*, Vancouver, Canada. July 16–21, 2006, pp. 927–934.

Chapter 4

Active Learning with Uncertainty

This chapter mainly introduces active learning, especially uncertainty-based active learning. An introduction to active learning is presented in Section 4.1. The voting entropy technique is discussed in Section 4.2. Maximum ambiguity–based active learning [1] and active learning approach to support vector machine [2] are discussed in Sections 4.3 and 4.4, respectively.

4.1 Introduction to Active Learning

As a learning approach, active learning [3–7] was originally proposed in the 1980s. Essentially, active learning is an iterative sampling technique that guides the selection of unlabeled samples (instances) to be labeled by a supervisor [8–10]. Generally, active learning is applied in the scenarios in which many instances are easily acquired, but labeling them is expensive and/or time-consuming [11]. In the framework of classification, the problem addressed by active learning is to improve the performance of the classifiers by labeling as few instances as possible.

As pointed out by Li and Sethi [12], an active learning problem can be modeled as a quintuple (L, U, C, S, Q), where $L = \{(x_i, y_i)|x_i \in R^d, y_i \in D, 1 \leq i \leq l\}$ is a labeled training set and D is a set of class labels. If the instances of L belong to K classes, then we can let $D = \{1, 2, \ldots, K\}$. $U = \{x_i|x_i \in R^d, l+1 \leq i \leq l+n\}$ is a set of unlabeled instances, in general, $n \gg l$. C is a classifier, that is, a classification algorithm. S is a supervisor also called oracle or annotator [8]. Q is a query function used to select the informative unlabeled instances from U. A general active learning

99

algorithm is presented in Algorithm 4.1 [10,12]. The intuitive diagram of active learning is given in Figure 4.1.

Generally, a typical active learning system is composed of two parts, that is, a learning algorithm and a query algorithm [6]. The training algorithm is to train a classifier with the current labeled data set, while the query algorithm is to select the informative instances from the unlabeled data set. According to the way that unlabeled instances are presented to the query algorithm, active learning methods can be roughly classified into two categories: pool-based active learning methods and stream-based active learning methods. In pool-based active learning methods [13], all unlabeled instances are available for the query algorithm, whereas in the stream-based active learning methods [4,14], the unlabeled instances are presented to the query algorithm one by one or block by block. From this perspective, stream-based active learning can be viewed as an online version of the pool-based active learning [15]. Because the pool-based active learning appears to be much more common than the other [8], we will focus discussion on this scenario.

In the pool-based active learning, uncertainty sampling and committee-based sampling are two major sampling schemes [15]. Uncertainty sampling [5] uses only one classifier to identify unlabeled instances; the classifier has the least confidence in classifying the unlabeled instances, while committee-based sampling [6,14] generates a committee of classifiers and selects unlabeled instances by the principle of

---

Algorithm 4.1: General Active Learning Algorithm

    Input: $L = \{(x_i, y_i)|x_i \in R^d, y_i \in D, 1 \leq i \leq l\}$, a labeled training set;
           $U = \{x_i|x_i \in R^d, l+1 \leq i \leq l+n\}$, an unlabeled sample set or pool;
           q, the number of samples to add to the training set at each iteration.
    Output: A classifier with good performance.
1 **while** (*The stop criterion is not satisfied*) **do**
2   Train a classifier C with the training set L;
3   **for** (*each sample $x \in U$*) **do**
4 | Calculate the user-defined measure or heuristic Q;
5   **end**
6   According to the score of the measure, rank the samples $x \in U$;
7   Select the most q informative samples;
8   Annotate the labels of the q selected samples by the supervisor or oracle S, let ΔL be the set of the q labeled samples;
9      $L = L + \Delta L$;
10      $U = U - \Delta L$;
11 **end**
12 Output the trained classifier C.

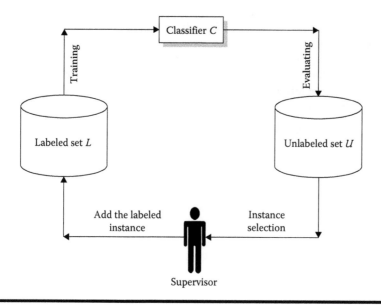

Figure 4.1 The diagram of active learning.

maximal disagreement among these classifiers, which is an uncertainty-based sampling with an ensemble [15,16]. In the next section, we will respectively discuss the two sampling schemes in detail.

Some researchers have investigated the stopping criterion [15,17–19]. In the framework of natural language processing, Vlachos [17] proposed a stop criterion for active learning using uncertainty-based sampling that does not require annotated data. Zhu et al. [15,18,19] proposed a confidence-based stop criteria, which can automatically determine when to stop the active learning process. Based on the combination of informativeness and representativeness, Huang et al. [20] proposed a novel stop criterion. Wang et al. [21] proposed stability-based stopping criterion. These criteria have their advantages and disadvantages, and all of them are tailored for the pool-based active learning approaches. It is a problem worth studying to establish the stop criteria for stream-based active learning approaches. Furthermore, by now, there is no omnipotent stop criterion that is suitable for different scenarios or applications.

Several papers have surveyed active learning from different perspectives [8,22,23] or from different application domains [10,24,25]. In recent years, active learning is mainly focusing on four aspects: (1) evaluation of the oracle with noisy and the selection of a reliable oracle, (2) batch mode active learning and the determination of a suitable batch size, (3) ensemble of active learning with different schemes, and (4) active learning for Big data.

4.2 Uncertainty Sampling and Query-by-Committee Sampling

In active learning, the essence is how to select the unlabeled instances for annotating. In this section, we introduce two popular sampling schemes: uncertainty sampling and query-by-committee (QBC) sampling.

4.2.1 Uncertainty Sampling

It is well known that uncertainty sampling [5] is the simplest and most commonly used query scheme. In this scheme, an active learner queries the instances that have the least certainty to label. The key issue of the uncertainty sampling is how to evaluate the uncertainty of the unlabeled instances. A general framework of the uncertainty sampling can be described in Algorithm 4.2 [5].

In step 4 of Algorithm 4.2, if we take different measure of uncertainty for unlabeled instances, then we can obtain different rules for selecting instances. Commonly used rules include the following.

4.2.1.1 Least Confident Rule [5]

This rule first applies probability learning model to estimate the posterior probability of unlabeled instances and then uses formula (4.1) to select instances:

$$x^* = \operatorname*{argmax}_{x} \left\{ 1 - P_\theta(\hat{y}|x) \right\}, \tag{4.1}$$

Algorithm 4.2: Algorithm for Uncertainty Sampling with a Single Classifier

---

    Input: $L = \{(x_i, y_i) | x_i \in R^d, y_i \in D, 1 \le i \le l\}$, a labeled training set;
            $U = \{x_i | x_i \in R^d, l+1 \le i \le l+n\}$, an unlabeled sample set or pool;
            q, the number of samples to add to the training set at each iteration.
    Output: A classifier with good performance.
1 Train an initial classifier C with the initial training set L;
2 **while** (*The stop criterion is not satisfied*) **do**
3   **for** (*each sample $x \in U$*) **do**
4 | Calculate its uncertainty;
5   **end**
6   Find the q instances for which the classifier C is least certain of class membership;
7   Let the oracle label the q instances;
8   Add the q labeled instances to L;
9   Train a new classifier C on the new L;
10 **end**
11 Output the trained classifier C.

---

where

θ is a probability learning model

$\hat{y} = \text{argmax}_x \{P_\theta(y|x)\}$ or the class label with the highest posterior probability under the model θ

4.2.1.2 Minimal Margin Rule [5]

The least confident rule only considers information about the most probable label [5], while the minimal margin rule can overcome this drawback, which can be formulated by

$$x^* = \underset{x}{\text{argmin}} \left\{ P_\theta(\hat{y}_1|x) - P_\theta(\hat{y}_2|x) \right\}, \tag{4.2}$$

where $\hat{y}_1$ and $\hat{y}_2$ are the first and second most probable class labels under the model θ, respectively.

4.2.1.3 Maximal Entropy Rule [5]

If the problems have very large label sets, the margin rule still ignores much of the output distribution for the remaining classes [5]. The maximal entropy rule can overcome the drawbacks mentioned earlier, which can be formulated by

$$x^* = \underset{x}{\text{argmax}} \left\{ -\sum_i P_\theta(y_i|x) \log_2 P_\theta(y_i|x) \right\}, \tag{4.3}$$

where y_i ranges over all possible labels.

In Algorithm 4.2, we use only one classifier to measure the uncertainty of the unlabeled instances. If we use multiple classifiers to do this measure, then we obtain QBC scheme, which will be discussed in the following subsection.

4.2.2 Query-by-Committee Sampling

QBC scheme was proposed by Seung et al. [6]. The QBC approach involves maintaining a committee $\mathcal{C} = \{\theta^{(c)}|1 \le c \le |\mathcal{C}|\}$ of models that are trained on the current labeled set L. Each committee member is then allowed to vote on the labels of query candidates. The most informative query is considered to be the instance about which they most disagree. The idea of QBC can be illustrated by Figure 4.2. The well-known multiple views sampling [26] (see Figure 4.3) is the variant of QBC.

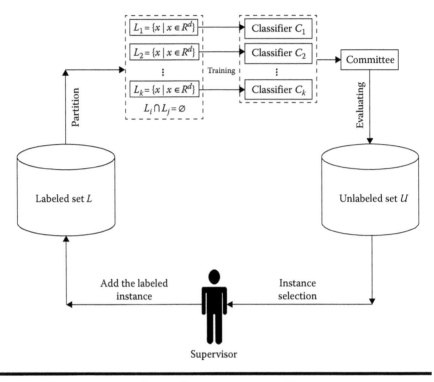

Figure 4.2   The diagram of query-by-committee sampling.

The voting entropy [14] and KL-divergence (KL: Kullback Leibler) [27] are two popular measures of uncertainty for unlabeled instances. The voting entropy is formulated by

$$x^* = \underset{x}{\operatorname{argmax}} \left\{ -\sum_i \frac{V(y_i)}{|\mathcal{C}|} \log_2 \frac{V(y_i)}{|\mathcal{C}|} \right\}, \tag{4.4}$$

where
   $|\mathcal{C}|$ is the number of members of committee $\mathcal{C}$
   $V(y_i)$ is the number of votes from which a label receives from the committee members

KL-divergence is formulated by

$$x^* = \underset{x}{\operatorname{argmax}} \left\{ \frac{1}{|\mathcal{C}|} \sum_{c=1}^{|\mathcal{C}|} D \left(P_{\theta^{(c)}} \| P_{\mathcal{C}} \right) \right\}, \tag{4.5}$$

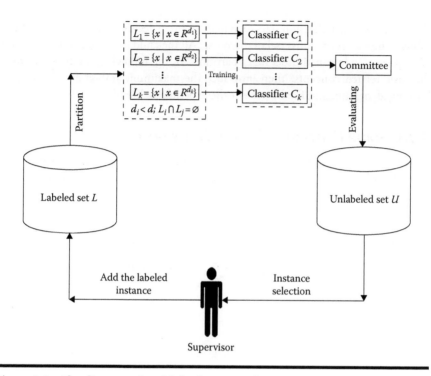

Figure 4.3   The diagram of multiple views sampling.

where

$$D\left(P_{\theta^{(c)}} \parallel P_{\mathcal{C}}\right) = \sum_i P_{\theta^{(c)}}(y_i|x) \log_2 \frac{P_{\theta^{(c)}}(y_i|x)}{P_{\mathcal{C}}(y_i|x)}. \tag{4.6}$$

In Equation (4.5), $\theta^{(c)}$ is the cth model in committee $\mathcal{C}$. In Equation (4.6), the definition of $P_{\mathcal{C}}(y_i|x)$ is given as

$$P_{\mathcal{C}}(y_i|x) = \frac{1}{|\mathcal{C}|} \sum_{c=1}^{|\mathcal{C}|} P_{\theta^{(c)}}(y_i|x). \tag{4.7}$$

4.3 Maximum Ambiguity–Based Active Learning

In this section, we introduce a sample selection algorithm [1], which selects samples with maximal ambiguity for induction of fuzzy decision tree. From Chapter 2, we know that fuzzy decision tree is an extension of crisp decision tree to uncertainty environments. Similar to a crisp decision tree, a fuzzy decision tree is a acyclic graph, in which each edge connects several nodes from parent node to child nodes.

Different from crisp decision tree, each node in fuzzy decision tree represents a fuzzy subset. The root is the universal of discourse. All the child nodes generated from the same parent node constitute a fuzzy partition. In the following, we first introduce the basic related concepts, then introduce the maximum ambiguity–based active learning algorithm, and finally present the experimental results.

4.3.1 Some Concepts of Fuzzy Decision Tree

Consider a certain node R that is a fuzzy set defined on the sample space S. Let $C = \{C_1, C_2, \ldots, C_k\}$ be the class label set. It means that C_i $(1 \le i \le k)$ is a fuzzy set defined on S for each i $(1 \le i \le k)$.

Definition 4.1 The relative frequency of R to every class is defined as

$$p_i = \frac{|C_i \cap R|}{|R|} = \frac{\sum_{j=1}^{n} \min\{C_i(e_j), R(e_j)\}}{\sum_{k=1}^{n} R(e_k)}, \tag{4.8}$$

where
$S = \{e_1, e_2, \ldots, e_n\}$
p_i $(1 \le i \le k)$ is considered as the degree of the implication $R \Rightarrow C_i$

Definition 4.2 If R is a leaf node, the classification ambiguity of R is defined as

$$Ambiguity(R) = \sum_{i=1}^{k} (p_i^* - p_{i+1}^*) \ln i, \tag{4.9}$$

where $(p_1, p_2, \ldots, p_k)$ is the relative frequency vector of R and $(p_1^*, p_2^*, \ldots, p_k^*)$ is the normalization of $(p_1, p_2, \ldots, p_k)$ with $1 = p_1^* \ge \cdots \ge p_i^* \ge p_{i+1}^* \ge \cdots \ge p_{k+1}^* = 0$.

Definition 4.3 If R is a non-leaf node having m child nodes $R_1, R_2, \ldots, R_m$, which are generated according to their corresponding values $V_1, V_2, \ldots, V_m$ of the expanding attribute F, that is, $R_i = R \cup V_i$ $(1 \le i \le m)$, we define the following weighted average ambiguity as the classification ambiguity of the non-leaf node R:

$$Ambiguity(R) = \sum_{i=1}^{m} w_i \times Ambiguity(R_i) = \sum_{i=1}^{m} \frac{|R_i|}{|R|} \times Ambiguity(R_i). \tag{4.10}$$

In the maximum ambiguity–based active learning algorithm, we define the ambiguity of a fuzzy decision as the averaged classification ambiguity of the root, which could be calculated recursively from the leaf nodes to the root according to Equations (4.9) and (4.10).

In crisp decision tree, when an unseen new instance is matched to the decision tree, the matching output of the decision tree is an exact class because only one rule matches the instance. While a new instance is matching to a fuzzy decision tree, the matching output is not a certain class label but a vector, each element of which represents the membership degree of the instance belonging to the corresponding class, respectively.

Definition 4.4 Let T be a fuzzy decision tree trained well and x be a new instance of which the class information is unknown. Matching the instance to the fuzzy decision tree T, we obtain a fuzzy set $\pi = (\pi_1, \pi_2, \ldots, \pi_k)$, in which each component represents the membership degree of x belonging to the corresponding class. Then the estimated ambiguity of x is defined as

$$EA(x) = Ambiguity(\pi), \tag{4.11}$$

where $Ambiguity(\pi)$ is given in formula (4.9).

4.3.2 Analysis on Samples with Maximal Ambiguity

Usually, sample selection aims to find those informative samples and add them to the training set to improve the performance of the current learner. Many existing sample selection algorithms are to select the misclassified samples, which are based on the idea that those misclassified samples are more helpful than those samples that are correctly classified regarding the improvement of the learning accuracy of the learner.

This idea can be extended to the uncertainty environment. The probably misclassified samples are usually in the vicinity of the decision boundary, which are difficult to classify by using the current learner. Here, we think that the samples that are with more classification ambiguity can provide more information to the learner.

To intuitively analyze the characteristics of the samples with maximal ambiguity, we take a simple demonstration of classification problem.

Consider a binary classification problem. Suppose that an instance is a point on the x-axis and its class label is determined by the function defined by

$$f(x) = e^{-(x-1)^2} - e^{-(x+1)^2}. \tag{4.12}$$

If $f(x) \geq 0$, the point will be classified to the first class with membership degree $C_1(x)$ that is evaluated by

$$C_1(x) = \frac{e^{-(x-1)^2}}{e^{-(x+1)^2} + e^{-(x-1)^2}}. \tag{4.13}$$

If $f(x) < 0$, the point will be classified to the second class with membership degree $C_2(x)$ that is evaluated by

$$C_2(x) = \frac{e^{-(x+1)^2}}{e^{-(x+1)^2} + e^{-(x-1)^2}}. \qquad (4.14)$$

Figure 4.4 gives the intuitive model of the binary classification problem. Figure 4.4a gives the points distribution and corresponding classification function; Figure 4.4b shows the membership degree of the points to every class. Clearly, we can get that $x = 0$ is the decision boundary of the classification problem. When $x > 0$, the membership degree of the point to the first class is bigger than that to the second class; thus it will be classified to C_1. When $x < 0$, the membership degree of the point to the first class is smaller than that to the second class; thus it will be classified to C_2. According to the membership degree function provided by formulae (4.13) and (4.14), we get the ambiguity shown in Figure 4.5.

It is clear to see that the points near the boundary $x = 0$ are with more ambiguity than those that are far away from $x = 0$. Usually, it is considered that the boundary points are easier to be misclassified by the learner than those far away from the

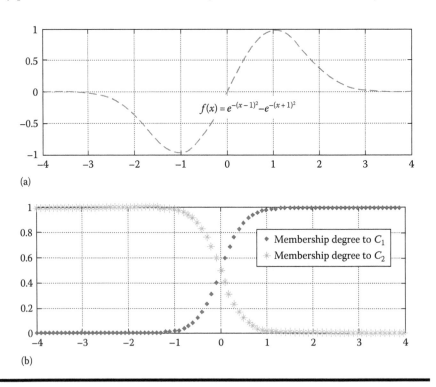

(a)

(b)

Figure 4.4 A simple model of two binary classification problem. (a) Classification function. (b) Membership degrees.

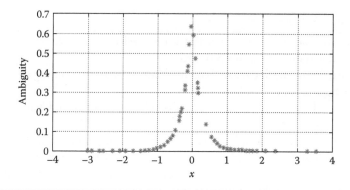

Figure 4.5   Ambiguity of the points.

boundary. And thus the boundary points are considered to be able to provide more information for current learner. Therefore, the sample with maximal classification ambiguity should be most informative.

4.3.3 Maximum Ambiguity–Based Sample Selection

In this section, we present maximum ambiguity–based sample selection algorithm named MABSS. The framework of this sample selection algorithm is described in Figure 4.6.

First, we randomly select a certain number of instances from original data set and submit them to experts for labeling. The labeled set is considered as the initial training set. Then we build a fuzzy decision tree using the training set and predict the unlabeled instances using the currently built decision tree. According to the prediction results (estimated ambiguity), we select one or some instances for annotation by domain experts. Finally, we add the selected instance(s) to the training set. The procedure will repeat several times until the number of the selected samples is up to the predefined threshold. The MABSS algorithm is presented in Algorithm 4.3.

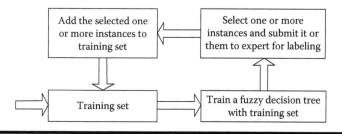

Figure 4.6   Framework of the maximum ambiguity–based sample selection algorithm.

Algorithm 4.3: MABSS Algorithm

Input: A, a data set, q, the predefined size of selected samples.

Output: A trained fuzzy decision tree.

1 Data partitions. Each data set is divided into three parts: training set, instance pool (short for pool), and testing set.
2 Training a fuzzy decision tree by the algorithm introduced in Chapter 2 or Min-A [28].
3 Estimating the memberships of each instance in the pool to each class by using the newly built fuzzy decision tree and getting its classification ambiguity.
4 Selecting the instance with the maximum classification ambiguity to label. Then moving it to the training set from the pool.
5 If the selected samples are less than the predefined size q, then repeat Steps 2–4, and select next instance; otherwise train a decision tree using the labeled samples and test the tree using testing set.
6 Output the trained fuzzy decision tree.

In the first step of Algorithm 4.3, the training set is used for building a classifier/learner that is used for selecting the next instance; instance pool is a set of unlabeled instances that provide candidate instances for the learner to select; testing set is used for testing the performance of the current classifier. In the experiments, we choose one from the five folds as testing set, one fold of the remaining as the training set, and the others as the instance pool.

With respect to the second step of Algorithm 4.3, in the experiments, each attribute is discretized into two values by Kohonet's feature mapping algorithm [28], and then each attribute is fuzzified into two linguistic terms by triangular fuzzification method [28]. The final data set is the 0.45-strong set of the fuzzified data sets, which means that the cut level is 0.45. In the growing of the decision tree, the truth level threshold is set as 0.85, which means that a leaf node is produced when the classification accuracy of a node is bigger than or equal to 0.85. In the following, we give some further notes on the MABSS algorithm.

Many sample selection algorithms such as IBL, CNN, and their extensions could not select samples from data sets without labels, because their selection mechanisms are associated with the class labels of the samples to be selected. Their selection results are directly dependent on the class labels of the samples. Thus, these algorithms could just condense the data set but could not reduce labeling cost.

Different from these algorithms, pool-based active learning methods do not have to know the class label of the instance before it is added to the training set, that is, during the selection procedure, there is no need to label all the instances in the pool. Thus, the experts just need to label the selected samples when they are added to the training set, which is just a small part of the whole samples in the data set.

Compared with the random selection mechanism, MABSS algorithm selects the samples with maximal classification ambiguity. It avoids labeling useless samples such as those that can be correctly classified without doubt. The samples with maximal classification ambiguity are usually in the neighborhood of the decision boundary and are considered that they could provide more information and make a more exact decision boundary. Thus, MABSS could get a more representative and smaller training set than the random selection method. The experimental results on data sets give a convincing evidence.

Compared with the existing work [29,30], there are the following main similarities and differences between them and MABSS. (1) Regarding class distribution information, Maytal et al. [29,30] used the class probability estimation, while MABSS used the possibility distribution. The difference between probability and possibility is given in Section 1.5. (2) Regarding the sample selection mechanism, the methods in [29,30] are based on variance of probability estimation, while MABSS is based on the ambiguity. (3) Both belong to a general methodology: uncertainty sampling [5].

4.3.4 Experimental Results

Generally, with respect to MABSS, there is no essential difference between the fuzzy and crisp label data sets, since the uncertainty comes from an estimated probability or possibility distribution and does not come from the original class labels. Thus, we conduct the following experiments on some UCI [31] data sets with crisp labels, which is a degenerated case of the setting.

We experimentally compare three selection methodologies: MABSS, uncertainty sampling [5], and random selection method in terms of the following five aspects: (1) the number of leaf nodes, (2) the number of nodes, (3) average depth of the tree, (4) classification accuracy on pool (called pool accuracy), and (5) classification accuracy on the testing set (called testing accuracy).

We adopt the acceptance/rejection sampling (short for A/R or AR) [32] to select samples randomly, which is presented in Algorithm 4.4.

The experiments are conducted on some selected UCI data sets with continuous attributes, the basic information of the selected data sets for experiments is summarized in Table 4.1.

In Table 4.1, the datum 699 in 699(683) about Breast denotes the number of records in original data set, while 683 denotes the number of records after removing some records with missing values, and so are 458(444) and 241(239).

In the following, we give an analysis on experimental results in detail. First, we explore the change tendencies of the performances of the trees as more and more selected samples are added to the training set and compare the trees trained from the same number of samples selected by different selection methods. When all samples in the pool are added to the training set, the trained tree is called a pool tree. The information of pool trees on selected data sets is listed in Table 4.2. In Table 4.2,

---

Algorithm 4.4: A/R Sampling (Random Selection Method)

    Input: An instance pool: $(e_1, e_2, \ldots, e_n)$, the degree of each sample to be
        selected: $w = (w_1, w_2, \ldots, w_n)$, where n is the number of instances in
        the pool.

    Output: The selected instance e^*.

1 Each element in w is divided by the sum of all the elements:
$w' = \frac{1}{\sum_{i=1}^{n} w_i}(w_1, w_2, \ldots, w_n)$.

2 Tag the border lines between adjacent subregions. For example, the border
between the first and second subregions is $\frac{w_1}{\sum_{i=1}^{n} w_i}$, and the border between

the k-th and $(k+1)$-th subregions is $\frac{\sum_{j=1}^{k} w_j}{\sum_{i=1}^{n} w_i}$.

3 Produce a double data between 0 and 1 randomly. If the data is bigger than
$\frac{\sum_{j=1}^{k} w_j}{\sum_{i=1}^{n} w_i}$ and smaller than or equal to $\frac{\sum_{j=1}^{k+1} w_j}{\sum_{i=1}^{n} w_i}$, then the k-th instance is
selected. We use e^* to denote the selected instance.

4 Label the class for e^* by experts and remove it from the pool.

5 Output e^* with its label.

L-Nodes denotes leaf nodes of the generated fuzzy decision tree, A-Depth denotes the average depth of the generated fuzzy decision tree, P-Accuracy denotes the accuracy of the pool trees, and T-Accuracy denotes the testing accuracy of the generated fuzzy decision tree.

As an example, we analyze the experimental results on Glass, which is a data set containing multiclass with unbalanced distribution F. In the experiment on Glass, we select 120 samples iteratively using MABSS and the random selection, respectively. The average experimental results are depicted in Figure 4.7.

In Figure 4.7, the horizontal axis is the number of selected samples, and the vertical axis is the corresponding measurements. The curves with bold legend "+" are the experimental results using MABSS, and the curves without legend are the results of random selection method. The dashed lines are the corresponding values of the pool trees.

Figure 4.7a shows the testing accuracies of the trees trained from samples selected by MABSS and random selection methods. Clearly we can see from Figure 4.7a that the testing accuracy of the random selection method is increasing all the time as more and more samples are added into the training set. This fact coincides with the idea that more training samples there are, the higher prediction ability is. But the curves with bold legend "+" ascend gradually initially, then descend, and finally converge to the testing accuracy of pool tree. The reason why the testing accuracy of MABSS increases at an early stage and decreases at a late stage is that (1) the selected instances are usually insufficient, (2) more representative instances exist in the pool at the

Table 4.1 Basic Information of the Selected UCI Data Sets for Experiments

Data Sets	Instances	Attributes	Data Type	Classes	Class Distribution	Missing Values
Glass	214	9	Real	6	70/76/17/13/9/30	None
Iris	150	4	Real	3	50/50/50	None
Wine	178	13	Real	3	59/71/48	None
Ecoli	336	7	Real	8	143/77/52/35/20/5/2/2	None
Wdbc	569	31	Real	2	357/212	None
Breast	699(683)	9	Integer	2	458(444)/241(239)	16
Ionosphere	351	34	Real	2	225/126	None
Haberman	306	3	Integer	2	225/81	None
Transfusion	748	4	Real	2	178/560	None
Bupa	354	6	Integer	2	145/200	None
Sonar	208	60	Real	2	111/97	None
Yeast	1484	8	Real	10	463/429/244/163/51/44/37/30/20/5	None
Waveform	5000	21	Real	3	1657/1647/1696	None
Spambase	4601	57	Real	2	2788/1813	None
Segmentation	2310	19	Real	7	330/330/330/330/330/330/330	None
Wine quality-white	4898	11	Real	7	5/175/880/20/163/1457/2198	None
Wine quality-red	1599	11	Real	6	18/199/638/10/53/681	None

Table 4.2   Information of Pool Trees

Data Sets	L-Nodes	Nodes	A-Depth	P-Accuracy	T-Accuracy
Glass	27.6200	57.9600	5.7549	0.6676	0.5305
Iris	3.1000	5.2000	1.7218	0.7553	0.7580
Wine	6.3200	11.8200	2.8171	0.8892	0.8654
Ecoli	17.3600	34.6000	4.8200	0.8264	0.7816
Wdbc	2.0000	3.0000	1.0000	0.9057	0.9004
Breast	2.0000	3.0000	1.0000	0.8914	0.8869
Ionosphere	3.6100	6.3000	2.0041	0.8862	0.8839
Haberman	3.8000	6.6000	2.0136	0.7549	0.7354
Transfusion	4.7800	9.0600	2.5390	0.7662	0.7612
Bupa	21.8100	42.7600	4.8904	0.6435	0.5823
Sonar	30.4500	65.960	7.1755	0.9163	0.6988
Yeast	53.0800	109.8700	6.6715	0.5307	0.4917
Waveform	1417	2956.6	14.2	0.9000	0.7500
Spambase	271.2455	804.5909	28.6000	0.8439	0.8223
Segmentation	76.0500	190.0750	13.2835	0.8168	0.8105
Wine quality-white	184.6800	406.7900	9.7200	0.5364	0.5013
Wine quality-red	189.6900	396.7800	9.0120	0.6544	0.5748

early stage, (3) MABSS effectively selects the representative and removes the similar samples, and (4) few samples exist at the late stage, and therefore, samples selected by MABSS may be with little representativeness, which leads to a little decrease of testing accuracy. Generally if the selected samples are sufficient, at the early stage of selection, the averaged performance gradually increases with the sample added, but when the exact true model is approximately found, the new added samples will not significantly influence the performance. This phenomenon indicates that the selected samples using MABSS could indeed select representative samples.

From another point of view, to get a predefined testing accuracy, the selected samples by MABSS are less than by the random selection method. For example, to get to the level of the testing accuracy (samples in the pool as training set, about 171 samples), we just need to select around 10 samples (25% samples as training set, about

53 samples) by using MABSS, while about 90 samples will be selected (62% samples as training set, about 133 samples) when using the random selection methodology.

Similar to Figure 4.7a, in Figure 4.7b, when more and more samples are selected to add to the training set, pool accuracies of the trees increase gradually and finally arrive in the training accuracy of the pool tree. Figure 4.7c and d describes the average depth of the tree and the number of nodes/leaf nodes, respectively. From Figure 4.7c and d, we can see that the sizes of the trees become larger when more and more samples are added into the training set and the size of the tree trained by the samples selected by using MABSS is a little larger than by using the random selection method.

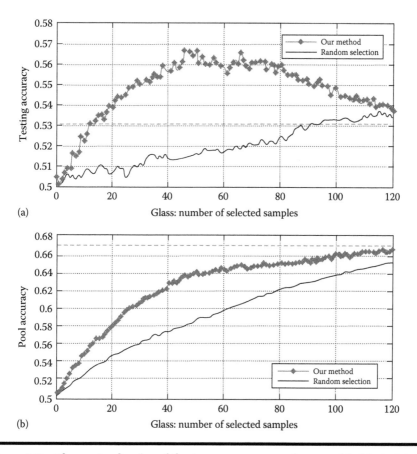

(a)

(b)

Figure 4.7   Change tendencies of the trees as more samples are added to training set using MABSS and random selection method on Glass. (a) Relationship between the testing accuracy and the number of selected samples and (b) relationship between the pool accuracy and the number of selected samples.   (*Continued*)

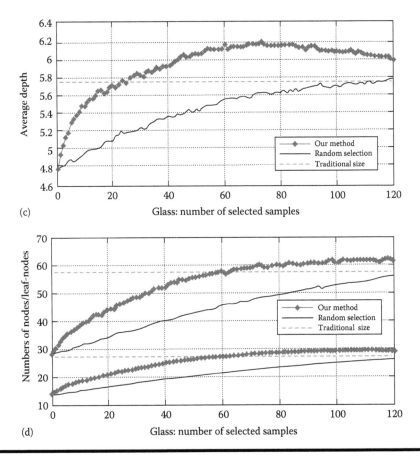

Figure 4.7 (*Continued*) Change tendencies of the trees as more samples are added to training set using MABSS and random selection method on Glass. (c) Relationship between the average depth and the number of selected samples and (d) relationship between the numbers of nodes/leaf-nodes and the number of selected samples. ■

We take record of the testing accuracies when the selected numbers are 30, 40, 50, 60, 70, 80, 100, and 120, respectively. They are shown in Table 4.3. Based on Table 4.3, the significant level and confidence interval are applied in the analysis. It is found that the rangeabilities are less than 0.005. To verify the differences between the two methods, the statistical significance testing is used. We get the conclusion that the testing accuracies of MABSS are 3.5%–4.3% higher than random selection when the number of selected samples is between 30 and 80.

We further analyze the experimental results on a larger data set. Figure 4.8 intuitively illustrates the experimental results on Spambase. As same as in Figure 4.7, the horizontal axis is the number of selected samples and the vertical axis is the

Table 4.3 Statistical Information of Testing Accuracies on Glass

No. of Samples	Selection Type	$\overline{X}$	S^2	n
30	MABSS	0.5501	0.0191^2	20
	Rand	0.5116	0.0175^2	20
	US	0.5313	0.0189^2	20
40	MABSS	0.5566	0.0185^2	20
	Rand	0.5135	0.0158^2	20
	US	0.5342	0.0135^2	20
50	MABSS	0.5660	0.0164^2	20
	Rand	0.5164	0.0199^2	20
	US	0.5389	0.0178^2	20
60	MABSS	0.5590	0.0145^2	20
	Rand	0.5171	0.0167^2	20
	US	0.5403	0.0168^2	20
70	MABSS	0.5609	0.0163^2	20
	Rand	0.5206	0.0152^2	20
	US	0.5432	0.0156^2	20
80	MABSS	0.5598	0.0170^2	20
	Rand	0.5247	0.0129^2	20
	US	0.5489	0.0189^2	20
100	MABSS	0.5488	0.0181^2	20
	Rand	0.5330	0.0187^2	20
	US	0.5464	0.0179^2	20
120	MABSS	0.5372	0.0130^2	20
	Rand	0.5339	0.0188^2	20
	US	0.5368	0.0158^2	20

corresponding measurements in Figure 4.8. The curves with bold legend "+" are the experimental results using MABSS, and the curves without legend are the results of the random selection method. The dashed lines are the corresponding values of the pool trees.

From Figure 4.8, we can see that the testing accuracies of the trees trained from samples selected by MABSS and random selection methods are gradually increased when more and more samples are added into the training set. Different from Figure 4.7a, the curves with bold legend "+" in Figure 4.8a are always increased during the whole process, and there is no descent stage. This fact is consistent with the assumption that the method could effectively select the representative samples if there exist sufficient instances and sufficient representative instances to be selected. One reason why both the curves of testing accuracies are below the testing accuracy of the pool tree is that the training set of both trees are far less than the training set of

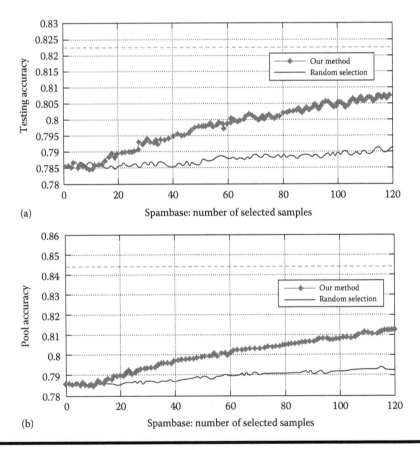

Figure 4.8 Experimental results on Spambase. (a) Relationship between the testing accuracy and the number of selected samples and (b) relationship between the pool accuracy and the number of selected samples. (*Continued*)

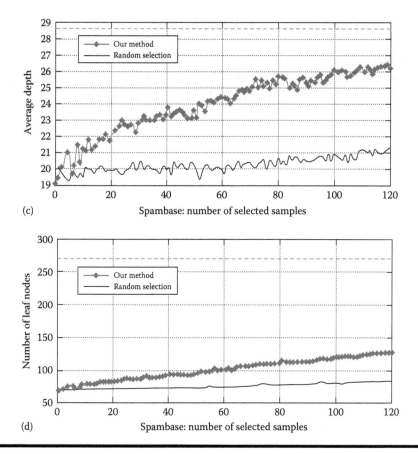

(c)

(d)

Figure 4.8 (*Continued*) Experimental results on Spambase. (c) Relationship between the average depth and the number of selected samples and (d) relationship between the numbers of leaf-nodes and the number of selected samples.

the pool tree. (The proportion is about 580:3680.) Another reason is that the model for Spambase is the most complex among the data sets, so more training samples are required to establish the model.

Finally, we compare the testing accuracies and the sizes of the trees trained from samples selected by the three methods when the number of selected samples is 60, and the statistical results are shown in Table 4.4 and Figure 4.9. In Table 4.4, U-Sampling denotes uncertainty sampling, and P-Tree denotes pool tree.

Table 4.4 shows a comparative result about the testing accuracy. On all data sets in Table 4.4, MABSS has a better testing accuracy than the other two methods, but is not always better than the pool tree. The reason is again explained as that MABSS can indeed select the representative samples if the instances in the pool are sufficient and the pool tree has a much bigger training set.

Table 4.4 Testing Accuracy of Three Sample Selection Methods

Data Sets	Rand (Mean/Var)	MABSS	U-Sampling	P-Tree
Glass	$0.5171/0.0167^2$	$0.5590/0.0145^2$	$0.5403/0.0168^2$	0.5305
Iris	$0.7572/0.0065^2$	$0.7789/0.0175^2$	$0.7589/0.0118^2$	0.7580
Wine	$0.8667/0.0123^2$	$0.8843/0.0093^2$	$0.8697/0.103^2$	0.8654
Ecoli	$0.7636/0.0120^2$	$0.7722/0.0150^2$	$0.7589/0.0128^2$	0.7816
Wdbc	$0.8984/0.0037^2$	$0.9229/0.0024^2$	$0.8712/0.0049^2$	0.9004
Breast	$0.8818/0.0052^2$	$0.9330/0.0104^2$	$0.9102/0.0089^2$	0.8869
Ionosphere	$0.8573/0.0066^2$	$0.8674/0.0062^2$	$0.8913/0.099^2$	0.8839
Haberman	$0.7312/0.0067^2$	$0.7372/0.0051^2$	$0.7335/0.0068^2$	0.7354
Transfusion	$0.7628/0.0028^2$	$0.7627/0.0021^2$	$0.7815/0.0056^2$	0.7612
Bupa	$0.5580/0.0107^2$	$0.5409/0.0100^2$	$0.5448/0.0108^2$	0.5823
Sonar	$0.6929/0.0175^2$	$0.6948/0.0172^2$	$0.6932/0.0119^2$	0.6988
Yeast	$0.4583/0.0066^2$	$0.4664/0.0053^2$	$0.4486/0.0156^2$	0.4917
Waveform	$0.6892/0.0094^2$	$0.6930/0.0142^2$	$0.6901/0.0135^2$	0.7500
Spambase	$0.7887/0.0139^2$	$0.8016/0.0126^2$	$0.7983/0.0115^2$	0.8223
Segmentation	$0.7794/0.0265^2$	$0.7839/0.0167^2$	$0.7809/0.0216^2$	0.8105
Wine quality-white	$0.4458/0.0173^2$	$0.4524/0.0141^2$	$0.4518/0.0169^2$	0.5013
Wine quality-red	$0.4942/0.0214^2$	$0.5056/0.0164^2$	$0.4987/0.0192^2$	0.5748

From Figure 4.9a and b, we can see that the size of the tree built by the samples selected by MABSS is a little larger than random selection in terms of the number of leaf nodes and the average depth of the tree, which means that the learned knowledge is more complete. The trees built on the samples selected by MABSS have less leaf nodes than pool trees especially when the pool trees are large such as yeast.

4.4 Active Learning Approach to Support Vector Machine

In this section, we introduce another sample selection algorithm [2] named IALPSVM (Informative Active Learning aPproach to Support Vector Machine). The IALPSVM algorithm aims at selecting the most informative instance from an unlabeled pool, which is nearest to the new hyperplane learnt from labeled training set

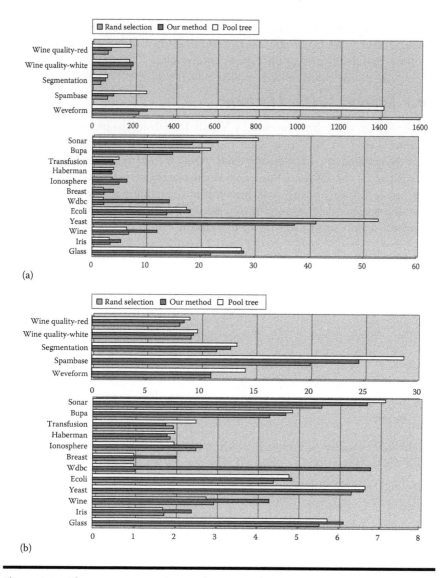

Figure 4.9 The average tree size on data sets of UCI. (a) Average number of leaf nodes. (b) Average depth.

and the instance itself. In the IALPSVM algorithm, a batch of unlabeled instances are selected by considering both the distance and the angular diversity in the batch. The advantages of the IALPSVM algorithm include two aspects: (1) Queries selected by IALPSVM can be better used in learning an optimal hyperplane compared with SVM active learning approach [33]. (2) It can guarantee that these queries are informative and valuable as they are near the final hyperplane as much as they could.

In the following, we first present brief reviews of SVM, SVM active learning, and semisupervised SVM batch mode active learning, then introduce the IALPSVM algorithm, and finally present the experimental results.

4.4.1 Support Vector Machine

SVM [34] is an algorithm proposed by Vapnik for solving the binary classification problems. Let $L = \{(x_i, y_i)|x_i \in R^n, y_i \in \{-1, 1\}(1 \leq i \leq l)\}$ be the training set. If the training set is linearly separable, SVM is looking for a hyperplane that can separate all the instances with a maximal margin. The equation of a hyperplane can be defined as $f(x) = 0$. Instances in the training set are mapped into a higher-dimensional feature space H_k by a mapping ϕ for nonlinear case. The primal optimization problem of SVM can be modeled by

$$\min_{\omega, b, \xi} \frac{1}{2} \| \omega \|^2 + C \sum_{i=1}^{l} \xi_i$$

$$s.t. \; y_i((\omega, \phi(x_i)) + b) \geq 1 - \xi_i$$

$$\xi_i \geq 0, i = 1, 2, \ldots, l \qquad (4.15)$$

where
  $\xi_i \; (1 \leq i \leq l)$ are the slack variables
  C is the trade-off parameter between maximal margin and minimal misclassification

Let the inner product of vectors in the feature space H_k be kernel function $k(\cdot, \cdot)$ and K the Gram matrix $K_{ij} = k(x_i, x_j)$. The optimal hyperplane can be modeled by

$$f(x) = (\omega^*, \phi(x)) + b^* = 0, \qquad (4.16)$$

where ω^* and b^* are the optimal solutions of the problem in Equation (4.15). We solve the optimization problem in Equation (4.15) by its dual form and can obtain

$$\omega^* = \sum_{i=1}^{l} \alpha_i^* y_i \phi(x_i)$$

$$b^* = y_j - \sum_{i=1}^{l} y_i \alpha_i^* k(x_i, x_j), \quad 0 < \alpha_j < C \qquad (4.17)$$

where
  α is the Lagrange multiplier
  α^* is the optimal solution of Equation (4.15)'s dual problem

The decision function is

$$\mathrm{sgn}(f(x)) = \mathrm{sgn}\left(\sum_{i=1}^{l} \alpha_i^* y_i k(x, x_i) + b^*\right). \qquad (4.18)$$

4.4.2 SVM Active Learning

SVM active learning [33] was proposed by Tong et al. and is recognized as the first technique of combining active learning with SVM. On the premise of all feature vectors' modulus being constant (e.g., $\phi(x) = 1$, for each x) in the feature space H, each feature vector $\phi(x)$ is on the surface of a hyper sphere in H, whose radius is equal to the constant mentioned earlier. Each labeled instance x in the training set L corresponds to a single hyperplane $(w, \phi(x) = 0)$, which intersects with the hyper sphere through the mapping feature vector $\phi(x)$ of x; each unit normal vector x of a hyperplane $(w, \phi(x) = 0)$ in H corresponds to a single point on the sphere. All normal vectors of hyperplanes, which can classify all instances in the training set L correctly, make up the version space. Three approximate approaches of bisecting the version space are proposed in [33]. They are Simple Margin, MaxMin Margin, and Ratio Margin, respectively. In the following, we briefly review the Simple Margin method which is the typical one of the three approaches.

First, Simple Margin approach learns an optimal hyperplane denoted by Equation (4.19) from all labeled instances in the training set L:

$$f^*(x) = (w^*, \phi(x)) + b^* = 0. \qquad (4.19)$$

Then such an unlabeled instance x^*, which is nearest to the hyperplane, is selected from the unlabeled set U for annotation. The x^* is selected with the following formula:

$$x^* = \underset{x \in U}{\mathrm{argmin}} \frac{|f^*(x)|}{\|w^*\|}. \qquad (4.20)$$

Then x^* is removed from the unlabeled set U and put into the labeled set L. After several iterations, a classifier $\mathrm{sgn}(f^{**}(x))$, which is learnt from the training set L, will be accurate enough to predict all unlabeled instances left in U.

Only one query x^* is found each time in SVM active learning's theory, which is unrealistic in practical application. So Tong and Koller [33] select a batch of queries each time using the same principle as mentioned earlier. That is, a batch of unlabeled instances, which are nearest to the hyperplane, are selected for annotation. However, experimental results show that such a batch mode instance selection approach often leads to redundancy in queries. Fortunately, this kind of redundancy can be eliminated by combining diversity measurement with the instance selection approach in the batch mode.

Algorithm 4.5: Incremental Batch Query Algorithm Based on SVM Active Learning

---

Input: An unlabeled instance pool U; a tradeoff parameter $\lambda \in [0, 1]$ between minimal distance and maximal angle; a predefined parameter m, which represents the number of instance in a batch.

Output: The selected instance subset S.

1 Let $S = \varnothing$.

2 **while** $(|S| \neq m)$ **do**

3 $\quad$ $x^* = \underset{x_i \in U-S}{argmin} \left(\lambda \frac{|f^*(x_i)|}{\|\omega^*\|} + (1-\lambda) \underset{x_j \in S}{\max} \, cos(\theta_{ij}) \right)$;

4 $\quad$ $S = S \cup \{x^*\}$;

5 **end**

6 Output S.

Different kinds of diversity measurements can be found in Brinker et al. [35–37]. Here we briefly review the angular diversity in Brinker [35]. We have known that each instance x corresponds to a hyperplane in the feature space. So the difference between each two instances can be weighed by the diversity of two instances' corresponding hyperplanes. Hyperplanes' diversities can be represented by the cosine value of intersection angles and can be calculated by the kernel function. Let θ_{ij} be the intersection angle of two hyperplanes corresponding to x_i and x_j. Let k be the kernel function. Then cosine of θ_{ij} can be evaluated by

$$\cos(\theta_{ij}) = \left(\frac{|k(x_i, x_j)|}{\sqrt{k(x_i, x_i)k(x_j, x_j)}} \right). \tag{4.21}$$

By incorporating the angular diversity proposed in Brinker [35], queries are selected by Algorithm 4.5 [35]. In Algorithm 4.5, f^* is the optimal function learnt on L, that is, $f^*(x) = 0$ is the optimal hyperplane learnt on L.

4.4.3 Semisupervised SVM Batch Mode Active Learning

Semisupervised SVM active learning was proposed by Hoi et al. [38] and can be recognized as an improvement of SVM active learning approach in Tong and Koller [33]. First, a data-dependent kernel function k is learnt by considering the geometric relationship of instances both in the labeled set L and the unlabeled set U. Let ϕ be the mapping function corresponding to the kernel function k. H_k represents the feature space. Then Hoi et al. [38] explain that the query's effect in Equation (4.20) is overestimated. The reason is that Equation (4.20) is proved to be equivalent to

$$x^* = \underset{x \in U}{\operatorname{argmin}} \; \underset{y \in \{-1,1\}}{\max} \; g(f^*, L \cup \{(x,y)\}, K). \tag{4.22}$$

In Equation (4.22), f^* is the optimal function learnt on L; g is the object function described by Equation (4.23) in the primal problem of SVM:

$$g(f^*, L, K) = \frac{1}{2} \|\omega^*\|^2 + C \sum \xi_i^*. \tag{4.23}$$

K represents the Gram matrix. x^* in Equation (4.22) is the most valuable instance on the premise of the hypothesis that f^* is unchanged even if one more instance (x,y) is put into the training set. So the query's effect in increasing the value of g is overestimated. Then a new instance selection approach with Equation (4.24) is proposed in Hoi et al. [38] to compensate this shortcoming by considering the changes of f when (x,y) is put into the training set:

$$x^* = \underset{x \in U}{\operatorname{argmin}} \; \underset{y \in \{-1,1\}}{\max} \; \underset{f \in H_k}{\min} \; g(f, L \cup \{(x,y)\}, K). \tag{4.24}$$

Equation (4.24) is a method of selecting one single query each time in Hoi et al. [38]. For semisupervised SVM batch mode active learning, another two approximate methods are proposed in Hoi et al. [38], in which a quadratic programming problem is solved in order to approximate the combinatorial optimization problem for the batch mode of Equation (4.24). Regarding the details of the two approximate methods, interested readers can refer to Hoi et al. [38].

4.4.4 IALPSVM: An Informative Active Learning Approach to SVM

In this section, we introduce IALPSVM. First of all, we state that query's each possible label does not affect SVM active learning approach's decision. That's the following theorem.

Theorem 4.1 Let f^* be the optimal function learnt on labeled instances in the training set L. U is the set of unlabeled instances. Then we have

$$x^* = \underset{x \in U}{\operatorname{argmin}} \; \frac{|f^*(x)|}{\|\omega^*\|} \iff x^* = \underset{x \in U}{\operatorname{argmin}} \; \underset{y \in \{-1,1\}}{\max} \; \frac{|f^*(x)|}{\|\omega^*\|}. \tag{4.25}$$

The equivalence (4.25) can be proved easily [2]. The motivation of changing (4.20) into the right part of Equation (4.25) is as follows. We want to prove that x's each possible label y does not affect the value $\frac{|f^*(x)|}{\|\omega^*\|}$ at all, so y has little effect on SVM active learning's decision of selecting x^* either. Here a new classifier is learnt after x^*

is labeled and put into the training set L in the IALPSVM algorithm. By considering the changes of f in Hoi et al. [38] when (x, y) is added into the training set, the right part of Equation (4.25) is changed into the following equation:

$$x^* = \underset{x \in U}{\text{argmin}} \ \underset{y \in \{-1,1\}}{\max} \ \frac{|f^{\sharp}(x)|}{\|w^{\sharp}\|}$$

$$f^{\sharp} = \underset{f \in H_k}{\text{argmin}} \ g(f, L \cup \{(x, y)\}, K). \tag{4.26}$$

The main idea hidden in Equation (4.26) is to select such a query x^*, which is nearest to the hyperplane learnt by both instances in L and the query x^* by considering its two possible labels. As is known, training instances around the hyperplane play important roles in constructing an optimal hyperplane. These instances can be support vectors or misclassified instances by the classifier. So queries should be selected from these instances. However, when a query x^* is labeled and put into the training set L to learn a new hyperplane, this new training instance may be far away from the new hyperplane and become dispensable. That is, we cannot assure that this new training instance is useful to the new hyperplane. However, query selected by Equation (4.26) is assured to be closest to the new hyperplane in the worst case of labels. Description of IALPSVM in selecting informative query is shown in the following.

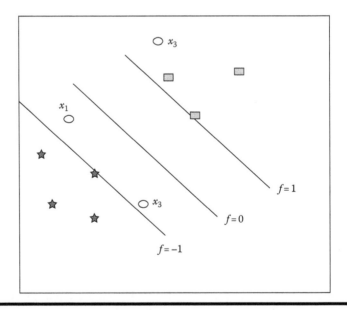

Figure 4.10 Initial instances and hyperplane. Squares and stars represent positive and negative instances in the labeled training set *L*. Circles are unlabeled instances in *U*.

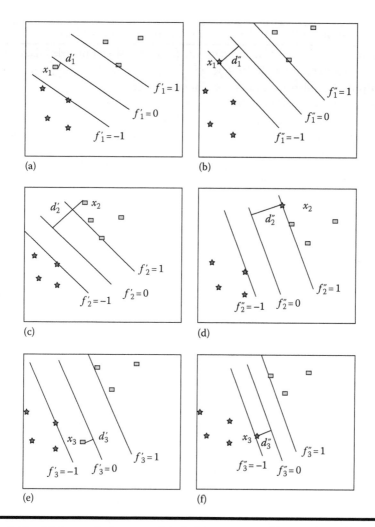

Figure 4.11 **Distances between unlabeled instances and hyperplanes by considering all possible labels. The label of x_i is taken as positive (or negative) in (a), (c), and (e) (or in (b), (d), and (f)). Hyperplanes $f_i' = 0$ and $f_i'' = 0$ are learnt from L and x_i. d_i' and d_i'' are distances between x_i and these two hyperplanes.**

Initial instances are shown in Figure 4.10. The equation of the optimal hyperplane learnt on L is $f = 0$. Margin is the distance between $f = 1$ and $f = -1$.

For each unlabeled instance x_i, we consider its two possible labels in Figure 4.11. For each unlabeled instance x_i, the values of distances can reflect the degree of importance in learning a hyperplane. As support vectors except outliers always lie close to

---

Algorithm 4.6: IALPSVM Algorithm for Choosing a Single Query

Input: L, a small-sized labeled data set; U, a large-sized unlabeled data set; V, a zero vector with size $1 \times |U|$.

Output: An unlabeled instance x^* for annotation.

1 **for** *(each instance x_i in U)* **do**
2   **for** *(x_i's each possible label $y \in \{-1, 1\}$)* **do**
3   Train SVM with the data set $L \cup \{(x, y)\}$ to get the optimal hyperplane $f^\sharp = 0$;
4   Compute the value of $\frac{|f^\sharp(x_i)|}{\|\omega^\sharp\|}$;
5   Let $V(i) = \max\left(V(i), \frac{|f^\sharp(x_i)|}{\|\omega^\sharp\|}\right)$;
6   **end**
7 **end**
8 Find the index ID of the minimal element of V;
9 Let $x^* = x_{ID}$;
10 $U = U - \{x^*\}$;
11 Output x^*.

---

the hyperplane, so queries should be close to the hyperplane and be the support vectors as much as possible. Only the larger one between d_i' and d_i'' is concerned in IALPSVM. From Figure 4.11, we can see that d_1'', d_2', and d_3'' are the larger distances corresponding to x_1, x_2, and x_3, respectively. The value of distance concerned in IALPSVM can weigh the degree of importance in x_i's worse case of labels. The final query is the instance whose corresponding larger distance is minimal. A comparison of d_1'', d_2', and d_3'' indicates that x_3 should be selected as the query for future annotation. x_i's each possible label plays an important role in the instance selection process of IALPSVM, which is different from SVM active learning. So instance selected by IALPSVM can be as useful as possible in constructing a new hyperplane. The algorithm is presented in Algorithm 4.6.

Next, we discuss how to apply IALPSVM to the batch mode in this section. We incorporate the angular diversity in Brinker [35] into IALPSVM in the batch mode. The corresponding algorithm is given in Algorithm 4.7.

4.4.5 Experimental Results and Discussions

4.4.5.1 Experiments on an Artificial Data Set by Selecting a Single Query Each Time

Two data sets are generated respectively from two Gaussian distributions centered at $(-8, -8)$ and $(8, 8)$ with the same variance 8. Each data set contains 500 instances. These two data sets compose the positive and negative classes that are plotted

---

Algorithm 4.7: IALPSVM Algorithm for Choosing a Batch of Queries

---

    Input: L, a small-sized labeled data set; U, a large-sized unlabeled data set; V, a zero vector with size $1 \times |U|$; λ, a trade-off parameter; n_0, the number of selected instances.

    Output: The selected instance subset S.

1 Let $S = \varnothing$ and $m = 0$.

2 **while** $(|S| \le n_0)$ **do**

3   **for** (*each instance x_i in $U - S$*) **do**

4   **for** (*x_i's each possible label $y \in \{-1, 1\}$*) **do**

5   Train SVM with the data set $L \cup \{(x, y)\}$ to get the optimal hyperplane $f^\sharp = 0$;

6   Compute the value of $\frac{|f^\sharp(x_i)|}{\|\omega^\sharp\|}$;

7   Let $V(i) = \max\left(V(i), \frac{|f^\sharp(x_i)|}{\|\omega^\sharp\|}\right)$;

8   **end**

9   **for** (*each instance x_j in S*) **do**

10   Compute $k_1 = \frac{|k(x_i, x_j)|}{\sqrt{k(x_i, x_i)k(x_j, x_j)}}$;

11   Let $m = \max(m, k_1)$;

12   **end**

13        $V(i) = V(i) + (1 - \lambda)m$;

14   **end**

15   Find the index ID of the minimal element of V;

16   Let $S = S \cup \{x_{ID}\}$;

17     $U = U - \{x_{ID}\}$;

18 **end**

19 Output S.

---

in Figure 4.12. Squares represent positive instances, and stars represent negative instances. So the whole data set contains 1000 instances in all. We select 0.2% instances (2 instances, 1 positive and 1 negative) randomly from the whole data set and put them into the labeled training set L (see Figure 4.13). For each of the experiments in the following, we assure that the labeled set L always contains at least one positive and one negative instances. The other 99.8% instances of the whole data set are put into unlabeled set U. We select one query each time for annotation by applying three approaches: SVM active learning [33], semisupervised SVM batch mode active learning (denoted by Equation (4.24)) (Hoi et al. [38]), and IALPSVM [2]. Each query is annotated and put into the labeled set L and eliminated from U. We do this 20 times for each of the three approaches. For all three approaches, the value of C is fixed to 1000, Gaussian kernel $k(x_1, x_2) = \exp\left(\frac{-\|x_1 - x_2\|^2}{2\sigma^2}\right)$ is used as

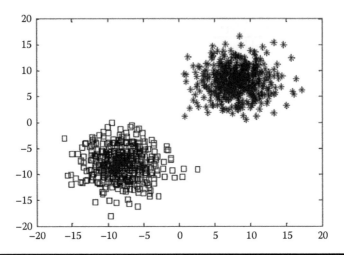

Figure 4.12   An artificial data set.

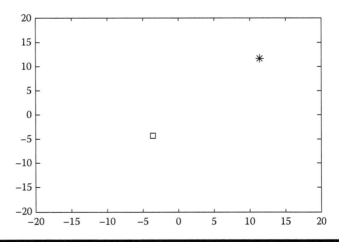

Figure 4.13   Initial labeled instances.

the kernel function, and the value of σ is fixed to 1. LIBSVM [39] toolbox is applied in all the experiments. Results are shown in Figures 4.14 through 4.16.

We can see from Figures 4.14 through 4.16 that instances selected by SVM active learning and semisupervised SVM batch mode active learning are nearly the same in distribution. These instances all lie around the centers tightly. However, instances selected by IALPSVM lie incompactly in the plane. This incompact distribution might represent a higher degree of diversity between instances selected to a certain extent. In this view, the result of IALPSVM is a little better than that of the other two approaches.

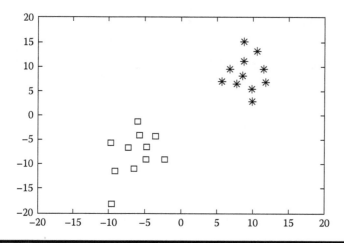

Figure 4.14 First 20 instances selected by support vector machine active learning approach.

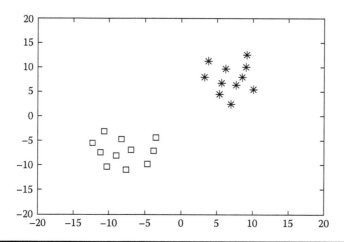

Figure 4.15 First 20 instances selected by Equation (4.24).

4.4.5.2 Experiments on Three UCI Data Sets by Selecting a Single Query Each Time

Three UCI data sets [31] (Dermatology, Ionosphere, and Thyroid Disease) are selected, and each data set is used separately as the whole data set in the experiments. The basic information of the three UCI data sets is shown in Table 4.5. Just like the experiment earlier, we select one query each time for annotation by using the three approaches, and parameters are set the same values as earlier except $\sigma = 5$ for all the approaches. The reason why we do the experiments here is that we want

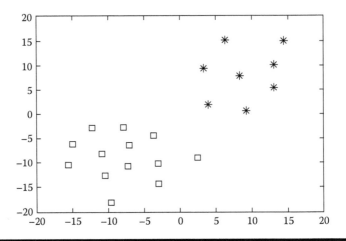

Figure 4.16   First 20 instances selected by IALPSVM.

Table 4.5   Basic Information of the Three UCI Data Sets

Data Set	♯ the Positive	♯ the Negative	♯ Attributes
Dermatology	171	187	34
Ionosphere	224	126	34
Thyroid disease	150	65	5

to compare the abilities of three approaches in choosing the informative unlabeled queries. Test accuracy is calculated for all the approaches on the remaining sets of unlabeled instances. All the experiments are repeated 10 times and the results are averaged. Experimental results are shown in Figures 4.17 through 4.19.

From Figures 4.17 through 4.19 we can see that, taking as a whole, test accuracy goes up along with the number of queries for most of the three approaches in the three data sets. In Dermatology data set, IALPSVM and semisupervised SVM batch mode active learning (denoted by Equation (4.24)) are nearly the same in performance, but IALPSVM can get the highest test accuracy in most of the times; SVM active learning is a little lower in Dermatology. In Ionosphere data set, and IALPSVM performs well most of the times, and IALPSVM and semisupervised SVM batch mode active learning (denoted by Equation (4.24)) can get the highest test accuracy in the end. In Thyroid Disease data set, although all the three approaches get nearly the same accuracy in the beginning, the accuracy of IALPSVM is a little higher than the other two approaches in the end. The semisupervised SVM

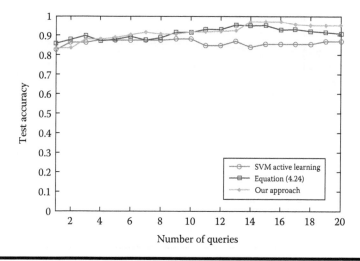

Figure 4.17   Test accuracy on Dermatology, first 20 queries is selected.

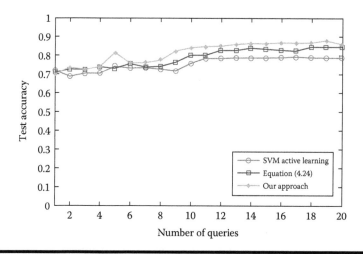

Figure 4.18   Test accuracy on Ionosphere, first 20 queries is selected.

batch mode active learning (denoted by Equation (4.24)) and SVM active learning are nearly the same in Thyroid.

Additionally, we also use correlation coefficient (cc) to measure the performance of the three approaches. This indicator can measure the correlation between the forecast result and the actual situation. The value cc is calculated with Equation (4.27). All the experiments are repeated 10 times and the results are averaged. Experimental results are shown in Figures 4.20 through 4.22.

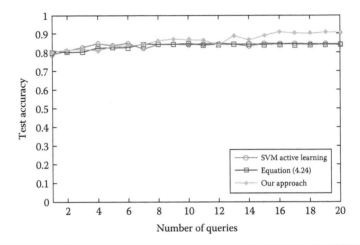

Figure 4.19   Test accuracy on Thyroid, first 20 queries is selected.

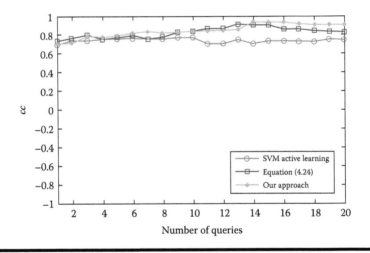

Figure 4.20   Value of correlation coefficient on Dermatology, first 20 queries is selected.

TP (or *FP*) is the number of positive (or negative) instances that are predicted as positive by the classifier; *TN* (or *FN*) is the number of negative (or positive) instances that are predicted as negative by the classifier. The value of *cc* ranges from −1 to 1, where 1 represents the forecast result is the same as the actual result and 0 represents the forecast result is a random prediction.

By comparing Figure 4.17 with Figure 4.20, Figure 4.18 with Figure 4.21, and Figure 4.19 with Figure 4.22, we can see that test accuracy and *cc* value go up and down in the same way, which means that test accuracy can be a valuable indicator

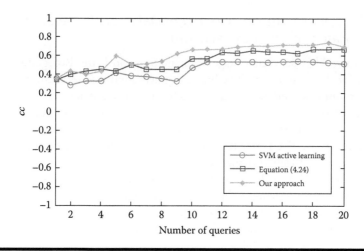

Figure 4.21 Value of correlation coefficient on Ionosphere, first 20 queries is selected.

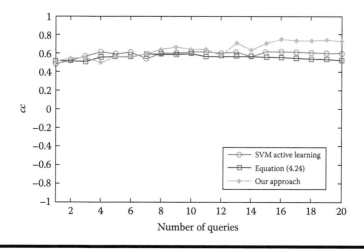

Figure 4.22 Value of correlation coefficient on Thyroid, first 20 queries is selected.

for measuring the performance of the three approaches. From Figures 4.20 through 4.22, we can see that forecast results of all the three approaches are much better in Dermatology than in other two data sets. IALPSVM can get the highest prediction results in all the three data sets:

$$cc = \frac{TP \times TN - FP \times FN}{\sqrt{(TP + FN)(TP + FP)(TN + FP)(TN + FN)}}. \tag{4.27}$$

4.4.5.3 Experiments on Two Image Data Sets by Selecting a Batch of Queries Each Time

Another two UCI data sets (Image Segmentation and Letter Recognition) are also selected for the experiments. The Image Segmentation data set is composed of two sets: the training set and the testing set. Each of two sets contains 7 classes of instances and each class contains 30 instances in the training set and 300 instances in the testing set. We merge three classes as the positive class, and other four classes as the negative class. The Letter Recognition data set contains 26 classes of instances corresponding to 26 letters in the alphabet. Each class contains at least 700 instances. We merge class "a" and "b" as positive class and class "c" and "d" as negative class. Other classes are eliminated. Then the whole data set is split randomly into the training set and the testing set of the same size. In this way both the training set and testing set are changed into two-class data sets. The basic information of the two UCI data sets is shown in Table 4.6.

We select 2% and 0.2% instances from the training set as the labeled instances for each image data set, and all other instances in the training set are seen as the unlabeled instances. As seen earlier, the labeled set contains at least one positive and one negative instance. A batch of queries is selected by the three approaches earlier. Batchsize is fixed to 5, and the value of σ is fixed to 1. Both the SVM active learning approach and IALPSVM have the parameter λ, the range of its value is set to be 10 numbers $\{0.1, 0.2, \ldots, 1.0\}$. The optimal value of k is the one by using which the approach can attain the highest test accuracy in the testing set after 10 batches of queries are annotated and put into the labeled set. Test accuracies of SVM active learning approach and IALPSVM on Image and Letter testing set are shown in Figures 4.23 through 4.26, respectively.

From the results of Image Segmentation data set in Figures 4.23 and 4.24, the optimal k can be either 0.3 or 0.7 for SVM active learning approach, whereas it can be either 0.3 or 0.5 for IALPSVM. So we set k to be 0.3 for both the two approaches. From the results of Letter Recognition data set in Figures 4.25 and 4.26, the optimal k is 0.2 for SVM active learning approach, and it can be either 0.7 or 0.8 for IALPSVM. So we set them to be 0.2 and 0.7, respectively.

Table 4.6   Basic Information of the Two UCI Data Sets

Data Set	♯ the Positive	♯ the Negative	♯ Attributes
Image training set	90	120	19
Image testing set	900	1200	19
Letter training set	777	771	16
Letter testing set	778	770	16

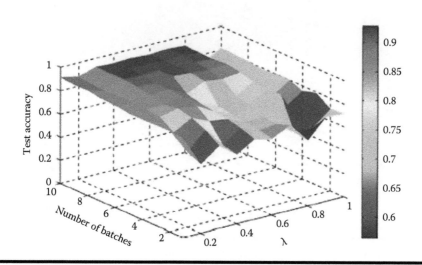

Figure 4.23 **Test accuracy of support vector machine active learning approach on Image.**

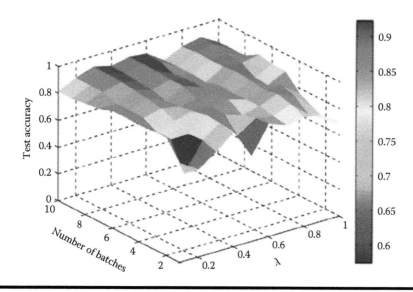

Figure 4.24 **Test accuracy of IALPSVM on Image.**

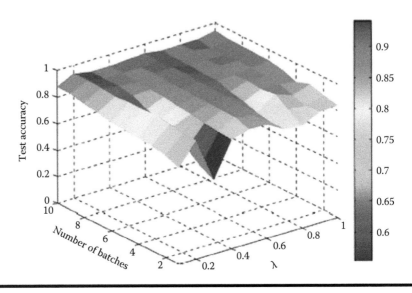

Figure 4.25 Test accuracy of support vector machine active learning approach on Letter.

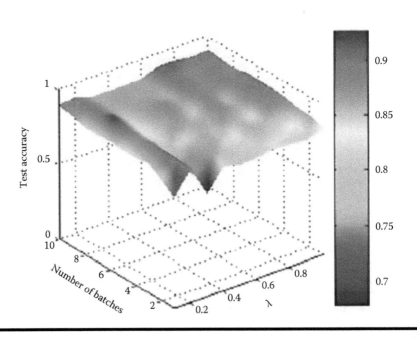

Figure 4.26 Test accuracy of IALPSVM on Letter.

After each parameter k of the two approaches is set to be the optimal value, these two approaches and semisupervised SVM batch mode active learning (denoted by Equation (4.24)) are compared in the precision of the testing set. *Precision* computed by (4.28) is the percentage of instances whose real labels are positive in instances whose labels the classifier believes are positive:

$$Precision = \frac{TP}{TP + FP}. \tag{4.28}$$

TP (or *FP*) is the number of positive (or negative) instances that are predicted as positive by the classifier. So the experiment process is as follows: each time a batch of queries selected by each of the three approaches are annotated and put into the labeled set, which is applied as the training set to learn a new classifier. Then the new classifier predicts instances in the testing set. Selected as the top returned instances are 50–150 unlabeled instances that are the most distant from the hyperplane. These instances are used to compute the precision. Experimental results of the three approaches on the two data sets are shown in Figures 4.27 through 4.36, respectively.

From the results of those three approaches in Figures 4.27 through 4.29, we can see that: let the number of top returned instances be fixed; precision of all the three approaches is not monotone increasing or decreasing when the number of batches is increasing. In other words, precisions of all the three approaches are changing unsteadily. Similar results can also be seen in Figures 4.32 through 4.34. However,

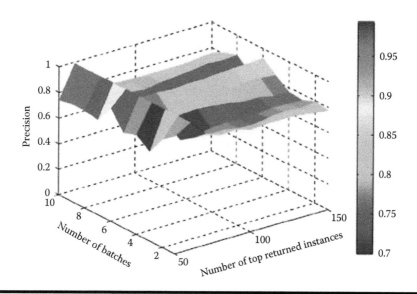

Figure 4.27   Precision of support vector machine active learning approach on Image.

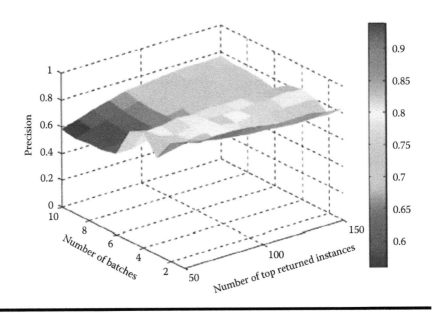

Figure 4.28 Precision of semisupervised support vector machine batch mode active learning (denoted by Equation (4.24)) on Image.

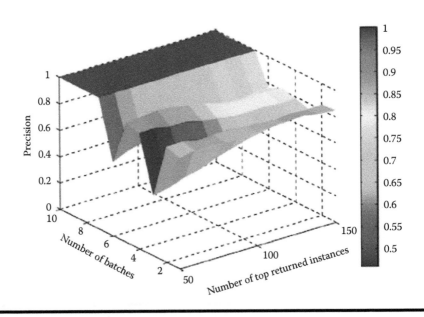

Figure 4.29 Precision of IALPSVM on Image.

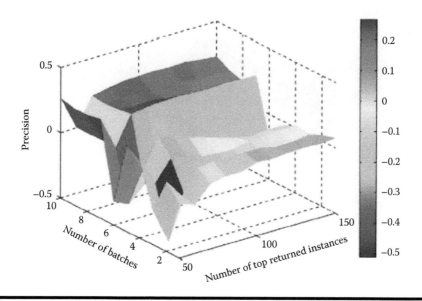

Figure 4.30 Precision of IALPSVM minus precision of support vector machine active learning approach.

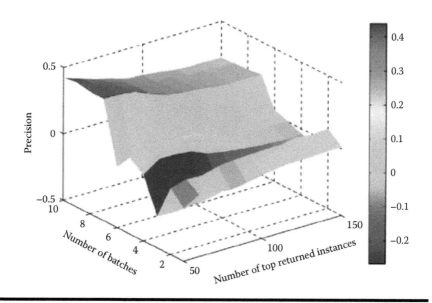

Figure 4.31 Precision of IALPSVM minus precision of semisupervised support vector machine batch mode active learning (denoted by Equation (4.24)).

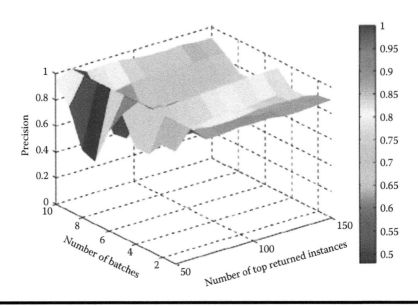

Figure 4.32   Precision of support vector machine active learning approach on Letter.

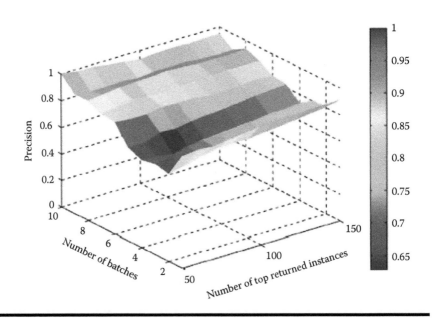

Figure 4.33   Precision of semisupervised support vector machine batch mode active learning (denoted by Equation (4.24)) on Letter.

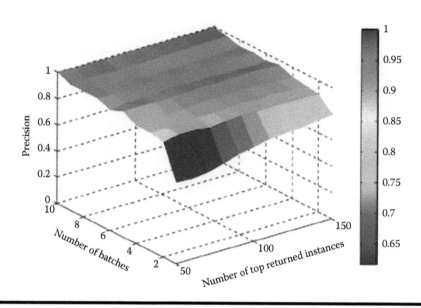

Figure 4.34 Precision of IALPSVM on Letter.

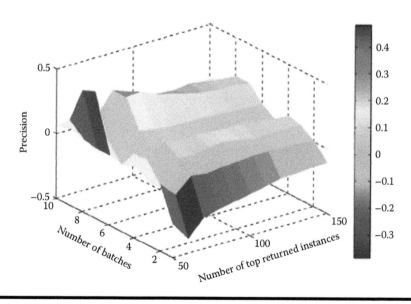

Figure 4.35 Precision of IALPSVM minus precision of support vector machine active learning approach.

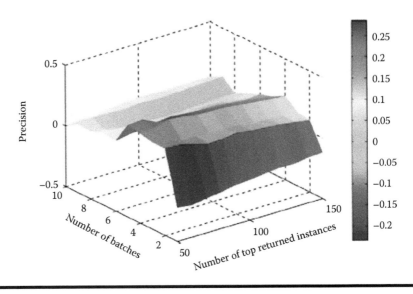

Figure 4.36 Precision of IALPSVM minus precision of semisupervised support vector machine batch mode active learning (denoted by Equation 4.24).

taken as a whole, precision of IALPSVM is increasing, whereas precision of SVM active learning approach only changes a little and precision of semisupervised SVM batch mode active learning (denoted by Equation (4.24)) even goes down in the last batch. This means that IALPSVM is a little better than the other two in precision when the number of instances in the labeled training set is growing. Results in Figures 4.30 and 4.31 show how much IALPSVM is higher than the other two approaches in precision. We can see that the values in Figures 4.30 and 4.31 are larger than zero in most cases.

From the results of three approaches in Figures 4.32 through 4.34, we can see that all the three approaches' precisions are increasing on the whole. Precision of SVM active learning approach is a little inferior to the other two approaches in Figure 4.35. IALPSVM is a little better than semisupervised SVM batch mode active learning (denoted by Equation (4.24)) in the beginning that can be seen in Figure 4.36. Semisupervised SVM batch mode active learning (denoted by Equation (4.24)) and IALPSVM reach an agreement in precision at the final phase.

Additionally, we also use values of cc to measure the performance of the three approaches on Image and Letter data set. Experimental results are shown in Figures 4.37 and 4.38.

From Figures 4.37 and 4.38, we can see that IALPSVM has better forecast ability on Image and Letter data sets in comparison with other two approaches. Especially on Image data set, the forecast result of IALPSVM can approach to the actual result for most cases. Forecast results of semisupervised SVM batch mode active learning

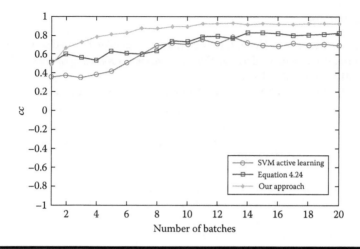

Figure 4.37 Correlation coefficient on Image, first 20 batches is selected.

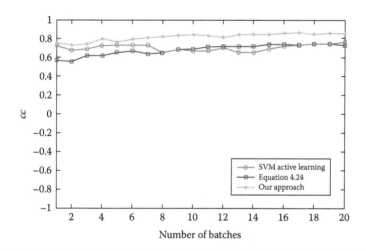

Figure 4.38 Correlation coefficient on Letter, first 20 batches is selected.

(denoted by Equation (4.24)) and SVM active learning approach are nearly the same on Letter data set, and prediction of IALPSVM is a little better than these two approaches.

In summary, queries selected by IALPSVM can be better used in learning an optimal hyperplane compared with SVM active learning approach and the approach in Hoi et al. [38]. It can be guaranteed that these queries are informative and valuable as they are near the final hyperplane as much as they could.

References

1. X. Z. Wang, L. C. Dong, J. H. Yan. Maximum ambiguity-based sample selection in fuzzy decision tree induction. *IEEE Transactions on Knowledge and Data Engineering*, 2012, 24(8):1491–1505.
2. L. S. Hu, S. X. Lu, X. Z. Wang. A new and informative active learning approach for support vector machine. *Information Sciences*, 2013, 244:142–160.
3. D. Angluin. Queries and concept learning. *Machine Learning*, 1988, 2:319–342.
4. D. Cohn, L. Atlas, R. Ladner. Improving generalization with active learning. *Machine Learning*, 1994, 15(2):201–221.
5. D. Lewis, W. Gale. A sequential algorithm for training text classifiers. In: *Proceedings of the ACM SIGIR Conference on Research and Development in Information Retrieval*, Dublin, Ireland. July 3–6, 1994, ACM/Springer, pp. 3–12.
6. H. S. Seung, M. Opper, H. Sompolinsky. Query by committee. In: *Proceedings of the ACM Workshop on Computational Learning Theory*, Pittsburgh, PA. July 27–29, 1992, pp. 287–294.
7. Y. Freund, H. S. Seung, E. Shamir et al. Selective sampling using the query by committee algorithm. *Machine Learning*, 1997, 28:133–168.
8. B. Settles. Active learning literature survey. Computer Sciences Technical Report 1648, University of Wisconsin-Madison. January 2010.
9. M. M. Crawford, D. Tuia, H. L. Yang. Active learning: Any value for classification of remotely sensed data? *Proceedings of the IEEE*, 2013, 101(3):593–608.
10. D. Tuia, M. Volpi, L. Copa et al. A survey of active learning algorithms for supervised remote sensing image classification. *IEEE Journal of Selected Topics in Signal Processing*, 2011, 5(3):606–617.
11. H. L. Yu, C. Y. Sun, W. K. Yang, et al. AL-ELM: One uncertainty-based active learning algorithm using extreme learning machine. *Neurocomputing*, 2015, 166:140–150.
12. M. Li, I. K. Sethi. Confidence-based active learning. *IEEE Transactions on Pattern Analysis and Machine Intelligence*, 2006, 28(8):1251–1261.
13. D. A. Cohn, Z. Ghahramani, M. I. Jordan. Active learning with statistical models. *Journal of Artificial Intelligence Research*, 1996, 4:129–145.
14. I. Dagan, S. Engelson. Committee-based sampling for training probabilistic classifiers. In: *Proceedings of the 12th International Conference on Machine Learning*, Massachusetts: Morgan Kaufmann, San Francisco, CA, July 9–12, 1995, pp. 150–157.
15. J. Zhu, H. Wang, E. Hovy et al. Confidence-based stopping criteria for active learning for data annotation. *ACM Transactions on Speech and Language Processing*, 2010, 6(3):1–24.
16. X. Zhu, P. Zhang, X. Lin et al. Active learning from stream data using optimal weight classifier ensemble. *IEEE Transactions on Systems, Man, and Cybernetics, Part B: Cybernetics*, 2010, 40(6):1607–1621.
17. A. Vlachos. A stopping criterion for active learning. *Computer Speech and Language*, 2008, 22(3):295–312.
18. J. Zhu, H. Wang, B. K. Tsou et al. Active learning with sampling by uncertainty and density for data annotations. *IEEE Transactions on Audio, Speech, and Language Processing*, 2010, 18(6):1323–1331.

19. J. Zhu, H. Wang, E. Hovy. Multi-criteria-based strategy to stop active learning for data annotation. In: *Proceedings of the 22nd International Conference on Computational Linguistics*, Manchester, UK. August 18–22, 2008, Vol. 1, pp. 1129–1136.

20. S. J. Huang, R. Jin, Z. H. Zhou. Active learning by querying informative and representative examples. *IEEE Transactions on Pattern Analysis and Machine Intelligence*, 2014, 36(10):1936–1949.

21. W. Wang, W. Cai, Y. Zhang. Stability-based stopping criterion for active learning. In: *2014 IEEE International Conference on Data Mining (ICDM)*, Shenzhen, China. December 14–17, 2014, pp. 1019–1024.

22. Y. Fu, X. Zhu, B. Li. A survey on instance selection for active learning. *Knowledge and Information Systems*, 2013, 35(2):249–283.

23. L. L. Sun, X. Z. Wang. A survey on active learning strategy. In: *Proceedings of the Ninth International Conference on Machine Learning and Cybernetics*, Qingdao, China, July 11–14, 2010, Vol. 1, pp. 161–166.

24. M. Wang, X. S. Hua. Active learning in multimedia annotation and retrieval: A survey. *ACM Transactions on Intelligent Systems and Technology*, 2011, 2(2):389–396.

25. G. Riccardi, D. Hakkani-Tür. Active learning: Theory and applications to automatic speech recognition. *IEEE Transactions on Speech and Audio Processing*, 2005, 13(4): 504–511.

26. I. Muslea, S. Minton, C. A. Knoblock. Active learning with multiple views. *Journal of Artificial Intelligence Research*, 2006, 27:203–233.

27. A. McCallum, K. Nigam. Employing EM in pool-based active learning for text classification. In: *Proceedings of the International Conference on Machine Learning (ICML)*, Massachusetts: Morgan Kaufmann, Madison, WI. July 24–27, 1998, pp. 359–367.

28. Y. F. Yuan, M. J. Shaw. Induction of fuzzy decision trees. *Fuzzy Sets and Systems*, 1995, 69(2):125–139.

29. S. T. Maytal, P. Foster. Active sampling for class probability estimation and ranking, *Machine Learning*, 2004, 54(2):153–178.

30. P. Melville, S. M. Yang, S. T. Maytal et al. Active learning for probability estimation using Jensen-Shannon divergence. In: *Proceedings of the 16th European Conference on Machine Learning (ECML)*, Porto, Portugal. October 3–7, 2005, pp. 268–279.

31. A. Frank, A. Asuncion. UCI machine learning repository. http://archive.ics.uci.edu/ml, June 19, 2010.

32. F. Olken, D. Rotem. Random sampling from databases: A survey. *Statistics and Computing*, 1995, 5(1):25–42.

33. S. Tong, D. Koller. Support vector machine active learning with applications to text classification. *Journal of Machine Learning Research*, 2001, 2:45–66.

34. V. N. Vapnik. *The Nature of Statistical Learning Theory*. Springer, New York, 1995.

35. K. Brinker. Incorporating diversity in active learning with support vector machines. In: *Proceedings of the 20th International Conference on Machine Learning*, Washington. August 21–24, 2003, pp. 59–66.

36. C. K. Dagli, S. Rajaram, T. S. Huang. Leveraging active learning for relevance feedback using an information theoretic diversity measure. In: *Proceedings of ACM Conference on Image and Video Retrieval*, Tempe, AZ. July 13–15, 2006, pp. 123–132.

37. Y. H. Guo, D. Schuurmans. Discriminative batch mode active learning. In: *Proceedings of Advances in Neural Information Processing Systems*, Vancouver, Canada. December 8–11, 2008, MIT Press, Cambridge, MA, pp. 593–600.

38. S. C. H. Hoi, R. Jin, J. Zhu. Semisupervised SVM batch mode active learning with applications to image retrieval. *ACM Transactions on Information Systems*, 2009, 27(3):1–19.

39. C. C. Chang, C.J. Lin. LIBSVM: A library for support vector machines. *ACM Transactions on Intelligent Systems and Technology*, 2011, 2:1–27.

Chapter 5

Ensemble Learning with Uncertainty

This chapter mainly introduces ensemble learning in the uncertainty environments. An introduction to ensemble learning is presented in Section 5.1. Bagging and boosting are presented in Section 5.2. In the next three sections, we will introduce multiple fuzzy decision trees [1], fusion of classifiers based on upper integral [2], and the relationship between fuzziness and generalization in ensemble learning [3].

5.1 Introduction to Ensemble Learning

Ensemble learning, in the framework of classification, is also known as classifier ensembles, multiple classifier systems, and multiple classifier combinations. It is an aggregation of several classifiers with some ensemble methods to form a final prediction. Ensemble learning generally provides better and/or more robust solutions in most applications due to the availability of more than one classifier [4]. The concept of ensemble learning is first introduced in the classification literature by Nilsson [5] and has subsequently been studied in several different forms, including stacking [6], boosting [7], and bagging [8]. In Section 5.2, we will briefly introduce bagging algorithm and boosting algorithm.

Ensemble learning mainly includes three phases [9]: (1) generation of base classifiers, (2) selection of base classifiers, and (3) integration of the selected base classifiers with some ensemble methods (see Figure 5.1). In the first phase, a pool of base classifiers is generated, and the pool may be composed of homogeneous classifiers (same base classifiers) or heterogeneous classifiers (different base classifiers); in the second phase, one or a subset of base classifiers is selected, while in the last phase, a final

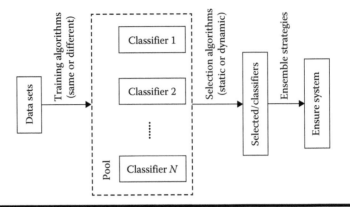

Figure 5.1   Three phases of ensemble learning.

decision is made by integrating the selected classifiers with an ensemble method. If all classifiers in the pool are used for aggregation, then there is no step of selection. Generally, the base classifiers should be accurate classifiers with some diversities. Dietterich explains in [10] that an accurate classifier is a classifier that has an error rate lower than the random guessing on new samples, while two classifiers are diverse if they make different errors on new samples. In other words, the idea of diversity is to generate classifiers that make different mistakes and, consequently, show some degree of complementarity. A comprehensive survey of different diversity measures and diversity creation methods can be found in the study by Kuncheva and Whitaker [11] and Brown et al. [12], respectively.

In the following, we will introduce some commonly used ensemble methods [13], including majority voting, weighted majority voting, the approach based on Dempster–Shafer theory of evidence, and fuzzy integral ensemble approach. The voting-based methods can be applied to any type of classifier, while others rely on specific outputs or specific interpretations of the output.

5.1.1 Majority Voting and Weighted Majority Voting

The concept of majority voting is simple and is easy to be implemented [4,14–16]. Let $T = \{(x_i, y_i) | x_i \in R^d, y_i \in \Omega, i = 1, 2, \ldots, n\}$ be a training set, $\Omega = \{\omega_1, \omega_2, \ldots, \omega_k\}$ be a set of class labels, and $L = \{L_1, L_2, \ldots, L_l\}$ be a pool of classifiers. Given a new sample x, each classifier L_i votes for a target class, the class that gets the highest number of votes will be selected, and the majority voting can be formulated by the following equation:

$$class(x) = \underset{c_i \in \Omega}{argmax} \left(\sum_j g(y_j(x), c_i) \right), \tag{5.1}$$

where

$y_j(x)$ is the classification of instance x by the classifier L_j

$g(\cdot, \cdot)$ is an indicator function defined as the following formula:

$$g(y, c) = \begin{cases} 1, & \text{if } y = c; \\ 0, & \text{if } y \neq c. \end{cases} \tag{5.2}$$

The weighted majority voting is to weight the classifiers proportionally to their accuracy performance on a validation set [17]. Mathematically, performance weighting can be formulated by the following equation:

$$w_i = \frac{1 - e_i}{\sum_{j=1}^{l} (1 - e_j)}, \tag{5.3}$$

where e_i is a normalization factor that is based on the performance evaluation of classifier L_i on a validation set.

5.1.2 Approach Based on Dempster–Shafer Theory of Evidence

This method uses the Dempster–Shafer theory of evidence for aggregating classifiers [13,18]. Specifically, this method uses the notion of basic probability assignment defined as formula (5.4) for a certain class w_i given the instance x

$$bpa(w_i, x) = 1 - \prod_{j=1}^{l} \left(1 - P_{L_j}(y = w_i | x)\right), \tag{5.4}$$

where

L_j denotes jth classifier

$P_{L_j}(y = w_i | x)$ denotes the posterior probability of y obtaining the value w_i given an instance x

Consequently, the selected class is the one that maximizes the value of the following belief function:

$$Bel(w_i, x) = \frac{1}{A} \times \frac{bpa(w_i, x)}{1 - bpa(w_i, x)}, \tag{5.5}$$

where A is a normalization factor defined as the following formula:

$$A = \sum_{w_i \in \Omega} \frac{bpa(w_i, x)}{1 - bpa(w_i, x)} + 1. \tag{5.6}$$

5.1.3 Fuzzy Integral Ensemble Approach

For $\forall x \in R^d$, the base classifier L_i assigns a class label to x from Ω. As given by Kuncheva [19], we may define the classifier output to be a k-dimensional vector with support degree of the classes, that is,

$$L_i(x) = (p_{i1}(x), p_{i2}(x), \ldots, p_{ik}(x)), \tag{5.7}$$

where $p_{ij}(x) \in [0, 1]$ $(1 \leq i \leq l; 1 \leq j \leq k)$ denotes the support degree given by classifier L_i to the hypothesis that x comes from class ω_j. Generally, $p_{ij}(x)$ is an estimate of the posterior probability $p(\omega_j|x)$. In the following, we will give some related definitions.

Definition 5.1   Given $L = \{L_1, L_2, \ldots, L_l\}$, $\Omega = \{\omega_1, \omega_2, \ldots, \omega_k\}$, and arbitrary testing sample x. The following matrix is called decision matrix:

$$DP(x) = \begin{bmatrix} p_{11}(x) & \cdots & p_{1j}(x) & \cdots & p_{1k}(x) \\ \vdots & \ddots & \vdots & \ddots & \vdots \\ p_{i1}(x) & \cdots & p_{ij}(x) & \cdots & p_{ik}(x) \\ \vdots & \ddots & \vdots & \ddots & \vdots \\ p_{l1}(x) & \cdots & p_{lj}(x) & \cdots & p_{lk}(x) \end{bmatrix}, \tag{5.8}$$

where
    the ith row of the matrix is the output of classifier L_i
    the jth column of the matrix is the support degree from classifiers $L_1, L_2, \ldots, L_l$
    for class ω_j

Definition 5.2   Given $L = \{L_1, L_2, \ldots, L_l\}$, let $P(L)$ be the power set of L and the fuzzy measure on L is a set function: $g : P(L) \rightarrow [0, 1]$, such that

(1) $g(\varnothing) = 1, g(L) = 1$
(2) For $\forall A, B \subseteq L$, if $A \subset B$, then $g(A) \leq g(B)$.

Definition 5.3   For $\forall A, B \subseteq L$, and $A \cap B = \varnothing$, g is called λ-fuzzy measure, if

$$g(A \cup B) = g(A) + g(B) + \lambda g(A)g(B), \tag{5.9}$$

where $\lambda > -1$ and $\lambda \neq 0$.

The value of λ can be determined with the following formula:

$$\lambda + 1 = \prod_{i=1}^{l}(1 + \lambda g^i).\tag{5.10}$$

Definition 5.4 Given $L = \{L_1, L_2, \ldots, L_l\}$. Let $g^i = g(\{L_i\})$ and $\forall L_i \in L.$ g^i is called fuzzy density of classifier L_i.

Definition 5.5 Given $L = \{L_1, L_2, \ldots, L_l\}$, g is the fuzzy measure on L; the Choquet fuzzy integral of function $h : L \rightarrow R^+$ with respect to g is defined as follows:

$$(C)\int h\,d\mu = \sum_{i=1}^{l}(h(L_i) - h(L_{i-1}))g(A_i),\tag{5.11}$$

where
$$0 \le h(L_1) \le h(L_2) \le \cdots \le h(L_l) \le 1, h(L_0) = 0$$
$$A_i \subseteq L, A_i = \{L_1, L_2, \ldots, L_i\}$$
$$g(A_0) = 0$$

Definition 5.6 Given $L = \{L_1, L_2, \ldots, L_l\}$, g is the fuzzy measure on L, $h : L \rightarrow [0, 1]$ be a function defined on L, and without loss of generality, suppose that $0 \le h(L_1) \le h(L_2) \le \cdots \le h(L_l) \le 1$. The Sugeno fuzzy integral of function h with respect to g is defined as follows:

$$(S)\int h(\cdot)g(\cdot) = \bigvee_{i=1}^{l}\left(h(L_i)\bigwedge g(A_i)\right),\tag{5.12}$$

where $A_i = \{L_1, L_2, \ldots, L_i\}$.

5.2 Bagging and Boosting

5.2.1 Bagging Algorithm

Bagging algorithm was proposed by Breiman [8] in 1996, which is based on the concept of bootstrap to construct ensembles. It consists in training different classifiers with boot-strapped replicas of the original training set. That is, a new data set is formed to train each classifier by randomly drawing (with replacement) instances from the original data set (usually, maintaining the original data set size).

Algorithm 5.1: Bagging

Input: T, a training set; m, number of iterations; n, Bootstrap size; I, weak learner.

Output: Bagged classifier: $H(x) = sign\left(\sum_{t=1}^{m} h_t(x)\right)$, where
$h_i(i = 1, 2, \ldots, m)$ are the induced classifiers, and $h_i \in [-1, 1]$.

1 **for** $(i = 1; i \leq m; i = i + 1)$ **do**
2 $\quad S_i = Random\text{-}Sample\text{-}Replacement(S, n)$;
3 $\quad h_i = I(S_i)$;
4 **end**
5 Output $H(x) = sign\left(\sum_{t=1}^{m} h_t(x)\right)$.

Hence, diversity is obtained with the resampling procedure by the usage of different data subsets. Finally, when an unknown instance is presented to each individual classifier, a majority or weighted vote is used to infer the class. Algorithm 5.1 shows the pseudocode for bagging [20].

5.2.2 Boosting Algorithm

Boosting algorithm [21] was designed by Schapire who has proved that a weak classifier can be boosted to a strong classifier in the sense of probably approximately correct learning framework. AdaBoost [22] is the most representative boosting algorithm. AdaBoost uses the whole data set to train each base classifier serially, but after each round, it gives more focus to instances that are incorrectly classified. In other words, it gives more focus to instances that are harder to classify; the focus is quantificationally measured by a weight, which initially is equal for all instances. After iterations, the weights of misclassified instances are increased; on the contrary, the weights of correctly classified instances are decreased. Furthermore, another weight is assigned to each individual base classifier depending on its overall accuracy, which is then used in the test phase; more confidence is given to more accurate classifiers. Finally, when a new instance is submitted, each classifier gives a weighted vote, and the class label is selected by majority. The AdaBoost algorithm for binary classification problem is described by Algorithm 5.2.

5.3 Multiple Fuzzy Decision Tree Algorithm

Motivated by multiple fuzzy attribute reducts, a multiple fuzzy decision tree algorithm named MFDT is proposed in [1]. In this section, we introduce this algorithm that is an ensemble learning approach. The component classifiers are fuzzy decision trees that are induced from different fuzzy attribute reducts with fuzzy ID3

Algorithm 5.2: AdaBoost Algorithm

Input: $T = \{(x_i, y_i) | x_i \in R^d, y_i \in \{-1, +1\}, 1 \le i \le n\}$, a training set; m,
   number of iterations; I, weak learner.

Output: Boosted classifier: $H(x) = sign\left(\sum_{i=1}^{m} \alpha_i h_i(x)\right)$, where
   $h_i\ (i = 1, 2, \ldots, m)$ are the induced classifiers, and $h_i \in [-1, 1]$;
   $\alpha_i\ (i = 1, 2, \ldots, m)$ are the corresponding assigned weights.

1 **for** $(j = 1; j \le n; j = j + 1)$ **do**
2 $\quad W_1(j) = \frac{1}{n}$;
3 **end**
4 **for** $(i = 1; i \le m; i = i + 1)$ **do**
5 $\quad h_i = I(S, W_i)$;
6 $\quad \varepsilon_i = \sum_{j, y_j \ne h_i(x_j)} W_i(j)$;
7 $\quad$ **if** $(\varepsilon_i > 0.5)$ **then**
8 $\quad\quad m = i - 1$;
9 $\quad$ **end**
10 $\quad \alpha_i = \frac{1}{2} ln\left(\frac{1-\varepsilon_i}{\varepsilon_i}\right)$;
11 $\quad$ **for** $(j = 1; j \le n; j = j + 1)$ **do**
12 $\quad\quad W_{i+1}(j) = W_i(j) \times e^{-\alpha_i h_i(x_j) y_j}$;
13 $\quad$ **end**
14 $\quad$ **for** $(i = 1; i \le m; i = i + 1)$ **do**
15 $\quad\quad$ Normalize W_i to be a proper distribution;
16 $\quad$ **end**
17 **end**
18 Output $H(x) = sign\left(\sum_{i=1}^{m} \alpha_i h_i(x)\right)$.

---

algorithm. Fuzzy integral is used as the ensemble method. MFDT has the following advantages. (1) It can be certainly guaranteed that the base classifiers have diversity. (2) The algorithm can make full use of complementary information of different fuzzy attribute reducts in a fuzzy information system and, consequently, can enhance the testing accuracy of the algorithm. One can find in Chapters 1 and 2, respectively, the basic concepts of rough sets [23–25] and fuzzy rough sets [26–28]. In this section, we directly present the MFDT algorithm.

5.3.1 Induction of Multiple Fuzzy Decision Tree

In this section, we introduce the algorithm of induction of multiple fuzzy decision tree, that is, MFDT algorithm that includes three phases: (1) calculate multiple fuzzy attribute reducts, (2) train fuzzy decision trees on the calculated multiple fuzzy attribute reducts by fuzzy ID3 algorithm, and (3) integrate the multiple trained fuzzy decision trees with fuzzy integral. The algorithm is presented in Algorithm 5.3.

> **Example 5.1** Give a small training data set shown in Table 5.1 and present the induction process of the algorithm.
>
> In this example, the universe of discourse is $X = \{x_1, x_2, \ldots, x_{16}\}$. *Outlook*, *Temperature*, *Humidity*, and *Wind* are four fuzzy conditional attributes; *Play* is a fuzzy decision attribute.
>
> The first phase of Algorithm 5.3 is to find several fuzzy attribute reducts of the fuzzy decision table shown in Table 5.1. The lower approximation needs to be determined. Consider the first attribute in Table 5.1. Set $R = \{Outlook\}$ produces the fuzzy partition: $U/R = \{\{Sunny\}, \{Cloudy\}, \{Rain\}\}$. Similarly, set $C = \{Play\}$ produces the fuzzy partition: $U/C = \{\{V\}, \{S\}, \{W\}\}$; set $B = \{Temperature\}$ produces the fuzzy partition: $U/B = \{\{Hot\}, \{Mild\}, \{Cool\}\}$; and set $R \cap B = \{Outlook\} \cap \{Temperature\}$ produces the fuzzy partition: $U/(R \cap B) = \{\{Sunny \cap Hot\}, \{Sunny \cap Mild\}, \{Sunny \cap Cool\}, \{Cloud \cap Hot\}, \{Cloud \cap Mild\}, \{Cloud \cap Cool\}, \{Rain \cap Hot\}, \{Rain \cap Mild\}, \{Rain \cap Cool\}\}$.
>
> To determine the fuzzy lower approximation of V with respect to R, each $F \in U/R$ must be taken into consideration. For $F = Sunny$, we have

$$\min\left(\mu_{Sunny}(x), \inf_{y \in U} \max\{1 - \mu_{Sunny}(y), \mu_V(y)\}\right)$$

$$= \min(\mu_{Sunny}(x), 0.0) = 0.0.$$

> Similarly, for $F = Cloudy$ and $F = Rain$, we can calculate $\min(\mu_{Cloudy}(x), 0.3)$ and $\min(\mu_{Rain}(x), 0.0)$. To calculate the extent to which an object x in the data set belongs to the fuzzy lower approximation of V with respect to R, the union of these values is calculated. For example, object x_1 belongs to $\underline{R}(V)$ with a membership of $\mu_{\underline{R}(V)}(x_1)$, and

$$\mu_{\underline{R}(V)}(x_1) = \sup\{\min(\mu_{Sunny}(x_1), 0.0), \min(\mu_{Rain}(x_1), 0.3),$$

$$\min(\mu_{Cool}(x_1), 0.1)\}$$

$$= 0.0.$$

> Likewise, for *Wind*, we have $\mu_{\underline{R}(S)}(x_1) = 0.3$ and $\mu_{\underline{R}(W)}(x_1) = 0.0$. Finally, the degree to which object x_1 belongs to the fuzzy positive region of *Play* with respect to R can be determined by considering the union of fuzzy lower approximations:

$$\mu_{POS_R(Play)}(x_1) = \sup_{X \in U/Play} \mu_{\underline{R}(X)}(x_1) = 0.3.$$

Algorithm 5.3: Multiple Fuzzy Decision Tree Algorithm

Input: A fuzzy decision table $FDT = (U, A \cup C, V, f)$, and a testing
instance x.

Output: The class of x.

1 // The first phase: calculate multiple fuzzy
attribute reducts.

2 **for** $(i = 1; i \leq d; i = i + 1)$ **do**

3   Select one fuzzy conditional attribute with the maximum $\gamma_{A_i}(C)$ as
candidate attribute of fuzzy attribute reduct. For the sake of convenience,
suppose A_1 is selected;

4 **end**

5 **for** $(j = 1; j \leq d; j = j + 1)$ **do**

6   Select another fuzzy conditional attribute with maximum
$\gamma_{A_1 A_j}(C)$ $(2 \leq j \leq d)$ and $\gamma_{A_1 A_j}(C) > \gamma_{A_1}(C)$, suppose that A_2 is
selected, hence A_1 and A_2 are two candidate attributes of fuzzy attribute
reduct;

7 **end**

8 **if** $(B_k = \{A_1, A_2, \ldots, A_k\}$ *is selected as candidate attributes of fuzzy attribute*
reduct and exist A_m $(k < m < d)$ *satisfying* $\gamma_{B_k \cup \{A_m\}}(C) > \gamma_{B_m}(C)$
$(m = k, k+1, \ldots, d))$ **then**

9   Several fuzzy attribute subsets $\{A_1, A_2, \ldots, A_{i-1}, A_p\}$ $(p = k, k+1, \ldots, d)$
are fuzzy attribute reducts, which are denoted by $FR_1, FR_2, \ldots, FR_l$;

10 **end**

11 // The second phase: train fuzzy decision trees on
the l calculated multiple fuzzy attribute
reducts by fuzzy ID3 algorithm.

12 **for** $(i = 1; i \leq l; i = i + 1)$ **do**

13   Train fuzzy decision tree on FR_i with fuzzy ID3 algorithm;

14 **end**

15 // The third phase: integrate the trained multiple
fuzzy decision trees with fuzzy integral.

16 **for** (*each testing instance x*) **do**

17   **for** $(i = 1; i \leq k; i = i + 1)$ **do**

18   Calculate $e_i = (c) \int f_i d\mu_i$;

19        $Class(x) = argmax_{1 \leq i \leq k}\{e_i\}$;

20   **end**

21 **end**

22 Output $Class(x)$.

Table 5.1 Small Training Set with Fuzzy Representation

x	Outlook			Temperature			Humidity		Wind		Play		
	Sunny	Cloudy	Rain	Hot	Mild	Cool	High	Normal	Strong	Weak	V	S	W
x_1	1.0	0.0	0.0	0.7	0.2	0.1	0.7	0.3	0.4	0.6	0.0	0.6	0.4
x_2	0.6	0.4	0.0	0.6	0.2	0.2	0.6	0.4	0.9	0.1	0.7	0.6	0.0
x_3	0.8	0.2	0.0	0.0	0.7	0.3	0.2	0.8	0.2	0.8	0.3	0.6	0.1
x_4	0.3	0.7	0.0	0.2	0.7	0.1	0.8	0.2	0.3	0.7	0.9	0.1	0.0
x_5	0.7	0.3	0.0	0.0	0.1	0.9	0.5	0.5	0.5	0.5	1.0	0.0	0.0
x_6	0.0	0.3	0.7	0.0	0.7	0.3	0.3	0.7	0.4	0.6	0.2	0.2	0.6
x_7	0.0	0.0	1.0	0.0	0.3	0.7	0.8	0.2	0.1	0.9	0.0	0.0	1.0
x_8	0.0	0.9	0.1	0.0	1.0	0.0	0.1	0.9	0.0	1.0	0.3	0.0	0.7
x_9	1.0	0.0	0.0	1.0	0.0	0.0	0.4	0.6	0.4	0.6	0.4	0.7	0.0
x_{10}	0.0	0.3	0.7	0.7	0.2	0.1	0.8	0.2	0.9	0.1	0.0	0.3	0.7
x_{11}	1.0	0.0	0.0	0.6	0.3	0.1	0.7	0.3	0.2	0.8	0.4	0.7	0.0
x_{12}	0.0	1.0	0.0	0.2	0.6	0.2	0.7	0.3	0.7	0.3	0.7	0.2	0.1
x_{13}	0.0	0.9	0.1	0.7	0.3	0.0	0.1	0.9	0.0	1.0	0.0	0.4	0.6
x_{14}	0.0	0.9	0.1	0.1	0.6	0.3	0.7	0.3	0.7	0.3	1.0	0.0	0.0
x_{15}	0.0	0.3	0.7	0.0	0.0	1.0	0.2	0.8	0.8	0.2	0.4	0.0	0.6
x_{16}	0.5	0.5	0.0	1.0	0.0	0.0	1.0	0.0	1.0	0.0	0.7	0.6	0.0

Similarly, for the remaining objects, we have

$$\mu_{POS_R(Play)}(x_2) = 0.3, \ \mu_{POS_R(Play)}(x_3) = 0.3, \ \mu_{POS_R(Play)}(x_4) = 0.3,$$

$$\mu_{POS_R(Play)}(x_5) = 0.3, \ \mu_{POS_R(Play)}(x_6) = 0.6, \ \mu_{POS_R(Play)}(x_7) = 0.6,$$

$$\mu_{POS_R(Play)}(x_8) = 0.1, \ \mu_{POS_R(Play)}(x_9) = 0.3, \ \mu_{POS_R(Play)}(x_{10}) = 0.6,$$

$$\mu_{POS_R(Play)}(x_{11}) = 0.3, \ \mu_{POS_R(Play)}(x_{12}) = 0.1, \ \mu_{POS_R(Play)}(x_{13}) = 0.1,$$

$$\mu_{POS_R(Play)}(x_{14}) = 0.1, \ \mu_{POS_R(Play)}(x_{15}) = 0.6, \ \mu_{POS_R(Play)}(x_{16}) = 0.3.$$

The degree of fuzzy dependency of C on $R = Outlook$ can be calculated by using these values, that is,

$$\gamma_{Outlook}(Play) = \frac{\sum_{x \in U} \mu_{POS_{Outlook}(Play)}(x)}{|U|} = \frac{5.2}{16} = 0.325.$$

Similarly, we can calculate the following three values:

$$\gamma_{Temperature}(Play) = 0.3, \quad \gamma_{Humidity}(Play) = 0.2, \quad \gamma_{Wind}(Play) = 0.2.$$

As attribute "*Outlook*" causes the greatest increase in fuzzy dependency degree, it is added to the set of fuzzy attribute reduct.

In order to calculate $\gamma_{\{Outlook\} \cap \{Temperature\}}(Play)$, we must first obtain the membership of each linguistic value in $R \cap B = U/\{\{Outlook\} \cap \{Temperature\}\}$; repeating the earlier calculating process, we can have

$$\gamma_{\{Outlook, Temperature\}}(Play) = 0.581, \quad \gamma_{\{Outlook, Humidity\}}(Play) = 0.588,$$

$$\gamma_{\{Outlook, Wind\}}(Play) = 0.525.$$

then the attribute "*Humidity*" is also added to the fuzzy attribute reduct candidate; now two attributes are added to the fuzzy attribute reduct candidates. Next, we continue to add another member of attributes to the fuzzy attribute reduct candidate:

$$\gamma_{\{Temperature, Outlook, Wind\}}(Play) = 0.563,$$

$$\gamma_{\{Temperature, Outlook, Humidity\}}(Play) = 0.613,$$

$$\gamma_{\{Outlook, Wind, Humidity\}}(Play) = 0.575,$$

while

$$\gamma_{\{Temperature, Outlook, Humidity, Wind\}}(Play) = 0.613.$$

Hence, we obtain the following three conditional fuzzy attribute reducts: {*Outlook, Temperature, Humidity*}, {*Outlook, Temperature, Wind*}, and {*Outlook, Wind, Humidity*}.

Table 5.2   Training Set of Fuzzy Samples Corresponding to Fuzzy Attribute Reduct 1

x	Outlook			Temperature			Humidity		Play		
	Sunny	Cloudy	Rain	Hot	Mild	Cool	High	Normal	V	S	W
x_1	1.0	0.0	0.0	0.7	0.2	0.1	0.7	0.3	0.0	0.6	0.4
x_2	0.6	0.4	0.0	0.6	0.2	0.2	0.6	0.4	0.7	0.6	0.0
x_3	0.8	0.2	0.0	0.0	0.7	0.3	0.2	0.8	0.3	0.6	0.1
x_4	0.3	0.7	0.0	0.2	0.7	0.1	0.8	0.2	0.9	0.1	0.0
x_5	0.7	0.3	0.0	0.0	0.1	0.9	0.5	0.5	1.0	0.0	0.0
x_6	0.0	0.3	0.7	0.0	0.7	0.3	0.3	0.7	0.2	0.2	0.6
x_7	0.0	0.0	1.0	0.0	0.3	0.7	0.8	0.2	0.0	0.0	1.0
x_8	0.0	0.9	0.1	0.0	1.0	0.0	0.1	0.9	0.3	0.0	0.7
x_9	1.0	0.0	0.0	1.0	0.0	0.0	0.4	0.6	0.4	0.7	0.0
x_{10}	0.0	0.3	0.7	0.7	0.2	0.1	0.8	0.2	0.0	0.3	0.7
x_{11}	1.0	0.0	0.0	0.6	0.3	0.1	0.7	0.3	0.4	0.7	0.0
x_{12}	0.0	1.0	0.0	0.2	0.6	0.2	0.7	0.3	0.7	0.2	0.1
x_{13}	0.0	0.9	0.1	0.7	0.3	0.0	0.1	0.9	0.0	0.4	0.6
x_{14}	0.0	0.9	0.1	0.1	0.6	0.3	0.7	0.3	1.0	0.0	0.0
x_{15}	0.0	0.3	0.7	0.0	0.0	1.0	0.2	0.8	0.4	0.0	0.6
x_{16}	0.5	0.5	0.0	1.0	0.0	0.0	1.0	0.0	0.7	0.6	0.0

Correspondingly, the three fuzzy reduced decision tables, Tables 5.2 through 5.4, are achieved, respectively.

Based on Tables 5.1 through 5.4, four fuzzy decision trees with $\alpha = 0.0$ and $\beta = 0.80$ are generated by fuzzy ID3 (see Figures 5.2 through 5.5).

A fuzzy decision tree can be converted into several rules. Based on the converted rules, we can determine the degree to which class a sample belongs. An object may be classified into different classes with different degrees. The classification for a given object is obtained according to the method in Yuan and Shaw [29].

Because the three fuzzy attribute reducts have important and different contributions to the fuzzy system, every fuzzy attribute reduct provides us with different aspects of a given fuzzy information system. To make full use of the information provided by every fuzzy attribute reduct, we use the method of multiple classifiers

Table 5.3 Training Set of Fuzzy Samples Corresponding to Fuzzy Attribute Reduct 2

x	Outlook			Temperature			Wind		Play		
	Sunny	Cloudy	Rain	Hot	Mild	Cool	Strong	Weak	V	S	W
x_1	1.0	0.0	0.0	0.7	0.2	0.1	0.4	0.6	0.0	0.6	0.4
x_2	0.6	0.4	0.0	0.6	0.2	0.2	0.9	0.1	0.7	0.6	0.0
x_3	0.8	0.2	0.0	0.0	0.7	0.3	0.2	0.8	0.3	0.6	0.1
x_4	0.3	0.7	0.0	0.2	0.7	0.1	0.3	0.7	0.9	0.1	0.0
x_5	0.7	0.3	0.0	0.0	0.1	0.9	0.5	0.5	1.0	0.0	0.0
x_6	0.0	0.3	0.7	0.0	0.7	0.3	0.4	0.6	0.2	0.2	0.6
x_7	0.0	0.0	1.0	0.0	0.3	0.7	0.1	0.9	0.0	0.0	1.0
x_8	0.0	0.9	0.1	0.0	1.0	0.0	0.0	1.0	0.3	0.0	0.7
x_9	1.0	0.0	0.0	1.0	0.0	0.0	0.4	0.6	0.4	0.7	0.0
x_{10}	0.0	0.3	0.7	0.7	0.2	0.1	0.9	0.1	0.0	0.3	0.7
x_{11}	1.0	0.0	0.0	0.6	0.3	0.1	0.2	0.8	0.4	0.7	0.0
x_{12}	0.0	1.0	0.0	0.2	0.6	0.2	0.7	0.3	0.7	0.2	0.1
x_{13}	0.0	0.9	0.1	0.7	0.3	0.0	0.0	1.0	0.0	0.4	0.6
x_{14}	0.0	0.9	0.1	0.1	0.6	0.3	0.7	0.3	1.0	0.0	0.0
x_{15}	0.0	0.3	0.7	0.0	0.0	1.0	0.8	0.2	0.4	0.0	0.6
x_{16}	0.5	0.5	0.0	1.0	0.0	0.0	1.0	0.0	0.7	0.6	0.0

fusion based on fuzzy integral to combine the outputs of the three fuzzy decision trees into a consensus result. In the following, based on Choquet integral, we will aggregate the outputs of the three fuzzy decision trees. Here, a fuzzy decision tree can be viewed as a fuzzy classifier.

First of all, we determine the fuzzy measures for every class. The important degree of every fuzzy decision tree to every class can be determined using Tables 5.5 through 5.7. They can be viewed as fuzzy densities. For example, the fuzzy density with respect to every class (V, S, W) of the fuzzy decision tree 1 is, respectively, 0.406, 0.419, and 0.481. The fuzzy densities of the other two fuzzy decision trees can similarly be obtained. Based on the fuzzy densities, the value λ for every class can be determined by expression (5.10). According to expression (5.9), the fuzzy measures of the three fuzzy decision tree classifiers can be achieved as in Table 5.8

Table 5.4 Training Set of Fuzzy Samples Corresponding to Fuzzy Attribute Reduct 3

x	Outlook Sunny	Cloudy	Rain	Humidity High	Normal	Wind Strong	Weak	Play V	S	W
x_1	1.0	0.0	0.0	0.7	0.3	0.4	0.6	0.0	0.6	0.4
x_2	0.6	0.4	0.0	0.6	0.4	0.9	0.1	0.7	0.6	0.0
x_3	0.8	0.2	0.0	0.2	0.8	0.2	0.8	0.3	0.6	0.1
x_4	0.3	0.7	0.0	0.8	0.2	0.3	0.7	0.9	0.1	0.0
x_5	0.7	0.3	0.0	0.5	0.5	0.5	0.5	1.0	0.0	0.0
x_6	0.0	0.3	0.7	0.3	0.7	0.4	0.6	0.2	0.2	0.6
x_7	0.0	0.0	1.0	0.8	0.2	0.1	0.9	0.0	0.0	1.0
x_8	0.0	0.9	0.1	0.1	0.9	0.0	1.0	0.3	0.0	0.7
x_9	1.0	0.0	0.0	0.4	0.6	0.4	0.6	0.4	0.7	0.0
x_{10}	0.0	0.3	0.7	0.8	0.2	0.9	0.1	0.0	0.3	0.7
x_{11}	1.0	0.0	0.0	0.7	0.3	0.2	0.8	0.4	0.7	0.0
x_{12}	0.0	1.0	0.0	0.7	0.3	0.7	0.3	0.7	0.2	0.1
x_{13}	0.0	0.9	0.1	0.1	0.9	0.0	1.0	0.0	0.4	0.6
x_{14}	0.0	0.9	0.1	0.7	0.3	0.7	0.3	1.0	0.0	0.0
x_{15}	0.0	0.3	0.7	0.2	0.8	0.8	0.2	0.4	0.0	0.6
x_{16}	0.5	0.5	0.0	1.0	0.0	1.0	0.0	0.7	0.6	0.0

where L_i ($1 \leq i \leq 3$) denotes the ith classifier and μ_i ($1 \leq i \leq 3$) denotes the ith class fuzzy measure.

And then, for every $x \in X$, a decision matrix can be determined based on the three fuzzy decision trees. Finally according to the Choquet integral (5.11), the vector of the output of the three fuzzy decision trees can be obtained. For example, for sample 1, the decision profile is as follows:

$$DP = \begin{bmatrix} & \mu_1 & \mu_2 & \mu_3 \\ L_1 & 0.2 & 0.7 & 0.0 \\ L_2 & 0.2 & 0.7 & 0.0 \\ L_3 & 0.4 & 0.0 & 0.0 \end{bmatrix}.$$

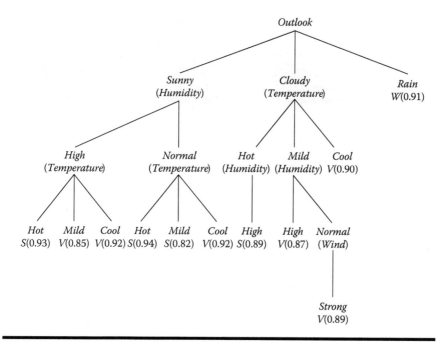

Figure 5.2 The fuzzy decision tree for Table 5.1.

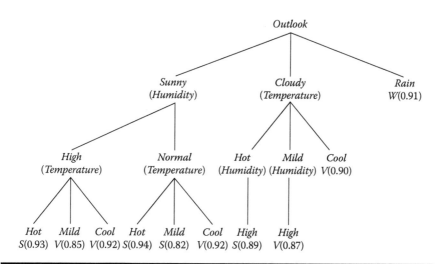

Figure 5.3 The fuzzy decision tree for Table 5.2.

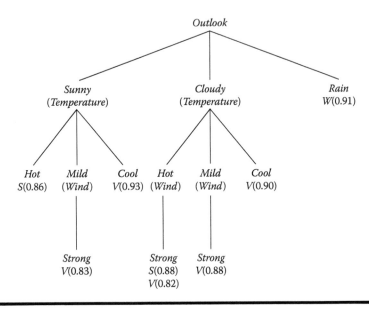

Figure 5.4   The fuzzy decision tree for Table 5.3.

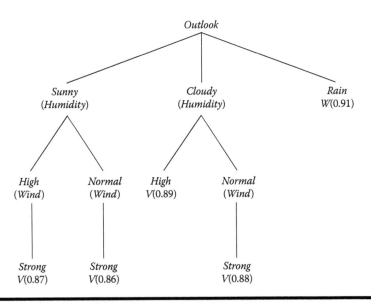

Figure 5.5   The fuzzy decision tree for Table 5.4.

Table 5.5 Membership of {Outlook} ∩ {Temperature} ∩ {Humidity}

x	Hot Sunny High	Hot Sunny Normal	Hot Cloudy High	Hot Cloudy Normal	Hot Rain High	Hot Rain Normal	Mild Sunny High	Mild Sunny Normal	Mild Cloudy High	Mild Cloudy Normal	Mild Rain High	Mild Rain Normal	Cool Sunny High	Cool Sunny Normal	Cool Cloudy High	Cool Cloudy Normal	Cool Rain High	Cool Rain Normal	v	s	w
x_1	0.7	0.3	0.0	0.0	0.0	0.0	0.2	0.2	0.0	0.0	0.0	0.0	0.1	0.1	0.0	0.0	0.0	0.0	0.0	0.6	0.4
x_2	0.6	0.4	0.4	0.4	0.0	0.0	0.2	0.2	0.2	0.2	0.0	0.0	0.2	0.2	0.2	0.2	0.0	0.0	0.7	0.6	0.0
x_3	0.0	0.0	0.0	0.0	0.0	0.0	0.2	0.7	0.2	0.2	0.0	0.0	0.2	0.3	0.2	0.2	0.0	0.0	0.3	0.6	0.1
x_4	0.2	0.2	0.2	0.2	0.0	0.0	0.3	0.2	0.7	0.2	0.0	0.0	0.1	0.1	0.1	0.1	0.0	0.0	0.9	0.1	0.0
x_5	0.0	0.0	0.0	0.0	0.0	0.0	0.1	0.1	0.3	0.1	0.0	0.0	0.5	0.5	0.3	0.3	0.0	0.0	1.0	0.0	0.0
x_6	0.0	0.0	0.0	0.0	0.0	0.0	0.0	0.0	0.3	0.3	0.3	0.7	0.0	0.0	0.3	0.3	0.3	0.3	0.2	0.2	0.6
x_7	0.0	0.0	0.0	0.0	0.0	0.0	0.0	0.0	0.0	0.0	0.3	0.2	0.0	0.0	0.0	0.0	0.7	0.2	0.0	0.0	1.0
x_8	0.0	0.0	0.0	0.0	0.0	0.0	0.0	0.0	0.1	0.8	0.1	0.2	0.0	0.0	0.0	0.0	0.0	0.0	0.3	0.0	0.7
x_9	0.4	0.6	0.0	0.0	0.0	0.0	0.0	0.0	0.0	0.0	0.0	0.0	0.0	0.0	0.0	0.0	0.0	0.0	0.4	0.7	0.0
x_{10}	0.0	0.0	0.3	0.2	0.7	0.2	0.0	0.0	0.2	0.2	0.2	0.0	0.0	0.0	0.1	0.1	0.1	0.1	0.0	0.3	0.7
x_{11}	0.6	0.3	0.0	0.0	0.0	0.0	0.3	0.3	0.0	0.0	0.0	0.0	0.1	0.1	0.0	0.0	0.0	0.0	0.4	0.7	0.0
x_{12}	0.0	0.0	0.2	0.2	0.0	0.0	0.0	0.0	0.6	0.3	0.0	0.0	0.0	0.0	0.2	0.2	0.0	0.0	0.7	0.2	0.1
x_{13}	0.1	0.2	0.1	0.7	0.1	0.0	0.1	0.2	0.1	0.3	0.0	0.0	0.0	0.0	0.3	0.0	0.0	0.0	0.0	0.4	0.6
x_{14}	0.0	0.0	0.1	0.1	0.1	0.1	0.0	0.0	0.6	0.3	0.1	0.1	0.0	0.0	0.3	0.3	0.1	0.1	1.0	0.0	0.0
x_{15}	0.0	0.0	0.0	0.0	0.0	0.0	0.0	0.0	0.0	0.0	0.0	0.0	0.0	0.0	0.2	0.3	0.2	0.7	0.4	0.0	0.6
x_{16}	0.5	0.0	0.5	0.0	0.0	0.0	0.0	0.0	0.0	0.0	0.0	0.0	0.0	0.0	0.0	0.0	0.0	0.0	0.7	0.6	0.0

Table 5.6 Membership of {Outlook} ∩ {Temperature} ∩ {Wind}

x	Hot Sunny Strong	Hot Sunny Weak	Hot Cloudy Strong	Hot Cloudy Weak	Hot Rain Strong	Hot Rain Weak	Mild Sunny Strong	Mild Sunny Weak	Mild Cloudy Strong	Mild Cloudy Weak	Mild Rain Strong	Mild Rain Weak	Cool Sunny Strong	Cool Sunny Weak	Cool Cloudy Strong	Cool Cloudy Weak	Cool Rain Strong	Cool Rain Weak	V	S	W
x_1	0.4	0.6	0.0	0.0	0.0	0.0	0.2	0.2	0.0	0.0	0.0	0.0	0.1	0.1	0.0	0.0	0.0	0.0	0.0	0.6	0.4
x_2	0.6	0.1	0.4	0.1	0.0	0.0	0.2	0.1	0.2	0.1	0.0	0.0	0.2	0.1	0.2	0.1	0.0	0.0	0.7	0.6	0.0
x_3	0.0	0.0	0.0	0.0	0.0	0.0	0.2	0.7	0.2	0.2	0.0	0.0	0.2	0.3	0.2	0.2	0.0	0.0	0.3	0.6	0.1
x_4	0.2	0.2	0.2	0.2	0.0	0.0	0.3	0.3	0.3	0.7	0.0	0.0	0.1	0.1	0.1	0.1	0.0	0.0	0.9	0.1	0.0
x_5	0.0	0.0	0.0	0.0	0.0	0.0	0.1	0.1	0.1	0.1	0.0	0.0	0.5	0.5	0.3	0.3	0.0	0.0	1.0	0.0	0.0
x_6	0.0	0.0	0.0	0.0	0.0	0.0	0.0	0.0	0.3	0.3	0.4	0.6	0.0	0.0	0.3	0.3	0.3	0.3	0.2	0.2	0.6
x_7	0.0	0.0	0.0	0.0	0.0	0.0	0.0	0.0	0.0	0.0	0.1	0.3	0.0	0.0	0.0	0.0	0.1	0.7	0.0	0.0	1.0
x_8	0.0	0.0	0.0	0.0	0.0	0.0	0.0	0.0	0.0	0.8	0.0	0.2	0.0	0.0	0.0	0.0	0.0	0.0	0.3	0.7	0.7
x_9	0.4	0.6	0.0	0.0	0.0	0.0	0.0	0.0	0.0	0.0	0.0	0.0	0.0	0.0	0.0	0.0	0.0	0.0	0.4	0.3	0.0
x_{10}	0.0	0.0	0.3	0.1	0.7	0.1	0.0	0.0	0.2	0.1	0.2	0.1	0.0	0.0	0.1	0.1	0.1	0.1	0.0	0.3	0.7
x_{11}	0.2	0.6	0.0	0.0	0.0	0.0	0.2	0.3	0.0	0.0	0.0	0.0	0.1	0.1	0.0	0.0	0.0	0.0	0.4	0.7	0.0
x_{12}	0.0	0.0	0.2	0.2	0.0	0.0	0.0	0.0	0.6	0.3	0.0	0.0	0.0	0.0	0.2	0.2	0.0	0.0	0.7	0.2	0.1
x_{13}	0.0	0.2	0.0	0.7	0.0	0.0	0.0	0.2	0.0	0.3	0.0	0.0	0.0	0.0	0.3	0.3	0.1	0.1	0.0	0.4	0.6
x_{14}	0.0	0.0	0.1	0.1	0.7	0.1	0.0	0.0	0.6	0.3	0.1	0.1	0.0	0.0	0.3	0.2	0.7	0.2	1.0	0.0	0.0
x_{15}	0.0	0.0	0.0	0.0	0.0	0.0	0.0	0.0	0.0	0.0	0.0	0.0	0.0	0.0	0.0	0.0	0.0	0.0	0.4	0.0	0.6
x_{16}	0.5	0.0	0.5	0.0	0.0	0.0	0.0	0.0	0.0	0.0	0.0	0.0	0.0	0.0	0.0	0.0	0.0	0.0	0.7	0.6	0.0

Table 5.7 Membership of {Outlook} ∩ {Humidity} ∩ {Wind}

x	Sunny High Strong	Sunny High Weak	Sunny Normal Strong	Sunny Normal Weak	Cloudy High Strong	Cloudy High Weak	Cloudy Normal Strong	Cloudy Normal Weak	Rain High Strong	Rain High Weak	Rain Normal Strong	Rain Normal Weak	V	S	W
x_1	0.4	0.6	0.3	0.3	0.0	0.0	0.0	0.0	0.0	0.0	0.0	0.0	0.0	0.6	0.4
x_2	0.0	0.6	0.0	0.0	0.0	0.4	0.0	0.0	0.0	0.0	0.0	0.0	0.7	0.6	0.0
x_3	0.2	0.8	0.1	0.1	0.2	0.2	0.1	0.1	0.0	0.0	0.0	0.0	0.3	0.6	0.1
x_4	0.3	0.3	0.2	0.2	0.3	0.7	0.2	0.2	0.0	0.0	0.0	0.0	0.9	0.1	0.0
x_5	0.5	0.5	0.5	0.5	0.3	0.3	0.3	0.3	0.0	0.0	0.0	0.0	1.0	0.0	0.0
x_6	0.0	0.0	0.0	0.0	0.3	0.3	0.0	0.3	0.4	0.6	0.3	0.3	0.2	0.2	0.6
x_7	0.0	0.0	0.0	0.0	0.0	0.0	0.0	0.0	0.1	0.8	0.1	0.2	0.0	0.0	1.0
x_8	0.0	0.0	0.0	0.0	0.0	0.2	0.0	0.2	0.0	0.8	0.0	0.8	0.3	0.0	0.7
x_9	0.4	0.4	0.6	0.4	0.0	0.0	0.0	0.0	0.0	0.0	0.0	0.0	0.4	0.7	0.0
x_{10}	0.0	0.0	0.0	0.0	0.3	0.1	0.1	0.1	0.7	0.1	0.1	0.1	0.0	0.3	0.7
x_{11}	0.0	0.7	0.2	0.3	0.0	0.0	0.0	0.0	0.0	0.0	0.0	0.0	0.4	0.7	0.0
x_{12}	0.0	0.0	0.0	0.0	0.3	0.7	0.3	0.3	0.0	0.0	0.0	0.0	0.7	0.2	0.0
x_{13}	0.1	0.0	0.2	0.0	0.1	0.0	0.8	0.0	0.0	0.0	0.0	0.0	0.0	0.4	0.6
x_{14}	0.0	0.0	0.0	0.0	0.7	0.3	0.1	0.1	0.1	0.1	0.1	0.1	1.0	0.0	0.0
x_{15}	0.0	0.0	0.0	0.0	0.0	0.0	0.0	0.0	0.0	0.0	0.8	0.2	0.4	0.0	0.6
x_{16}	0.0	0.5	0.0	0.0	0.0	0.5	0.0	0.0	0.0	0.0	0.0	0.0	0.7	0.6	0.0

Table 5.8 Fuzzy Measures of Three Classifiers and Their Combinations

Three Classifiers and Their Combinations	μ_1	μ_2	μ_3
L_1	0.406	0.419	0.481
L_2	0.413	0.438	0.463
L_3	0.406	0.375	0.463
$L_1 L_2$	0.735	0.765	0.725
$L_1 L_3$	0.730	0.715	0.725
$L_2 L_3$	0.735	0.730	0.776
$L_1 L_2 L_3$	1.00	1.00	1.00

According to Equation (5.11), we have

$$e_V = 0.2 \times (1 - 0.735) + 0.2 \times (0.735 - 0.460) + 0.4 \times 0.460 = 0.28$$
$$e_S = 0.0 \times (1 - 0.765) + 0.7 \times (0.765 - 0.419) + 0.4 \times 0.419 = 0.54$$
$$e_W = 0.0$$

so the vector of the output is (0.28, 0.54, 0.00). Selecting the class with the highest membership as the class label, we infer that sample x_1 belongs to class S.

The classification results by fuzzy decision tree 1 and classification results by fusion of other three fuzzy decision trees are shown in Table 5.9. Among the 16 training cases, 14 cases are correctly classified (samples 2 and 16 are not correctly classified) by the method used by Wang et al. [1] of the three fuzzy decision trees fusion. The classification accuracy is 87.5%, greater than the original classification (75%) by fuzzy decision tree 1 (samples 2, 8, 13, and 16 are not correctly classified). The true degree of the fuzzy rules is more than 80%. Obviously, the classification accuracy is improved after aggregating the three fuzzy decision trees. A fuzzy attribute reduct is an important set of attributes, and every fuzzy attribute reduct provides us with different aspects of the system. By aggregating their outputs, the classification accuracy can be improved.

5.3.2 Experiment on Real Data Set

A data set is obtained by collecting 212 medical CT images from Baoding local hospital. All CT images are classified into two classes, that is, normal class and abnormal class. The data set has 170 normal cases and 42 abnormal cases. Totally, 35 features

Table 5.9 Comparison Classification Results among Known Data, Fuzzy Decision 1, and Ensemble of Classifiers

	Classification Results Known in Training Data			Classification Results with Fuzzy Decision 1			Classification Results with Ensemble of Classifiers		
x	*V*	*S*	*W*	*V*	*S*	*W*	*V*	*S*	*W*
x_1	0.0	0.6	0.4	0.2	0.7	0.0	0.28	0.54	0.00
x_2	0.7	0.6	0.0	0.2	0.6	0.0	0.36	0.46	0.00
x_3	0.3	0.6	0.1	0.3	0.7	0.0	0.27	0.36	0.00
x_4	0.9	0.1	0.0	0.7	0.3	0.0	0.59	0.23	0.00
x_5	1.0	0.0	0.0	0.5	0.1	0.0	0.58	0.04	0.00
x_6	0.2	0.2	0.6	0.3	0.0	0.7	0.22	0.13	0.70
x_7	0.0	0.0	1.0	0.0	0.0	1.0	0.00	0.00	1.00
x_8	0.3	0.0	0.7	0.1	0.0	0.1	0.07	0.00	0.10
x_9	0.4	0.7	0.0	0.0	0.6	0.0	0.16	0.64	0.00
x_{10}	0.0	0.3	0.7	0.2	0.3	0.7	0.20	0.22	0.51
x_{11}	0.4	0.7	0.0	0.3	0.6	0.0	0.24	0.46	0.00
x_{12}	0.7	0.2	0.1	0.6	0.2	0.0	0.56	0.15	0.00
x_{13}	0.0	0.4	0.6	0.1	0.0	0.1	0.07	0.04	0.10
x_{14}	1.0	0.0	0.0	0.6	0.1	0.1	0.64	0.08	0.10
x_{15}	0.4	0.0	0.6	0.3	0.0	0.7	0.30	0.00	0.70
x_{16}	0.7	0.6	0.0	0.5	0.5	0.0	0.20	0.37	0.00

are initially selected. They are 10 symmetric features, 9 texture features, and 16 statistical features including mean, variance, skewness, kurtosis, energy, and entropy.

We use the cross-validation procedure. Each data set is randomly partitioned into 10 disjoint subsets; each size is $m/10$ where m is the number of examples of the data set. The procedure is then conducted 10 times, each time using a different one of these subsets as the validation (testing) set and combining the other nine subsets

Table 5.10   Experimental Results Compared with Fuzzy ID3 on a Real Data Set

Algorithms	Training Accuracy	Testing Accuracy
Single fuzzy ID3	0.93	0.91
MFDT algorithm	0.98	0.97

for the training set. The training and testing accuracies are then averaged. For each time, the experimental procedure is the following:

1. Fuzzify the data set according to a specified fuzzification procedure that is selected in this experiment as the triangular membership forms given in Yuan and Shaw [29], and then generate a single fuzzy decision tree.
2. Calculate all fuzzy attribute reducts with Algorithm 5.3 (actually, the first phase of Algorithm 5.3).
3. Train a fuzzy decision tree on each reduct with the fuzzy ID3 algorithm.
4. Convert each fuzzy decision tree into a set of fuzzy IF-THEN rules and calculate the corresponding training and testing accuracies.
5. Fuse the individual outputs of each fuzzy decision tree with Algorithm 5.3 (actually, the third phase of Algorithm 5.3).

The experimental results (averaged training and testing accuracies for 10 times) together with the results given by the single fuzzy ID3 are summarized as in Table 5.10. Averagely, the experimental results show that the fusion of multiple decision trees with respect to different reducts of attributes is superior to the single decision tree induction (single fuzzy ID3).

5.4 Fusion of Classifiers Based on Upper Integral

In this section, we introduce another ensemble learning method: fusion of classifiers based on upper integral [2]. In this method, we use extreme learning machine (ELM) [30,31] as base classifier. However, different from the general methods, the upper integral is not considered as a tool of classifier fusion, but it is considered as a tool to improve any existing classifier fusion operator. It has been proved that the method can improve the performance of classifier fusion.

5.4.1 Extreme Learning Machine

ELM is an algorithm proposed by Huang et al. for training single-hidden layer feed-forward network (SLFN). It randomly chooses the input weights and hidden node biases and analytically determines the output weights of SLFNs. The key superiority of ELM is that it needs no iterations, which dramatically reduces the computational time for training the model in comparison with other classical methods (such as support vector machine [SVM] [32] and back-propagation (BP) algorithm [33] and its variants, for instance, [Levenberg–Marquardt] algorithm [34]). ELM has much better generalization performance with much faster learning speed.

Given a training data set, $T = \{(x_i, y_i) | x_i \in R^d, y_i \in R^k, i = 1, 2, \ldots, n\}$, where x_i is a $d \times 1$ input vector and y_i is a $k \times 1$ target vector, an SLFN with m hidden nodes is formulated as

$$f(x_i) = \sum_{j=1}^{m} \beta_j g(w_j \cdot x_i + b_j), \quad i = 1, 2, \ldots, n, \qquad (5.13)$$

where

$w_j = (w_{j1}, w_{j2}, \ldots, w_{jd})^T$ is the weight vector connecting the jth hidden node with the input nodes

b_j is the threshold of the jth hidden node

w_j and b_j are randomly assigned

$\beta_j = (\beta_{j1}, \beta_{j2}, \ldots, \beta_{jm})^T$ is the weight vector connecting the jth hidden node with the output nodes

The parameters β_j $(j = 1, 2, \ldots, m)$ may be estimated by least-square fitting with the given training data set T, that is, satisfying

$$f(x_i) = \sum_{j=1}^{m} \beta_j g(w_j \cdot x_i + b_j) = y_i. \qquad (5.14)$$

Equation (5.14) can be written in a more compact format as

$$H\beta = Y, \qquad (5.15)$$

where

$$H = \begin{bmatrix} g(w_1 \cdot x_1 + b_1) & \cdots & g(w_m \cdot x_1 + b_m) \\ \vdots & \cdots & \vdots \\ g(w_1 \cdot x_n + b_1) & \cdots & g(w_m \cdot x_n + b_m) \end{bmatrix}$$

$$\beta = (\beta_1^T, \ldots, \beta_m^T)^T \qquad (5.16)$$

and

$$Y = (y_1^T, \ldots, y_n^T)^T. \qquad (5.17)$$

H is the hidden layer output matrix of the network, where the jth column of H is the jth hidden nodes output vector with respect to inputs $x_1, x_2, \ldots, x_n$, and the ith row of H is the output vector of the hidden layer with respect to input x_i. If the number of hidden nodes is equal to the number of distinct training samples, the matrix H is

---

Algorithm 5.4: ELM Algorithm

    Input: Training data set $T = \{(x_i, y_i) | x_i \in R^d, y_i \in R^k, i = 1, 2, \ldots, n\}$, an
       activation function g, and the number of hidden nodes m.
    Output: weights matrix β.
1 **for** $(j = 1; j \leq m; j = j + 1)$ **do**
2 | Randomly assign input weights w_j;
3 **end**
4 Calculate the hidden layer output matrix H;
5 Calculate output weights matrix $\beta = H^\dagger Y$;
6 Output β.

---

square and invertible, and SLFNs can approximate these training samples with zero error. But generally, the number of hidden nodes is much less than the number of training samples. Therefore, H is a nonsquare matrix and one cannot expect an exact solution of the system (5.15). Fortunately, it has been proved by Huang et al. [31] that SLFNs with random hidden nodes have the universal approximation capability and the hidden nodes could be randomly generated. The least-square fitting is to solve the following equation:

$$\min_{\beta} = \|H\beta - Y\|. \tag{5.18}$$

The smallest norm least-squares solution of (5.18) may be easily obtained:

$$\hat{\beta} = H^\dagger Y, \tag{5.19}$$

where $H^\dagger$ is the Moore–Penrose generalized inverse of matrix H [35]. The ELM is presented in Algorithm 5.4.

5.4.2 Multiple Classifier Fusion Based on Upper Integrals

In Section 5.1.3, we introduced the fuzzy integral ensemble method. Different from this method, in this section, we introduce a novel ensemble method based on upper integral, which is a type of fuzzy integrals proposed by Wang et al. [36]. The approach is motivated by the definition of upper integrals, which can be considered as a mechanism of maximizing potential efficiency of classifier combination. The goal of the approach is to improve the classification performance of a fusion operator based on upper integrals. It is worth noting that, in the approach, the upper integral itself is not considered as a tool of classifier fusion but it is considered as a tool to improve any existing classifier fusion operator. Specifically, given a group of individual classifiers trained from a set of samples and a fusion operator, we regard the classification accuracies of individual classifiers and their combinations as the efficiency measure, which avoids almost the difficulty of determining fuzzy measures. The upper integral plays a role of assigning suitable proportion of sample to different individual classifiers and their combinations to obtain the maximum classification efficiency. It computes how many samples will be allocated to some of individual classifiers and their combinations by solving an optimization problem derived from the upper integral. This implies a proportion of sample allocation for a given set of samples. Based on this proportion, some oracles are used to determine which samples will be allocated to those individual classifiers and their combinations. Given a sample, the oracle of a combination of classifiers first predicts the possibility with which the combination can correctly classify the sample. Then, the sample is allocated to the combination with maximum possibility. When the number of samples allocated to a combination attains the proportion, the allocation to this combination stops, and the allocations to other combinations continue until all samples are allocated. After the allocation, those classifiers perform the classification of the set of samples, which is the final classification result. Next, we first introduce the related concepts of upper integral, then present the method of classifier fusion based on upper integral, and finally present the experimental results.

5.4.2.1 Upper Integral and Its Properties

Definition 5.7 Let $X = \{x_1, x_2, \ldots, x_n\}$ be a nonempty set, $P(X)$ be the power set of X, $\mu : P(X) \rightarrow [0, +\infty)$ be an efficiency measure, and $f : X \rightarrow [0, +\infty)$ be a function. The upper integral of f with respect to a nonadditive set function μ is defined as

$$(U) \int f \, d\mu = \sup \left\{ \sum_{j=1}^{2^n-1} a_j \, \mu(A_j) \mid \sum_{j=1}^{2^n-1} a_j \chi_{A_j} = f \right\}, \qquad (5.20)$$

where

χ_{A_j} is the characteristic function of set A_j

$a_j \geq 0$, $A_j = \bigcup_{i:j_i=1} \{x_i\}$, j is expressed in binary digits as $j_n j_{n-1} \ldots j_1$, $j = 1, 2, \ldots, 2^{n-1}$

The value of the upper integral $(U) \int f \, d\mu$ is the solution of the following linear programming problem [36]:

$$\max z = \sum_{j=1}^{2^n-1} a_j \mu_j$$

$$\text{s.t.} \quad \sum_{j=1}^{2^n-1} a_j \chi_{A_j}(x_i) = f(x_i), \quad i = 1, 2, \ldots, n$$

$$a_j \geq 0, \quad j = 1, 2, \ldots, 2^n - 1,$$

where $\mu_j = \mu(A_j)$, $j = 1, 2, \ldots, 2^n - 1$, and $a_1, a_2, \ldots, a_{2^n-1}$ are unknown parameters. The n constraints here can also be rewritten as

$$\sum_{j:x \in A_j \subset X} a_j = f(x) \qquad \forall x \in X.$$

The upper integrals have the following properties:

1. For any $c \in [0, +\infty)$, $(U) \int cf \, d\mu = c(U) \int f \, d\mu$.
2. $(U) \int f \, d\mu \leq (U) \int g \, d\mu$ if $f(x) \leq g(x)$ for every $x \in X$.
3. $(U) \int f \, d\mu \leq (U) \int f \, d\nu$ if $\mu(A) \leq \nu(A)$ for every $A \subseteq X$.
4. $(U) \int f \, d\mu = 0$ if and only if for every set A with $\mu(A) > 0$, there exists $x \in A$ such that $f(x) = 0$, that is, $\mu(\{x | f(x) > 0\}) = 0$.

Generally, fuzzy integrals are not linear, that is, the equality

$$(U) \int (af + bg) d\mu = a(U) \int f \, d\mu + b(U) \int g \, d\mu$$

may not be true, where a, b are two constants and f, g are integrands. Therefore, fuzzy integrals are called nonlinear integrals sometimes. For simplicity, we hide the type of integrals here. The following sample [36] shows that the upper integral has a very intuitive and natural explanation.

> **Example 5.2** Three workers, x_1, x_2, and x_3, are engaged in producing the same kind of products. Their efficiencies (products per day) of working alone and their joint efficiencies are listed in Table 5.11. These efficiencies can be regarded as a nonnegative set function μ defined on the power set of $X = \{x_1, x_2, x_3\}$ with

Table 5.11 Values of Efficiency Measure μ in Example 5.2

Set (Combination)	Value of μ(Efficiency)
$\{x_1\}$	5
$\{x_2\}$	6
$\{x_1, x_2\}$	14
$\{x_3\}$	8
$\{x_1, x_3\}$	7
$\{x_2, x_3\}$	16
$\{x_1, x_2, x_3\}$	18

Table 5.12 Values of Function f in Example 5.2

x_i	$f(x_i)$
$\{x_1\}$	10
$\{x_2\}$	15
$\{x_3\}$	7

$\mu(\varnothing) = 0$ (the meaning is that there are no products if there is no worker). Here, $14 = \mu(\{x_1, x_2\}) > \mu(\{x_1\}) + \mu(\{x_2\}) = 5 + 6$ means that x_1 and x_2 have a good cooperation, while $7 = \mu(\{x_1, x_3\}) < \mu(\{x_1\}) + \mu(\{x_3\}) = 5 + 8$ and even $7 = \mu(\{x_1, x_3\}) < \mu(\{x_3\}) = 8$ mean that x_1 and x_3 have a very bad relationship and they are not suitable for working together. Suppose that x_1 works for 10 days, x_2 for 15 days, and x_3 only for 7 days. Also we suppose that the manager can arrange their working in any combination, working alone or together in some way. The question now is how to arrange their working schedule such that the total products are maximized. It can be solved through the following linear programming problem:

$$\max z = 5a_1 + 6a_2 + 14a_3 + 8a_4 + 7a_5 + 16a_6 + 18a_7$$

$$s.t. \; a_1 + a_3 + a_5 + a_7 = 10$$

$$a_2 + a_3 + a_6 + a_7 = 15$$

$$a_4 + a_5 + a_6 + a_7 = 7$$

$$a_j \geq 0, \quad j = 1, 2, \ldots, 7.$$

The optimal schedule is as follows: x_1 and x_2 work together for 10 days, x_2 works with x_3 for 5 days, and x_3 works alone for 2 days. The relevant number of total products is 236. This value is just the upper integral $(U) \int f \, d\mu$, where f is listed in Table 5.12.

5.4.2.2 A Model of Classifier Fusion Based on Upper Integral

This section introduces a new model for classifier fusion based on the upper integral. The new model, which is totally different from the existing fuzzy integral–based models, gives a sample assignment schedule regarding how many and which samples should be assigned to individual classifiers and their combinations, instead of the upper integral being aggregation operators.

5.4.2.2.1 Efficiency Measure

Suppose that we are considering n classifiers, denoted by $X = \{x_1, x_2, \ldots, x_n\}$. Let $P(X)$ be the power set of X. Then, each element of $P(X)$ will denote a combination of classifiers, and it is clear there are totally $2^n - 1$ combinations (excluding the empty set). For instance, $\{x_1\}$ denotes that the classifier works singly, and $\{x_1, x_3, x_4\}$ denotes the three classifiers work together. We first need to define an efficiency measure on $P(X)$.

Let T be the training set. Then, each classifier has a training accuracy on T, and therefore, the value of the efficiency measure on a single classifier can be defined as the training accuracy, that is, the correct rate of classification. Furthermore, suppose that we have a basic fusion operator such as average. Then, applying the fusion operator to a combination of classifiers on T, we can obtain a correct classification rate of the classifier combination on T, which is defined as the value of the efficiency measure on the classifier combination. In this way, the efficiency measure is defined as

$$\mu(A) = \begin{cases} 0 & \text{if } A = \varnothing \\ \text{Accuracy of } A \text{ on } T & \text{if } A \text{ is a nonempty subset of } X, \end{cases}$$

where A denotes either a single classifier or a group of classifiers. It is worth noting that the definition of efficiency measure depends on a training set and a basic fusion operator for groups of classifiers.

5.4.2.2.2 Integrand

Since we are considering a finite space of classifiers $X = \{x_1, x_2, \ldots, x_n\}$, the integrand is a function defined on X, to be exact, an n-dimensional vector $(y_1, y_2, \ldots, y_n)$ where y_i is the proportion of samples submitted to the classifier x_i ($1 \leq i \leq n$) to classify. The goal is to determine this integrand. Why is an assignment of samples needed? It can be seen clearly from the following example that an appropriate assignment will improve the classification accuracy in some case. Suppose there are 10 samples $\{s_1, s_2, \ldots, s_{10}\}$ and 3 classifiers $\{x_1, x_2, x_3\}$, the best combination $\{x_1, x_3\}$ has the highest accuracy that correctly classifies 7 samples $\{s_3, s_4, s_5, s_6, s_7, s_8, s_9\}$ and classifier, x_2, correctly classifies 6 samples $\{s_1, s_2, s_3, s_5, s_6, s_8\}$ and s_{10} cannot be correctly classified by any of combinations/classifiers. Then, an appropriate assignment of samples will obtain higher accuracy than 0.8, which is the highest accuracy. Assigning $\{s_3, s_4, s_5, s_6, s_7, s_8, s_9\}$ to combination $\{x_1, x_3\}$ and $\{s_1, s_2\}$ to classifier x_2, the final accuracy is 0.9. Or assigning $\{s_4, s_6, s_7, s_8, s_9\}$ to combination $\{x_1, x_3\}$ and $\{s_1, s_2, s_3, s_5\}$ to classifier x_2, the final accuracy is 0.9 too. Under some conditions an appropriate assignment could obtain higher performance than the best combination or classifier. That is, it can improve the performance of classification through the samples that are correctly classified by some combinations and misclassified by other combinations that are assigned to appropriate combination.

Noting the definition of upper integrals given in Definition 5.7, we find that the value of integral expresses the highest classification efficiency for singly and jointly using classifiers $x_1, x_2, \ldots, x_n$. Specifically, the integral value denotes the highest classification efficiency and the process of computing the integral specifies a way to achieve the highest value by assigning how many samples to single classifiers and how many samples to their combinations. Here, a key point we need to explicitly specify is the following. Suppose that p $(0 < p < 1)$ is the accuracy of a single classifier x_i and there exist N samples to be classified; then we will not assign all the N samples to x_i but will assign only t $(t \leq pN)$ samples to x_i. It is similar to the case of a combination. Further in the next subsection, we will discuss which samples will be assigned to single classifiers and their combinations.

Assuming that the efficiency measure μ is known already, the function f can be determined by the following optimization:

$$\max (U) \int \{y_1, y_2, \ldots, y_n\} d\mu$$
$$\text{s.t. } y_j \leq \overline{\mu}_j, \quad j = 1, 2, \ldots, n, \tag{5.21}$$

where y_j denotes the proportion of samples to be assigned to classifier x_j including samples to single x_j and to combinations containing x_j and $\overline{\mu}_j = \frac{n_+}{|T|}$ is the proportion of samples in the training set that are correctly classified by the single classifier x_j or any combination containing x_j, that is, n_+ is the number of samples correctly classified at least by one of the combinations containing x_j. The inequality restriction means that samples should be assigned to a classifier or combination that can correctly classify.

The optimization problem (5.21) can be transferred to the following equation:

$$\max (U) \int \{y_1, y_2, \ldots, y_n\} d\mu = \sum_{i=1}^{2^n-1} a_i \mu_i$$
$$\text{s.t. } y_j = \sum_{i|b_j=1} a_i \leq \overline{\mu}_j, \quad j = 1, 2, \ldots, n \tag{5.22}$$
$$a_i \geq 0, \quad i = 1, 2, \ldots, 2^n - 1,$$

where the number i has a binary expression $b_n b_{n-1} \cdots b_1$ and b_j is the jth bit. The classifier combination corresponding to a_i is $\{x_k | b_k = 1, k = 1, 2, \ldots, n\}$. The models (5.21) and (5.22) have such a weakness that samples for evaluating the accuracy may be counted more than once. To avoid this, we can add one more restriction:

$$\sum_{i=1}^{2^n-1} a_i = 1.$$

That is, instead of Equation (5.22) we can use Equation (5.23) to avoid the repeated counting of samples:

$$\max (U) \int \{y_1, y_2, \ldots, y_n\} d\mu = \sum_{i=1}^{2^n-1} a_i \mu_i$$

$$s.t. \quad y_j = \sum_{i|b_j=1} a_i \leq \overline{\mu}_j, \quad j = 1, 2, \ldots, n$$

$$\sum_{i=1}^{2^n-1} a_i = 1$$

$$a_i \geq 0, \quad i = 1, 2, \ldots, 2^n - 1.$$

(5.23)

The optimization problem (5.23) is a linear programming problem and is easy to numerically solve. The nonzero a_i in the solution indicates the proportion of tested samples for the combination $\{x_k | b_k = 1, k = 1, 2, \ldots, n\}$ to classify. The solution of Equation (5.23) results in integrand $f = \{y_1, y_2, \ldots, y_n\}$.

The classification accuracy of the upper integral–based fusion system is no less than that of any individual base classifier, provided the oracles are correct. The following is a brief mathematical proof for this statement.

Proposition 5.1   *The classification accuracy of upper integral–based fusion system is not less than that of any combination of classifiers, provided the oracles are correct.*

Proof: If the combination of classifiers A has the highest accuracy p, $\mu(A) = p$. Let the corresponding unknown parameter $a_A = p$ and the sum of values of some other unknown parameters be $1 - p$. It is a feasible solution of optimization problem (5.23). If the oracles are correct, $p \times N$ tested samples are correctly classified by the combination A, where N is the number of testing samples. At least the accuracy of upper integral–based fusion system is $(p \times N)/N = p$. The proof is completed.

The conclusion is suitable for the case where the sum of $\overline{\mu}_j$'s is no less than 1. Note that the value of the problems (5.22) and (5.23) is not the accuracy of the model. The value of the problem (5.23) is $\sum_{i=1}^{2^n-1} a_i \mu_i$, which is called classification efficiency, and the accuracy of the upper integral model with correct oracles is $\sum_{i=1}^{2^n-1} a_i$.

5.4.2.2.3 Oracles

We have discussed how to obtain the efficiency measure and the integrand for the upper integral–based classifier fusion under the assumption that a training set and a basic fusion operator are given. In fact, the integrand gives the proportions of samples that are assigned to different combinations of classifiers. The remaining problem is which samples should be assigned to different individual classifiers and their combinations. We employ an oracle to solve this problem. Given a sample, the oracle of a combination of classifiers first predicts the possibility with which the combination can correctly classify the sample. Then, the sample is allocated to the combination with maximum possibility. When the number of samples allocated to a combination attains the proportion a_i from the solution of the optimization problem (5.23), the allocation to this combination stops. The allocations to other combinations continue until all samples are allocated.

Practically, the oracle can be obtained by training. Let T be the training set. Based on the training set T and a basic fusion operator, each combination of classifiers (including each single classifier) will have a training accuracy. Let X_C be an arbitrary combination of classifiers with accuracy p ($0 < p < 1$). Intuitively, it means that there are $(p|T|)$ samples correctly classified by X_C and $((1 - p)|T|)$ samples incorrectly classified by X_C. Consider the $(p|T|)$ samples as positive samples and the $((1 - p)|T|)$ samples as negative samples; we can train a new classifier that is regarded as the oracle for the combination X_C. For example, $X_C = \{x_1, x_3\}$. If the sample O is classified correctly by combination $\{x_1, x_3\}$, the target output of the oracle for the sample O will be "1." Contrarily, if the sample O is misclassified by combination $\{x_1, x_3\}$, the target output of the oracle for the sample O should be "0." Note that the correct or misclassification is based on the result of fused classification of classifiers x_1 and x_3. For unseen sample "O," if the oracle corresponding combination $X_C = \{x_1, x_3\}$ output is most close to "1," we choose the classification of combination $\{x_1, x_3\}$ as system output. Summarizing the earlier discussions, we briefly list the scheme of upper integral–based classifier fusion as Algorithm 5.5.

5.4.2.3 Experimental Results

5.4.2.3.1 Comparison with Boosting/Bagging

In order to confirm well the upper integral–based model of fusion, an empirical study is performed in this section. Ten benchmark data sets are respectively selected from the UCI machine learning repository [37]. The size of data sets varies from 150 to 20,000, and the detailed information is summarized in Table 5.13.

All the simulations are carried out in MATLAB® 2007 environment running on an Intel T2400, 1.83 GHz CPU. The upper integral fusion model is compared with boosting [7] and bagging [8]. In the experiment, a 10-fold cross-validation is repeated 20 times on each data set. Both bagging and boosting contain 100 base classifiers. To compare with bagging, the upper integral model uses the 100 base classifiers trained by bagging and the basic fusion operator is majority vote. Similarly, in comparing with boosting, the upper integral model uses the 100 base classifiers

---

Algorithm 5.5: Upper Integral Based Classifier Fusion

Input: T, a training set, S, a the testing set, $X = \{x_1, x_2, \ldots, x_n\}$, a group of base classifiers, F, a fusion operator, L, a training algorithm for 2-class problem.

Output: Classification results of all tested samples.

1 For each $A \subseteq X$, compute $\mu(A) = \frac{n_A}{|T|}$, where n_A is the number of samples classified correctly by A based on F;

2 Build and solve the optimization problem (5.23) to determine the integrand;

3 According to the solution of problem (5.23), combinations (including single base classifier) corresponding to nonzero a_i are chosen to classify unseen samples, and a_i is the proportion of samples in testing set S that is assigned to the corresponding combination;

4 Train oracles for all chosen combinations by using algorithm L;

5 According to the trained oracles, a sample in S is assigned to the combination which has not reached its proportion and has the highest possibility to correctly classify the sample;

6 Let the combination classify the assigned sample based on F;

7 Calculate the final classification results;

8 Repeat Steps 5–7 until all samples in S are classified.

Table 5.13   Specification of Classification Data Sets

Data Sets	#Attributes	#Classes	#Samples
Iris	5	3	150
Breast Cancer	10	2	683
Tic-Tac-Toe	9	2	958
Ionosphere	34	2	351
Pima	8	2	768
Heart	10	2	270
Wine	13	3	178
Sonar	60	2	208
Letter	17	26	20,000
Waveform + noise	41	3	5,000

trained by boosting and the basic fusion operator is weighted majority vote where the weights are determined during the training of boosting. Here, the upper integral only considers the single base classifiers and combinations that consist of two or three base classifiers (not all possible combinations). The parameters in efficiency measure increase exponentially with the number of base classifiers. When the number of base classifiers is small, we can consider all the combinations. It is difficult to find the optimal solution of problem (5.23) when it is large. It is needed to balance the accurate solution and the feasibility.

The four types of base classifiers, that is, ELM, conventional BP single-layer neural networks, ELM with Gaussian kernel (ELM-kernel) [38], and least-square support vector machine (LS-SVM; available at http://www.esat.kuleuven.ac.be/sista/lssvmlab/), are, respectively, implemented in the verification experiment. For the ELM and BP, the transfer function is fixed as hyperbolic tangent sigmoid. The number of hidden neurons used in each data set is determined by a 10-fold cross-validation on each data set. The number that achieves the best average cross-validation accuracy will be selected for ELM and BP, respectively. Through observing the performance with different numbers, the appropriate step, such as 5, 10, and 50, can be adopted to search the best number of hidden neurons. In general, the performance will quickly increase with more hidden neurons, so the step could be larger. When the growth of accuracy slowed, a smaller step is adopted. When a turning point appears, the number of hidden neurons is chosen as the best. In order to achieve good generalization performance, the cost parameter C and kernel parameter γ of ELM-kernel and LS-SVM need to be chosen appropriately. For each data set, we have used 50 different values of C and 50 different values of γ, resulting in a total of 2500 pairs of (C, γ). The 50 different values of C and γ are $\{2^{-24}, 2^{-23}, \ldots, 2^{24}, 2^{25}\}$. We conduct a 10-fold cross-validation on each data set and select the pair of (C, γ) for ELM-kernel and LS-SVM, respectively, which achieves the best average cross-validation accuracy. The results are shown in Tables 5.14 and 5.15.

As seen from Table 5.14, the performance of three fusion systems, the upper integral fusion, bagging, and boosting, with ELMs is higher than that of fusion system with BPs on 10 data sets. This is in conformity with the conclusions by Huang et al. [31]. Table 5.15 shows that the accuracies with ELM-kernel are higher or similar to those with LS-SVM. It tallies with the result by Huang et al. [38]. It also shows that the performance of fusion system is dependent on the performance of base classifier. The performance of the upper integral model is higher or similar to that of bagging/boosting on 10 data sets. It shows that the upper integral model can obtain higher or similar performance to that of bagging/boosting. It demonstrates that the upper integral model could capture the interaction between base classifiers and make good use of the interaction through assigning tested samples to different individual classifiers and their combinations. That is, the upper integral could be used to

Table 5.14 Comparison of Three Fusion Schemes for Extreme Learning Machine and Back-Propagation (the Correct Rate)

Data Sets	ELM				BP			
	Upper Integral–Based Boosting	Boosting	Upper Integral–Based Boosting	Bagging	Upper Integral–Based Boosting	Boosting	Upper Integral–Based Boosting	Bagging
Iris	0.9839	0.9728	0.9831	0.9696	0.9481	0.9377	0.9565	0.9367
Breast Cancer	0.9591	0.9472	0.9529	0.9394	0.9312	0.9172	0.9310	0.9138
Tic-Tac-Toe	0.9247	0.9102	0.9321	0.9001	0.9216	0.9056	0.9251	0.8914
Ionosphere	0.8566	0.8301	0.8596	0.8313	0.8369	0.8194	0.8330	0.8217
Pima	0.7912	0.7686	0.7891	0.7532	0.7493	0.7287	0.7384	0.7181
Heart	0.8438	0.8273	0.8451	0.8191	0.8215	0.7967	0.7962	0.7771
Wine	0.9418	0.9281	0.9469	0.9327	0.9287	0.9016	0.9188	0.8962
Sonar	0.8567	0.8289	0.8626	0.8310	0.8207	0.8003	0.8167	0.7983
Letter	0.9519	0.9307	0.9462	0.9265	0.9172	0.9002	0.9207	0.8963
Waveform + noise	0.8528	0.8319	0.8487	0.8261	0.8231	0.8173	0.8279	0.8031

Table 5.15 Comparison of Three Fusion Schemes for Extreme Learning Machine with Gaussian Kernel and Least-Square Support Vector Machine (the Correct Rate)

Data Sets	ELM-Kernel				LS-SVM			
	Upper Integral–Based Boosting	Boosting	Upper Integral–Based Boosting	Bagging	Upper Integral–Based Boosting	Boosting	Upper Integral–Based Boosting	Bagging
Iris	0.9867	0.9818	0.9868	0.9791	0.9840	0.9848	0.9721	0.9672
Breast Cancer	0.9731	0.9519	0.9687	0.9421	0.9811	0.9569	0.9756	0.9512
Tic-Tac-Toe	0.9473	0.9123	0.9369	0.9316	0.9252	0.9105	0.9312	0.9123
Ionosphere	0.8901	0.8672	0.8965	0.8758	0.8749	0.8470	0.8629	0.8427
Pima	0.8015	0.7826	0.7971	0.7763	0.7992	0.7768	0.7868	0.7529
Heart	0.8672	0.8429	0.8722	0.8511	0.8709	0.8321	0.8531	0.8247
Wine	0.9887	0.9856	0.9818	0.9796	0.9869	0.9835	0.9872	0.9813
Sonar	0.8824	0.8526	0.8768	0.8449	0.8794	0.8376	0.8830	0.8427
Letter	0.9839	0.9775	0.9881	0.9768	0.9773	0.9556	0.9801	0.9610
Waveform + noise	0.8774	0.8496	0.8887	0.8687	0.8808	0.8521	0.8783	0.8592

improve existing fusion model. The base classifiers in boosting have stronger inter-action than those in bagging. In application, the base classifiers could be designed through other ways and the basic fusion operator can be others.

5.4.2.3.2 Comparison with Existing Fuzzy Integral Models

In this subsection, we experimentally compare the approach with existing fuzzy inte-gral models. The basic fusion operator in the approach is the average and the upper integral is used to improve the classifier fusion system by assigning tested samples to different classifier groups. Choquet integral, which is a type of most frequently used fuzzy integrals due to its simplicity and availability [36], is here selected as the fusion operator in comparison with the approach. Three methods are used to determine the fuzzy measures for Choquet integral model. The first one (written as λ-measure 1) is the λ-measure which is given by $g^i = \frac{p_i}{\sum_{j=1}^{n} p_j}$, where p_i is the accuracy of the ith classifier. The second (written as λ-measure 2) is λ-measure determined according to the following equation [39]:

$$g^{ij} = \frac{p_{ij}}{\sum_{s=1}^{n} p_{sj}}, \tag{5.24}$$

where p_{ij} is the accuracy of the ith classifier classifying samples from j class. The λ-measure $g^j = \{g^{1j}, g^{2j}, \ldots, g^{nj}\}$ is used to determine the possibility of samples belonging to jth class.

The third method to determine fuzzy measure is the genetic algorithm [40,41]. The population size is 100. The genetic algorithm is used to determine λ-measure (written as GAλ) and regular fuzzy measure ($2^n - 1$ unknown parameters, written as GARegular).

Tenfold cross-validation is repeated 20 times on each data set. Ten ELMs are trained as the base classifier for both Choquet integral and the approach. The results are listed in Table 5.16.

From Table 5.16 one can view that (1) the training for λ-measures 1 and 2 is extremely fast, (2) the training time of upper integral model is much shorter than that of genetic algorithm, (3) the performance of λ-measure 1 is the lowest, (4) the performance of λ-measure 2 is better than that of λ-measure 1 but worse than that of λ-measure determined by genetic algorithm, (5) the performance of upper integral is the highest on 7 out of 10 data sets, and (6) the performance of regular fuzzy measure determined by genetic algorithm is highest on 3 out of 10 data sets (but their time complexity of training is much higher than the approach by Feng and Wang [2]). Moreover, it is worth noting that the time complexity for training GARegular fuzzy measures is exponentially increasing with the number of base classifiers. Considering both the accuracy and the training complexity, we experimentally validate that the approach in Feng and Wang [2] is superior to the fusion model based on Choquet integral.

Table 5.16 Comparison of Upper Integral Model with Existing Fuzzy Integral Models

Data Sets	Upper Integral		λ-Measure 1		λ-Measure 2		GAλ		GARegular	
	Accuracy	Time(s)	Accuracy	Time(s)	Accuracy	Time(s)	Accuracy	Time(s)	Accuracy	Time(s)
Iris	0.956	4	0.928	0.1	0.934	0.1	0.949	57	0.957	21
Breast Cancer	0.894	9	0.841	0.1	0.850	0.1	0.860	167	0.874	132
Tic-Tac-Toe	0.937	9	0.887	0.1	0.905	0.1	0.911	419	0.921	423
Ionosphere	0.808	5	0.748	0.1	0.767	0.1	0.778	138	0.788	111
Pima	0.708	6	0.655	0.1	0.671	0.1	0.682	201	0.692	171
Heart	0.712	8	0.673	0.1	0.672	0.1	0.686	109	0.697	89
Wine	0.754	4	0.725	0.1	0.737	0.1	0.746	77	0.755	45
Sonar	0.793	5	0.771	0.1	0.772	0.1	0.784	61	0.797	30
Letter	0.875	16	0.825	0.1	0.848	0.1	0.854	892	0.867	555
Waveform + noise	0.781	11	0.745	0.1	0.761	0.1	0.770	743	0.773	411

5.5 Relationship between Fuzziness and Generalization in Ensemble Learning

In the framework of classification, generalization ability of a classifier refers to its capability to correctly classify unseen samples drawn from the distribution same as that of the training set. In this section, we will reveal a relationship between generalization and uncertainty. Specifically, we will present the investigation on the relationship between generalization abilities and fuzziness of base classifiers in ensemble learning [3]. One way to investigate this relation is the analysis on boundary points including their fuzziness and their classification performance. Accordingly, next we first discuss the classifier's generalization from the viewpoint of boundary points and their side effect on classification performance.

5.5.1 Classification Boundary

5.5.1.1 Boundary and Its Estimation Given by a Learned Classifier

Generally, a hypersurface in n-dimensional space can partition the input space into disjoint subsets called decision regions, and each region has points (samples) belonging to the same class. Decision boundary usually refers to the hypersurface between decision regions with different classes. In many real classification problems, the real decision boundary objectively exists but is usually unknown. One purpose of learning for classification problem is to find an approximation of the real boundary such that the difference between the real boundary and its estimation is as small as possible. The difference between the real boundary and its estimated boundary is called approximation error, and a training algorithm is required to find the estimated boundary. An ideal algorithm tries to make the error equal to zero but practically it is impossible. The estimated boundary is usually acquired based on a classifier, which is gotten by training a set of samples according to a training algorithm.

Theoretically, the estimated boundary can be determined if the classifier has been trained well. It means that we can obtain the class label of each sample in the considered area if the classifier has been well trained. For some classifiers the mechanism to obtain the label of a sample is clear. In these cases the estimated boundary is explicitly expressed by a certain formula. A simple illustration to indicate these cases is the linear boundary of decision.

Consider a binary classification task with $y = \pm 1$ labels. When the training samples are linearly separable, we can set the parameters of a linear classifier so that all the training samples are classified correctly. Let w denote a vector orthogonal to the decision boundary and b denote a scalar offset term; then we can write the decision boundary as

$$w^T x + b = 0. \tag{5.25}$$

A typical case of Equation (5.25) is the classifier given by SVM for linearly separable samples. It is easy to judge whether a sample is near to or far from the boundary. The distance between a sample and the boundary is computed as $|w^T x + b|$. A certain threshold value imposed on the distance can be used to judge whether a sample near to or far from the boundary.

Some classifiers do not have a clear mechanism to obtain the class label for each sample. In other words, we can use the trained classifier to calculate the label for each sample, but the pertinent formula cannot be provided explicitly. One example of this case is the Bayes' decision boundary [42]. Given a sample x, a prior probability $P(y_i)$ of class, and the conditional probability $p(x|y_i)$, we convert the prior probability to the posteriori probability $p(y_i|x)$ through Bayes' theorem. The Bayes' decision rules are as follows:

$$\begin{cases} x \in \text{class } y_1, & \text{if } P(y_1)p(x|y_1) > P(y_2)p(x|y_2); \\ x \in \text{class } y_2, & \text{if } P(y_1)p(x|y_1) < P(y_2)p(x|y_2). \end{cases} \tag{5.26}$$

This decision boundary for a two-class problem can be determined by the point locus $\{x|P(y_1)p(x|y_1) - P(y_2)p(x|y_2) = 0\}$, which is difficult to be explicitly expressed as a formula except for few certain special data distributions.

Another example of this situation is the fuzzy K-nearest neighbors' (K-NN) classifier [43] that outputs a vector of class membership. Each component of the vector is a number in [0, 1], representing a membership of the sample belonging to the corresponding class. If the components are equal to either 0 or 1, then it degrades to the traditional K-NN. Fuzzy K-NN acquires the membership of a sample x by the formula

$$\mu(x) = \frac{\sum_{j=1}^{K} \mu_{ij} \| x - x_j \|^{-2(m-1)}}{\sum_{j=1}^{K} \| x - x_j \|^{-2(m-1)}}, \tag{5.27}$$

where $(\mu_1(x), \mu_2(x), \ldots, \mu_k(x))^T$ is a membership vector (and the other symbols remain to be specified in next subsection). Its decision boundary is the locus $\{x|\mu_1^* = \mu_2^*\}$ where $(\mu_1^*(x), \mu_2^*(x), \ldots, \mu_k^*(x))$ is a permutation of $(\mu_1(x), \mu_2(x), \ldots, \mu_k(x))^T$ in a decreasing order. Obviously, it is impossible to explicitly express the classification boundary.

These two examples indicate that it is difficult to judge whether a sample is near to or far from the boundary when the boundary cannot be explicitly expressed as a formula.

Due to the difference between classifier design objectives, the estimated boundary is dependent strongly on the selection of classifier for the same training set. The difference between estimated boundary and real boundary is considered as a key index to evaluate the generalization performance of a classifier. The good estimated decision boundary could give an insight into a high-performance classifier design, which cannot be supplied only by accuracy. It can be applied to select proper classifiers, to discover possible overfitting, and to calculate the similarity among the models generated by different classifiers.

For a well-trained classifier with high performance, it is reasonable to believe that the estimated boundary has sufficiently approximated the real boundary. But since the real boundary is unknown, it is hard to judge which one is better based only on estimated boundaries. Therefore, there is a need to find new index to measure the generalization. Perhaps the ability of a classifier correctly classifying boundary samples is a crucial index.

5.5.1.2 Two Types of Methods for Training a Classifier

Usually, there are two types of classifiers. One can explicitly provide the analytic formula of the estimated decision boundary, while the other cannot but provide the approximation by locus of some points. SVM and fuzzy K-NN are two typical representatives of both types, respectively.

SVMs select a boundary according to the maximization of margin, which is based on statistical learning theory [44]. SVM supposes an implicit function φ mapping the data from the input space X into a high-dimensional feature space F. The mapping is associated with a kernel function $K(x_i, x_j)$, which satisfies $K(x_i, x_j) = (\varphi(x_i), \varphi(x_j))$, where x_i and x_j, respectively, denote the ith and jth training samples and $(\cdot, \cdot)$ denotes the inner product. The decision boundary is explicitly given by

$$f(x) = \text{sgn}\left(\sum_{i=1}^{n} \alpha_i y_i K(x, x_j) + b\right), \qquad (5.28)$$

where α_i and b are unknown parameters that are determined by solving a quadratic programming.

Fuzzy K-NN classifier [43] considers fuzzy classification problems and assigns each unseen sample x with a membership vector that can be determined by using the neighbors' class memberships and evaluating the distances between x and its K nearest neighbors. For every training sample, fuzzy K-NN assumes that the class information has been given by the memberships of the sample belonging to the predefined classes. Let $(\mu_1(x), \mu_2(x), \ldots, \mu_k(x))^T$ denote the output vector that fuzzy K-NN outputs for an unseen sample x, where $\mu_i(x) \in [0, 1]$ is the membership of x belonging to the ith class. The $\mu_i(x)$ is given by formula (5.27) where $x_j \in X$ is a labeled training sample that falls in the set of K nearest neighbors of the unseen sample x; $(\mu_{ij})_{j=1,2,\ldots,K} \in [0, 1]$ is the known class membership of x_j to the ith class y_i; $\| x - x_j \|$ is the distance between x and x_j; and m is a parameter to adjust the weights that indicate the neighbors' contribution to the membership value. As the parameter m is increasing, the neighbors are more evenly weighted, and their relative distances from the sample being classified have less effect.

It is worth noted that if we only know the class label of each training sample, that is, μ_{ij} is equal to either 0 or 1, then formula (5.27) will degenerate and can be considered as the weighted summation of samples in the K nearest neighbors that belong to the ith class, where the weight is the inverse of the distance between the sample and its neighbors. In this book, we focus on the second type of classifiers mentioned earlier.

5.5.1.3 Side Effect of Boundary and Experimental Verification

It is experimentally observed that, for classification problems with continuous attributes in supervised learning, a sample near to boundary usually has the statistical testing error higher than a sample positioned far from boundary. Here, the boundary refers originally to real one, which is replaced by an estimated boundary encountered in real-world problems. We call this phenomenon a side effect of boundary. The classifier we use in this section to estimate the boundary is fuzzy K-NN. As mentioned in Section 5.5.1, judging whether a sample is located near to or far from the boundary is more difficult for fuzzy K-NN than for other classifiers that have an explicit expression of the boundary.

The following simple simulation confirms the side effect phenomenon for a known boundary. Consider a 2-class problem in the $x - y$ plane and suppose that the real boundary is given by the function $y = \cos(2x)$ via the following rule: a sample (x, y) is considered as positive if $y > \cos(2x)$ and negative if $y < \cos(2x)$. The boundary is shown in Figure 5.6a. Uniformly, we select 200 samples from the rectangular area $\{(x, y)| -\pi < x < \pi, -2 < y < 2\}$ to form a sample set from which we randomly select 70% as the training set. Since the real boundary is known, we artificially split the entire set of all samples as two categories: samples near to boundary $\{(x, y)||y - \cos(2x)| < 0.5\}$ and sample far from boundary $\{(x, y)||y - \cos(2x)| > 0.5\}$. Using fuzzy K-NN ($K = 5$) to train a classifier and then apply it to classify the samples near to and far from the boundary, respectively, we have the experimental result that the classification error rate for samples near to boundary is 20% while the error rate for samples far from boundary is zero. Figure 5.6b clearly shows the experimental result.

More numerical experiments are conducted to confirm this side effect phenomenon for the fuzzy K-NN classifier on a number of selected data sets that are obtained from UCI machine learning repository [37] and summarized in Table 5.17. Basically, the experiments have three steps: (1) training the classifiers and estimating boundaries, (2) splitting all samples as two categories, that is, samples near to or far from boundaries, and (3) computing the classification error rates, respectively, for the two categories. A difficulty for the three steps is how to estimate the boundary and then judge a sample near to or far from the boundary for fuzzy K-NN. We have a simple scheme to overcome this difficulty for fuzzy K-NN without an explicit expression of the estimated boundary. Since the output of fuzzy K-NN for

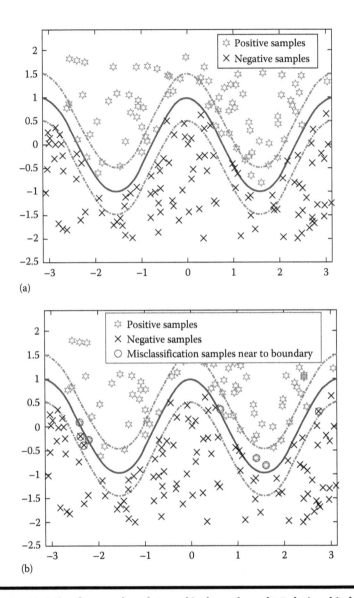

Figure 5.6 (a) A simple two-class data and its boundary. (b) Relationship between the real boundary and the classification error.

a sample is a vector $(\mu_1, \mu_2, \ldots, \mu_n)^T$ in which the component is a number in [0,1] representing the membership of the sample belonging to the corresponding class, we estimate its boundary as $\{x | \mu_1(x) = \mu_2(x) = 0.5\}$ for a 2-class problem and define the distance between the boundary and a sample with output $(\mu_1, \mu_2)^T$ as $(|\mu_1 - 0.5| + |\mu_2 - 0.5|)$. In this way, a threshold can also be set to judge a sample

Table 5.17 Data Sets Used in Experiments

Data Sets	N_{sample}	N_{cat}	N_{con}	N_{class}
Banknote	1372	0	4	2
Blood	748	0	4	2
Breast Cancer	263	9	0	2
Cleveland Heart	297	7	6	2
Diabetes	768	8	0	2
Flare Solar	144	9	0	2
German	1000	7	13	2
Glass	214	10	0	6
Heart	270	7	6	2
Housing	506	1	12	2
Ionosphere	351	0	34	2
New Thyroid	215	0	5	3
Parkinsons	195	0	22	2
Seeds	210	7	3	3
Sonar	208	0	60	2
Vowel	990	0	10	11
Wall-Following	5456	0	2	4
Wdbc	569	0	9	2
Wholesale	440	0	7	2
Yeast	1484	0	8	10

near to or far from the boundary. Experimental results are listed in Table 5.18 from which one can see that the classification error rate for samples near to boundaries is much higher than that for samples located far from boundaries.

Note: In Table 5.17, N_{sample} indicates number of samples; N_{cat} indicates number of categorical features; N_{con} indicates number of continuous features; and N_{class} indicates number of classes. In Table 5.18, $N_{MSNTB}(Err)$ indicates number of samples near to boundary; $N_{MSFFB}(Err)$ indicates number of samples far from boundary; and *Err* indicates error rate.

Table 5.18   Experimental Results for the Fuzzy *K*-NN Classifier

Data Sets	N_{MSNTB} (Err)	N_{MSFFB} (Err)	Threshold
Banknote	0 (0.0000)	0 (0.0000)	1.0000
Blood	38 (0.3393)	21 (0.1858)	0.8499
Breast Cancer	12 (0.3077)	8 (0.2000)	0.6340
Cleveland Heart	15 (0.3750)	3 (0.0600)	0.6821
Diabetes	45 (0.3913)	17 (0.1466)	0.6238
Flare Solar	8 (0.3636)	5 (0.2273)	0.3115
German	44 (0.2933)	26 (0.1733)	0.6118
Glass	1 (0.0312)	0 (0.0000)	1.6667
Heart	7 (0.1842)	4 (0.0930)	0.7355
Housing	23 (0.3026)	8 (0.1053)	0.8299
Ionosphere	10 (0.1887)	2 (0.0377)	1.0000
New Thyroid	4 (0.1250)	0 (0.0000)	1.3333
Parkinsons	4 (0.1379)	1 (0.0333)	1.0000
Seeds	6 (0.1935)	0 (0.0000)	1.3333
Sonar	9 (0.2903)	1 (0.0312)	0.8425
Vowel	9 (0.0608)	1 (0.0067)	1.7618
Wall-Following	19 (0.0232)	3 (0.0037)	1.5000
Wdbc	14 (0.1647)	2 (0.0233)	1.0000
Wholesale	8 (0.1212)	2 (0.0303)	1.0000
Yeast	118 (0.5291)	75 (0.3363)	1.6000

5.5.2 Fuzziness of Classifiers

In Section 1.2, we discussed the fuzziness of fuzzy sets. If $B = \{\mu_1, \mu_2, \ldots, \mu_n\}$ be a fuzzy set, the fuzziness of B can be measured by

$$E(B) = -\frac{1}{n} \sum_{i=1}^{n} (\mu_i \log \mu_i + (1 - \mu_i) \log(1 - \mu_i)). \qquad (5.29)$$

This section first investigates the classifiers fuzziness and then discusses the fuzziness's impact on misclassification.

5.5.2.1 Fuzziness of Classifier

Given a set of training samples $\{x_i\}_{i=1}^n$, a fuzzy partition of these samples assigns the membership degrees of each sample to the k classes. The partition can be described by a membership matrix $U = \left(\mu_{ij}\right)_{k \times n}$, where $\mu_{ij} = \mu_i(x_j)$ denotes the membership of the jth sample x_j belonging to the ith class. The elements in the membership matrix have to obey the following properties:

$$\sum_{i=1}^k \mu_{ij} = 1, 0 < \sum_{j=1}^n \mu_{ij} < n, \mu_{ij} \in [0, 1]. \tag{5.30}$$

Therefore, once the training procedure of a classifier is completed, the membership matrix U upon the n training samples can be obtained. For the jth sample x_j, the trained classifier will give an output vector represented as a fuzzy set $\mu_j = (\mu_{1j}, \mu_{2j}, \ldots, \mu_{kj})$. Based on (5.29), the fuzziness of the trained classifier on x_j is given by

$$E(\mu_j) = -\frac{1}{k} \sum_{i=1}^k (\mu_{ij} \log \mu_{ij} + (1 - \mu_{ij}) \log(1 - \mu_{ij})), \tag{5.31}$$

and furthermore, the fuzziness of the trained classifier can be given as follows:

$$E(U) = -\frac{1}{kn} \sum_{i=1}^k \sum_{j=1}^n (\mu_{ij} \log \mu_{ij} + (1 - \mu_{ij}) \log(1 - \mu_{ij})). \tag{5.32}$$

Equation (5.32) defines the fuzziness of a trained classifier that has fuzzy vector output. It plays a key role to investigate the classifier's generalization. From the previous definition, one can view that the fuzziness of a trained classifier is actually defined as the averaged fuzziness of the classifier's outputs on all training samples. In other words, it is the training fuzziness of the classifier. The most reasonable definition of a classifier's fuzziness should be the averaged fuzziness over the entire sample space including training samples and unseen testing samples. However, the fuzziness for unseen samples is generally unknown, and for any supervised learning problem, there is a well-acknowledged assumption, that is, the training samples have a distribution identical to the distribution of samples in the entire space. And therefore, we use Equation (5.32) as the definition of a classifier's fuzziness.

5.5.2.2 Relationship between Fuzziness and Misclassification

To observe the relationship between misclassified samples and their fuzziness, Ripley's synthetic data set [45] is utilized in the following experiment. There are

250 two-dimensional samples in the data set. Moreover, the samples are generated from mixtures of two Gaussian distributions. From Figure 5.7a we can visualize the data set.

The number of neighbors used in the fuzzy K-NN classifier, that is, the value of K in the experiment, ranges from 2 to 50 with a step size of 1. The experimental

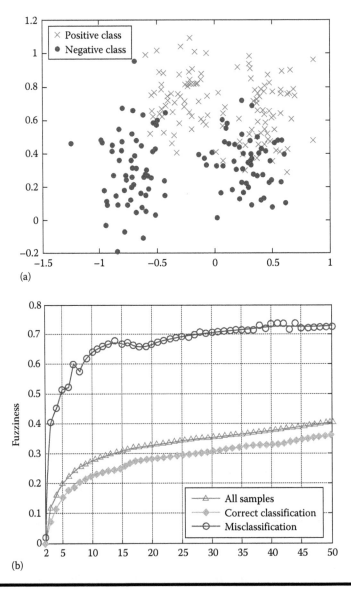

Figure 5.7 **(a) Ripley's synthetic data set. (b) Fuzziness of fuzzy K-nearest neighbors produced for the Ripley's synthetic data set.**

results are shown in Figure 5.7b, where we report the averaged fuzziness over (1) the set of correctly classified samples, (2) the set of all samples, and (3) the set of misclassified samples. For the fuzzy K-NN classifier, the values of fuzziness reported over misclassified samples are significantly higher than the values reported for the correctly classified samples.

To further verify the relationship between fuzziness and misclassification, more experiments are conducted on the 20 benchmark data sets taken from the UCI machine learning repository [37]. Two illustrations are shown in Figure 5.8 where one still can see that the fuzziness on misclassified samples is much larger than that on correctly classified samples, which once again experimentally confirms the mentioned relationship. One worth noting point is that the mentioned relationship is not sensitive to the classifier change. That is, the relationship still holds if the classifier training algorithm changes from one to another.

5.5.2.3 Relationship between Fuzziness and Classification Boundary

Furthermore, from the study on relationship between fuzziness and misclassification, it is found that samples with higher fuzziness are near to the classification boundary while samples with lower fuzziness are relatively far from the classification boundary. The following experiment gives an illustration in which the fuzzy K-NN is still used as the classifier, the data set is also the Ripley's synthetic data, and the number of neighbors for fuzzy K-NN is fixed as 20. The misclassified samples and the classification boundary are demonstrated in Figure 5.9a. Figure 5.9b shows the 50 samples with highest value of fuzziness. It can be observed from Figure 5.9 that both the misclassified samples and the samples with the larger fuzziness are all near to the classification boundary.

Furthermore regarding the fuzzy K-NN classifier, the following Proposition 5.2 relates a sample's fuzziness to the distance between the sample and the classification boundary.

Proposition 5.2   *For a 2-class problem, let D_1 be the distance between the sample x_1 and the classification boundary, while D_2 be the distance between the sample x_2 and boundary. Moreover, μ and σ are the outputs of the classifier on x_1 and x_2, respectively. If $D_1 \leq D_2$, then the fuzziness of x_1 is no less than that of x_2, that is, $E(\mu) \geq E(\sigma)$.*

Proof: Let the outputs of the trained classifier on x_1 and x_2 be $\mu = (\mu_1, \mu_2)^T$ and $\sigma = (\sigma_1, \sigma_2)^T$, respectively. According to the distance metric defined in previous section, we have $D_1 = |\mu_1 - 0.5| + |\mu_2 - 0.5|$ and $D_2 = |\sigma_1 - 0.5| + |\sigma_2 - 0.5|$. The value of D_1 keeps unchanged if the values of μ_1 and μ_2 are exchanged, while the value of D_2 keeps fixed if the values of σ_1 and σ_2 are exchanged. Therefore, without

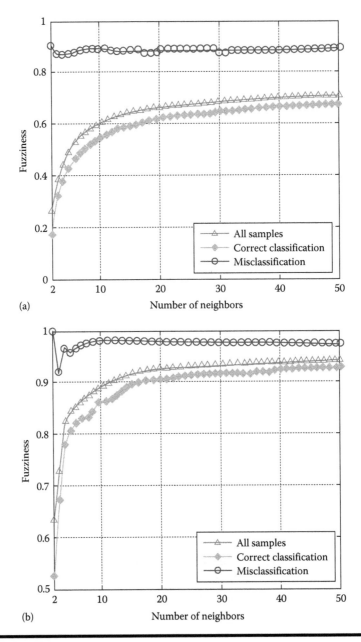

Figure 5.8 Relationship between fuzziness and misclassification on the two benchmark data sets. (a) Diabetes. (b) Flare solar.

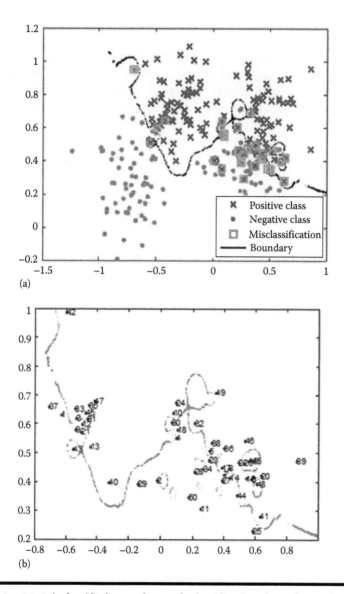

Figure 5.9 (a) Misclassified samples and classification boundary. (b) The 50 samples with highest values of fuzziness.

losing generality, we suppose that $\mu_1 \geq \mu_2$ and $\sigma_1 \geq \sigma_2$. It implies that $\mu_1 \geq 0.5$ and $\sigma_1 \geq 0.5$, which result in $D_1 = 2(\mu_1 - 0.5)$ and $D_2 = 2(\sigma_1 - 0.5)$. Since $D_1 \leq D_2$, we have $\mu_1 \leq \sigma_1$. According to Theorem 1.4, we have $E(\mu_1) \geq E(\sigma_1)$. Since $E(\mu_1) = E(\mu_2)$ and $E(\sigma_1) = E(\sigma_2)$, we finally obtain $E(\mu) = E(\mu_1) \geq E(\sigma) = E(\sigma_1)$.

5.5.2.4 Divide and Conquer Strategy

As the experimental observation, we find that the risk of misclassification increases as the fuzziness of training samples gets larger while the risk is relatively decreasing as the fuzziness of training samples gets statistically smaller. This analysis on misclassification risk inspires us to handle samples with large fuzziness separately from samples with small fuzziness. For most classification problems, samples with more fuzziness are more difficult to be correctly classified in comparison with samples having less fuzziness. Equivalently to say, that boundary points are more difficult to be correctly classified in comparison with inner points. However, the boundary points are often more important than inner points for most classification problems. The idea is to use a usual classifier to deal with the samples with less fuzziness while to use a particularly trained classifier to cope with the samples exhibiting higher fuzziness. This is the strategy of divide and conquer.

According to the magnitude of fuzziness, all samples are categorized as two groups. One group is of high fuzziness while the other is of low fuzziness. A lot of experiments on both simulated data and on real data sets have been conducted to verify the difference of performance (the correct classification rate) between the two groups. As an example, Figure 5.10 gives four illustrations that clearly indicate the significant difference upon the Ripley's synthetic, Diabetes, Flare Solar, and German data sets. The experimental results show that, upon all data sets, the difference is significant for any number of neighbors K ($1 < K < 50$).

One may argue that the difference tells nothing about the improvement of classification performance because samples that users are really interested in are the ones with high fuzziness. In fact this difference is to make users pay particular attention to samples with high fuzziness and to tell users that the classification for samples with small fuzziness is much possibly correct even they use a simple trained classifier. Without loss of generality, we will report in the following the handling strategy of high-fuzziness samples separating from the low-fuzziness samples and the improvement the strategy brings.

5.5.2.5 Impact of the Weighting Exponent m on the Fuzziness of Fuzzy K-NN Classifier

It is obvious to see from (5.27) that the output of fuzzy K-NN classifier with respect to a sample is a membership vector. Each component of the membership vector depends on m ($m > 1$), the parameter of weighting exponent. Since the fuzziness of a classifier is computed based on the membership vectors, and therefore, the fuzziness changes with value of parameter m, fuzzy K-NN approaches the traditional K-NN as m is decreasingly tending to one. We experimentally examine the impact of m on the fuzziness of fuzzy K-NN classifier on the 20 selected data sets. All experiments show a consistent trend for the change of fuzziness value in fuzzy K-NN classifiers with different weighting exponent m. It can be observed from Figure 5.11 that the

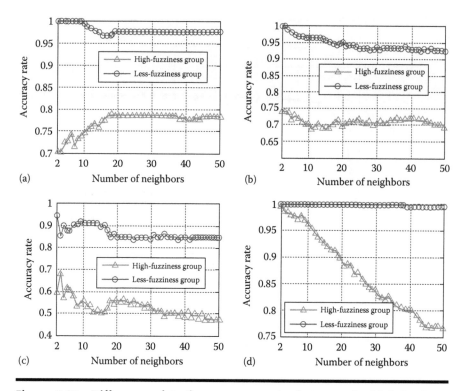

Figure 5.10 Difference of testing accuracy rates between the high-fuzziness group and low-fuzziness group. (a) Ripley. (b) Diabetes. (c) Flare solar. (d) German.

fuzziness of fuzzy K-NN drastically increases as m increases from 1.05 to 4, and the increase of fuzziness of fuzzy K-NN classifier becomes more saturated as $m > 8$.

5.5.3 Relationship between Generalization and Fuzziness

In this section, we will discuss the key issue, that is, the relationship between the generalization of a classifier and the fuzziness of the classifier. We first present the definition of generalization and its estimation, then present the classifier selection, then give the explanation based on extreme (max/min) fuzziness, and finally present the experimental results.

5.5.3.1 Definition of Generalization and Its Elaboration

Generally, the task of a learning model is to construct a function $f(x)$ based on a training set $T = \{(x_i, y_i), 1 \leq i \leq n\}$ in order to approximate an objective function $f(x)$ at future observations of x. The use of $f(x)$ to approximate $F(x)$ on future

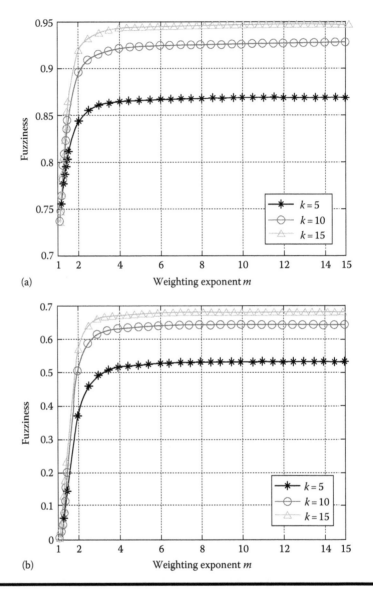

(a)

(b)

Figure 5.11 Impact of the weighting exponent *m* on the fuzziness of fuzzy *K*-NN classifier. (a) Flare solar. (b) German.

observations is called "generalization." The learned function $f(x)$ is called a classifier for classification problems. The difference between $f(x)$ and $F(x)$ is called generalization error that is considered as the measure of generalization ability of the involved learning model.

Theoretically, the generalization error can be investigated from many different angles. One typical method is to estimate an upper bound for the generalization error. The true generalization error reported on the entire input space can be denoted as $R_{true} = \int_S [f(x) - F(x)]^2 p(x)dx$, where S denotes the entire input space and $p(x)$ is the probability density function of input x. Since both target outputs and distributions of the unseen samples are unknown, it is impossible to compute R_{true} directly. Many researchers want to find an upper bound to estimate the generalization error. For example, from the angle of structural risk minimization, Vapnik [46] gave a bound that depends on the training error and the complexity of the classifier. Here, the complexity of a classifier is described by the size of training set and the VC dimension of a function group including the learned function $f(x)$.

Experimentally, the generalization error is often verified by observing the prediction accuracy of a classifier on a set of samples, called testing samples, that are not used in the process of training the classifier. This is the testing accuracy, which is regarded as the most crucial index for experimentally measuring the generalization of a classifier. This section makes an attempt to study on the generalization of a classifier from a new viewpoint. Different from search for an upper error bound, we try to find a relationship between the generalization of a classifier and the fuzziness of the classifier outputs. The relationship is expected to provide some useful guidelines for improving the generalization ability of a classifier.

5.5.3.2 Classifier Selection

When the membership μ_j of a fuzzy set A is equal to 0.5 for all j, the fuzziness of the fuzzy set attains the maximum. The fuzziness maximization implies that, for drawing a fuzzy set as the conclusion, we prefer a fuzzy set with bigger fuzziness to other fuzzy sets. In other words, we consider that an event with much uncertainty (fuzziness) will bring us more information when it occurs [47].

We now consider the output of a trained classifier. Suppose that there are k classes and the output of the classifier for an unseen sample can be represented as $\mu = (\mu_1, \mu_2, \ldots, \mu_k)^T$ in which each component is the degree of the unseen sample belonging to the corresponding class. The final class label C_{i0} for the unseen sample is determined by $i_0 = \text{argmax}_{1 \leq i \leq k}\{\mu_i\}$. The basic idea is described in Figure 5.12, where classifiers A and B denote two trained classifiers, respectively.

Focusing on Figure 5.12, we consider the two classifiers having the same training accuracy but generally having the different predictive accuracy. The problem is which one has the better generalization?

It is impossible to provide a general answer since it depends on the specific problem. Nevertheless, from the viewpoint of *traditional* pattern recognition, one

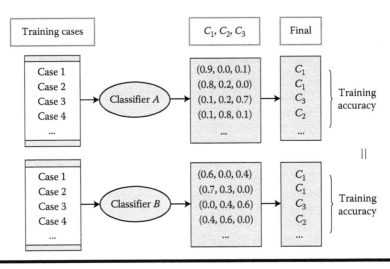

Figure 5.12   The idea of the approach by Wang et al. [3].

definitely prefers the classifier A. The reason is at least twofold. The first is that the uncertainty in the training set for classifier A is smaller than for classifier B. People always prefer the one with the lower uncertainty since it seems making the decision easier. The second is that classifier A has the training accuracy same as classifier B. In fact, in many approaches to the design of classifiers, the design objective to be optimized is usually the one associated with some constraints using which we tend to minimize the uncertainty of the entries of the output vector while retaining accuracy on the training set. Implicitly, it acknowledges that, for two classifiers with the same training accuracy, the one with the lower uncertainty has better generalization than the classifier with the higher uncertainty level. However, through a large number of experiments carried out for classification problems with complex and highly nonlinear boundaries or without a clearly delineated boundary, we found that this traditional viewpoint is not always true. Here, we propose an alternative that, for some types of classification problems, classifiers with higher uncertainty for the training set exhibit higher generalization abilities.

5.5.3.3 Explanation Based on Extreme (max/min) Fuzziness

We recall the crux of the training algorithm as follows. Basically, the idea of this algorithm is very simple. First, we generate an ensemble of base classifiers, and then from this ensemble, we find the first l classifiers with the highest fuzziness values while keeping an acceptable individual training accuracy.

5.5.3.3.1 Training Phase

Suppose that we have had a training algorithm for generating an ensemble of classifiers by setting up different parameters of this algorithm. Given a training set, we first generate an ensemble of classifiers based on the training algorithm. With respect to any sample x_j, each classifier is required to have an output vector $\mu_j = (\mu_{1j}, \mu_{2j}, \ldots, \mu_{kj})^T$. According to Equation (5.32), the fuzziness level is computed for each classifier. We sort these classifiers in a decreasing order based on the fuzziness magnitudes of these classifiers and select the first l classifiers with highest fuzziness while keeping an acceptable individual training accuracy. Here, the fuzzy K-NN is used as the classifier generation algorithm.

5.5.3.3.2 Reasoning Phase

For any testing sample, match this sample to each of l trained classifiers and getting l vectors in which the component represents a possibility of the sample belonging to the corresponding class. Take an average for each component of the l vectors and assign the class label with maximum component to the considered sample.

Basically, this algorithm is to raise the fuzziness during the classifier training process under the condition that an acceptable training accuracy is kept. The central idea behind this algorithm is that, regarding the improvement of generalization performance, the classifiers with big fuzziness play a key role. This idea is identical to the discussion in Section 1.5.1 regarding the relationship between boundary area and high-fuzziness samples. Section 1.5.1 provides us with a result that basically samples near to boundary have the outputted fuzziness higher than samples far from boundary. Usually, we believe that samples near to boundary are more difficult to be correctly classified than samples far from boundary. The idea implies such a preference that we would like to select classifier C_1 if, for two classifiers C_1 and C_2, C_1 can correctly classify a set of boundary samples (denoted by A) and C_2 can correctly classify another set of boundary samples (denoted by B), the number of samples in A is as same as in B, and samples in A are nearer to boundary than samples in B averagely. One may argue that, for a classification problem with simple real boundary, this sufficient consideration of boundary points will give a very complex boundary, which possibly results in the overfitting phenomenon. In fact, for classification problems with simple boundaries such as the linearly separable cases, the fuzziness of a well-trained classifier is usually very small. But for classification problems with complex boundaries, experimental results do not show the overfitting. Interestingly, this idea coincides with the following maximum fuzziness principle.

5.5.3.3.3 Maximum Fuzzy Entropy Principle [47]

Consider a reasoning process that includes a number of parameters to be determined. With respect to a given fact, the reasoning conclusion will be a parametric fuzzy set, which implies that the reasoning conclusion can be changed with diverse parameters. We prefer the parametric fuzzy set with maximum fuzziness (to other fuzzy sets) as the reasoning conclusion, subject to the given constraints.

We have the following explanations and remarks regarding the maximum fuzziness principle in classifier generalization improvement.

Remark 5.1: Why does the fuzziness maximization improve the generalization capability of a classifier? Intuitively, we can offer the following explanation. The explanation is similar to that by Wang and Dong [47]. Suppose that there is a classification problem with k classes and x is an object to be classified. If there is not any additional available information for classification, the most reasonable classification result for x should be that the membership degree of x belonging to each of the k classes is identical (i.e., $1/k$). This can be achieved by maximizing the entropy of x, according to the maximum entropy principle in traditional probability theory. If some additional information for classification is available (i.e., there exists a training set in which each example's class is known and an acceptable training accuracy is required to be kept), then in order to get a reasonable and fair classification for x, we should maximize the fuzziness of x subject to some constraints; each constraint represents that a training example can be classified correctly. These constraints mean that the available information for classification has been utilized but there still exist uncertain factors such that the classification for other objects is uncertain. A reasonable way to handle the remaining uncertain information for classification is to use the maximum uncertainty principle. The reasonable and fair classification for x is expected to result in an increase of generalization capability.

Remark 5.2: The maximum fuzziness principle is more suitable for classifiers in which the classification uncertainty exists inherently. These cases indicate that the problem may be of crisp classification but its essence of classes for samples is fuzzy. For example, a crisp classification problem in which any positive (negative resp.) sample has several negative (positive resp.) nearest neighbors will definitely have not a boundary that separates one class of samples from another even with a very low correct rate of classification. In this way, every sample associated with a vector (μ_1, μ_2) (representing the possibilities of the sample belonging to each of both classes, respectively) is more reasonable and more accurate than that associated with a crisp class label. The maximum fuzziness principle makes a classifier to output a vector (μ_1, μ_2) with μ_1 and μ_2 approaching 0.5 rather than with μ_1 and μ_2 approaching either 0 or 1.

Remark 5.3: Since x is an object remaining to classify, we do not know its components before matching x to the trained classifier and further we cannot directly maximize its fuzziness. Noting that any supervised learning algorithm has a fundamental assumption that the training set is a sampling from a population of examples and the testing set has the distribution identical to the training set, it is reasonable that we replace the fuzziness maximization of x over the entire sample space with that over the training set. Unfortunately, so far we still have not yet a formal mathematical formulation for this explanation on maximum fuzziness.

Remark 5.4: The acceptability threshold is referring to the acceptable training accuracy rate that is problem dependent. Usually, it is defined by users. Experimentally, we find that this threshold is sensitive to the output of the approach by Wang et al. [3]. The ensemble of classifiers with high maximum fuzziness is obtained by selecting individual classifiers that are required to have a training accuracy rate over the threshold. And therefore, the ensemble varies with the change of threshold value. We experimentally find that the approach by Wang et al. [3] has a better performance when the threshold is smaller in comparison with a big threshold for a given learning problem. One explanation may be that for a smaller threshold the individual classifier with high fuzziness will have more chance to be selected, which will enhance the diversity of the ensemble.

5.5.3.4 Experimental Results

To validate the training and reasoning algorithm presented in Section 5.5.3, three classifiers, that is, the fuzzy K-NN, the fuzzy ELM, and the fuzzy decision tree (DT), are utilized to generate the base classifier ensemble. For a given training set and an integer l, we first train l fuzzy K-NN classifiers by varying the value of K from 2 to $l + 1$ with a step of 1, l fuzzy ELM classifiers by repeating the random weight l times, and l fuzzy DTs by varying the leaf level and the parameters of triangular memberships, respectively. Once the training procedure of the l fuzzy classifiers has been completed, these classifiers are sorted in a descending order according to their fuzziness values. Then, the first 10 base classifiers with highest fuzziness values and the last 10 base classifiers with the lowest fuzziness values are selected, respectively.

Two mechanisms of validation are selected. The first is the hold-out validation (70–30), namely, for each data set, 70% samples are randomly chosen for training while the rest 30% are used for testing. The second is the DOB-SCV (distribution optimally balanced-standard stratified cross validation) validation scheme [48] in which the concept of class neighbor is used to generate the partition for increasing the randomness and uniformity of samples.

The averaged training and testing accuracy rates together with their corresponding standard deviations are recorded. Furthermore, the paired t-test is conducted to examine whether the performance improvement achieved by the ensemble of classifiers with high fuzziness over the ensemble of classifiers with low fuzziness is statistically significant. Experimental results do not show significant difference between the two validation mechanisms except for two data sets with imbalanced classes. The experimental results for DOB-SCV validation and their statistical analyses, including paired t-test and Wilcoxon signed rank test [49,50], are listed in Tables 5.19 and 5.20.

Table 5.19 Training Accuracy (%) of Three Fuzzy Classifiers (F-KNN, F-ELM, F-DT) with Different Fuzziness

Data Sets	Fuzzy K-NN (Low Fuzziness) Acc_{Train}	Fuzzy K-NN (High Fuzziness) $Acc_{Train}(P_1, P_2)$	Fuzzy ELM (Low Fuzziness) Acc_{Train}	Fuzzy ELM (High Fuzziness) $Acc_{Train}(P_1, P_2)$	Fuzzy DT (Low Fuzziness) Acc_{Train}	Fuzzy DT (High Fuzziness) $Acc_{Train}(P_1, P_2)$
Banknote	100 ± 0.00	$99.77 \pm 0.22(1.431E-004, 4.883E-004)$	100 ± 0.00	$100 \pm 0.00(1, 1)$	93.15 ± 1.06	$95.86 \pm 0.64(6.487E-009, 1.316E-004)$
Blood	86.63 ± 1.13	$79.43 \pm 0.76(1.409E-015, 8.782E-005)$	84.86 ± 0.80	$81.89 \pm 0.72(1.380E-012, 8.696E-005)$	76.73 ± 0.33	$77.95 \pm 0.87(2.855E-011, 2.130E-005)$
Breast Cancer	88.83 ± 1.60	$79.43 \pm 1.11(1.357E-012, 8.720E-005)$	97.73 ± 0.93	$87.98 \pm 1.27(1.811E-017, 8.720E-005)$	77.49 ± 1.88	$91.86 \pm 1.31(1.209E-016, 8.696E-005)$
Cleveland Heart	99.93 ± 0.18	$93.33 \pm 1.00(4.514E-016, 8.282E-005)$	99.83 ± 0.24	$92.71 \pm 1.26(5.143E-016, 8.211E-005)$	86.64 ± 3.57	$99.35 \pm 0.53(6.206E-012, 8.720E-005)$
Diabetes	90.08 ± 0.56	$81.86 \pm 0.93(4.922E-14, 8.782E-005)$	87.12 ± 0.80	$82.07 \pm 1.19(4.455E-015, 8.832E-005)$	77.17 ± 1.10	$84.17 \pm 1.27(1.016E-014, 8.807E-005)$
Flare Solar	76.65 ± 2.54	$66.20 \pm 1.11(7.869E-018, 8.858E-005)$	85.50 ± 2.72	$84.95 \pm 2.39(0.061, 0.056)$	76.05 ± 2.31	$79.05 \pm 2.24(8.393E-006, 1.847E-004)$
German	99.76 ± 0.18	$89.57 \pm 0.77(4.279E-025, 8.832E-005)$	86.13 ± 0.68	$80.03 \pm 0.78(4.187E-017, 8.820E-005)$	79.34 ± 4.49	$98.81 \pm 0.51(4.189E-014, 8.858E-005)$
Glass	100 ± 0.00	$100 \pm 0.00(0.3299, 1)$	100 ± 0.00	$99.53 \pm 0.50(4.103E-004, 9.766E-004)$	93.11 ± 3.33	$96.76 \pm 1.50(2.747E-005, 1.803E-004)$
Heart	99.60 ± 0.38	$91.14 \pm 1.43(1.866E-016, 8.745E-005)$	99.86 ± 0.24	$92.46 \pm 1.36(1.803E-015, 8.609E-005)$	77.35 ± 1.26	$99.07 \pm 1.27(1.544E-025, 8.414E-005)$
Housing	100 ± 0.00	$100 \pm 0.00(1, 1)$	97.54 ± 0.64	$92.17 \pm 0.89(5.586E-014, 8.820E-005)$	83.57 ± 1.10	$92.71 \pm 0.73(1.839E-018, 8.795E-005)$
Ionosphere	97.29 ± 0.50	$85.08 \pm 2.52(7.193E-022, 8.858E-005)$	99.74 ± 0.20	$96.12 \pm 0.82(5.219E-014, 8.560E-005)$	99.89 ± 0.20	$93.92 \pm 0.86(1.312E-014, 8.832E-05)$
New Thyroid	100 ± 0.00	$98.00 \pm 0.61(8.653E-012, 6.757E-005)$	100 ± 0.00	$99.73 \pm 0.34(0.002, 0.008)$	81.00 ± 2.87	$93.80 \pm 1.18(2.286E-007, 0.002)$
Parkinsons	100 ± 0.00	$100 \pm 0.00(1, 1)$	100 ± 0.00	$97.11 \pm 0.83(2.814E-012, 7.557E-005)$	84.15 ± 1.21	$99.19 \pm 0.90(2.223E-022, 8.271E-005)$
Seeds	90.82 ± 1.58	$91.09 \pm 1.43(0.0029, 0.0079)$	100 ± 0.00	$99.73 \pm 0.34(0.002, 0.008)$	87.11 ± 1.61	$95.27 \pm 1.31(4.227E-012, 8.646E-005)$
Sonar	89.38 ± 1.78	$81.22 \pm 2.57(5.249E-012, 8.795E-005)$	100 ± 0.00	$98.68 \pm 0.74(1.904E-007, 1.019E-004)$	99.12 ± 0.00	$98.11 \pm 0.79(0.003, 0.006)$
Vowel	98.40 ± 0.48	$95.12 \pm 0.84(3.480E-015, 8.770E-005)$	97.92 ± 0.52	$88.66 \pm 1.18(2.003E-017, 8.832E-005)$	95.75 ± 0.71	$97.41 \pm 0.50(2.364E-006, 0.002)$
Wall-Following	98.64 ± 0.08	$98.25 \pm 0.12(1.215E-016, 8.832E-005)$	95.55 ± 0.24	$94.41 \pm 0.19(1.884E-016, 8.708E-005)$	50.09 ± 0.35	$51.47 \pm 0.55(3.674E-010, 8.8575-005)$
Wdbc	99.72 ± 0.26	$99.77 \pm 0.18(0.0217, 0.0242)$	98.31 ± 0.36	$97.13 \pm 0.44(7.498E-010, 8.696E-005)$	91.79 ± 0.73	$95.26 \pm 0.37(2.852-008, 0.002)$
Wholesale	100 ± 0.00	$100 \pm 0.00(1, 1)$	97.87 ± 0.63	$93.89 \pm 0.68(9.567E-017, 8.487E-005)$	82.56 ± 2.09	$83.40 \pm 2.01(0.026, 0.037)$
Yeast	50.95 ± 1.29	$59.19 \pm 0.86(6.750E-018, 8.807E-005)$	69.03 ± 0.68	$63.14 \pm 0.69(2.110E-016, 8.770E-005)$	55.74 ± 1.29	$60.27 \pm 1.33(1.033E-011, 8.845-005)$

Table 5.20 Testing Accuracy(%) of Three Classifiers (F-KNN, F-ELM, F-DT) with Different Fuzziness

Data Sets	Fuzzy K-NN (Low Fuzziness) Acc_{Train}	Fuzzy K-NN (High Fuzziness) $Acc_{Train}(P_1, P_2)$	Fuzzy ELM (Low Fuzziness) Acc_{Train}	Fuzzy ELM (High Fuzziness) $Acc_{Train}(P_1, P_2)$	Fuzzy DT (Low Fuzziness) Acc_{Train}	Fuzzy DT (sHigh Fuzziness) $Acc_{Train}(P_1, P_2)$
Banknote	99.95 ± 0.10	99.66 ± 0.40(0.006, 0.023)	100 ± 0.00	100 ± 0.00(1, 1)	93.28 ± 1.08	95.66 ± 1.09(4.941E−007, 1.316E−004)
Blood	66.33 ± 2.66	74.27 ± 1.66(2.806E−012, 8.745E−005)	74.16 ± 2.12	77.67 ± 1.85(1.137E−005, 1.489E−004)	76.27 ± 0.34	77.09 ± 1.29(0.012, 0.013)
Breast Cancer	66.94 ± 3.79	72.50 ± 2.47(8.425E−006, 4.899E−004)	51.94 ± 6.58	72.06 ± 4.06(1.286E−010, 8.758E−005)	73.88 ± 2.66	75.75 ± 4.68(2.123E−007, 8.330E−005)
Cleveland Heart	85.22 ± 2.88	82.72 ± 2.20(6.917E−006, 0.001)	83.67 ± 3.43	82.06 ± 2.82(1.840E−010, 8.795E−005)	81.83 ± 2.80	79.83 ± 3.33(0.009, 0.017)
Diabetes	72.51 ± 1.61	74.37 ± 2.16(0.003, 0.001)	73.27 ± 2.34	76.39 ± 2.64(3.383E−010, 8.758E−005)	73.77 ± 2.03	73.40 ± 2.12(0.376, 0.370)
Flare Solar	61.70 ± 3.85	66.02 ± 0.90(8.727E−005, 7.204E−004)	37.05 ± 7.19	39.66 ± 6.66(0.108, 0.169)	58.98 ± 4.92	63.98 ± 4.29(9.104E−006, 1.924E−004)
German	73.50 ± 2.13	74.17 ± 1.28(0.175, 8.795E−005)	75.07 ± 1.80	75.83 ± 1.70(0.066, 0.048)	72.41 ± 1.34	72.89 ± 1.96(0.396, 0.408)
Glass	98.64 ± 1.19	98.18 ± 1.36(0.083, 0.001)	67.65 ± 6.82	86.29 ± 4.46(2.732E−009, 8.832E−005)	87.27 ± 5.02	88.56 ± 3.59(0.198, 0.238)
Heart	80.19 ± 3.91	84.14 ± 3.50(1.493E−005, 0.006)	68.77 ± 5.82	79.57 ± 3.68(1.499E−008, 8.597E−005)	75.93 ± 3.89	77.47 ± 3.42(0.046, 0.060)
Housing	80.56 ± 3.33	80.98 ± 2.75(0.418, 0.370)	87.09 ± 2.02	86.70 ± 2.06(0.368, 0.359)	83.99 ± 2.65	86.21 ± 2.27(0.001, 0.001)
Ionosphere	84.29 ± 2.84	84.81 ± 2.51(2.734E−011, 8.858E−005)	85.43 ± 3.05	89.95 ± 2.69(1.892E−004, 9.426E−004)	84.34 ± 3.34	83.95 ± 3.88(1.562E−005, 1.697E−004)
New Thyroid	92.54 ± 4.21	87.08 ± 3.40(6.917E−006, 1.379E−004)	77.39 ± 5.07	86.00 ± 4.52(4.428E−006, 2.180E−004)	78.46 ± 4.53	92.62 ± 1.75(1.681E−006, 0.002)
Parkinsons	85.33 ± 2.79	85.75 ± 3.13(0.514, 0.247)	72.42 ± 9.23	89.42 ± 2.93(2.312E−007, 8.795E−005)	84.75 ± 2.31	93.17 ± 2.96(5.370E−012, 8.536E−005)
Seeds	90.87 ± 2.41	91.90 ± 2.82(0.019, 0.0002)	79.37 ± 4.89	76.43 ± 1.70(2.478E−013, 8.745E−005)	87.14 ± 3.13	92.78 ± 2.84(7.266E−008, 1.282E−004)
Sonar	81.41 ± 4.59	85.44 ± 3.61(0.015, 0.007)	72.27 ± 8.27	81.64 ± 4.44(2.797E−006, 2.459E−004)	75.28 ± 9.17	82.66 ± 4.67(3.745E−007, 8.832E−005)
Vowel	96.82 ± 1.19	93.45 ± 1.67(5.360E−010, 8.782E−005)	89.69 ± 1.59	90.36 ± 2.41(1.141E−014, 8.832E−005)	86.33 ± 2.13	89.06 ± 1.75(4.517E−004, 0.002)
Wall-Following	98.66 ± 0.25	98.91 ± 0.34(1.914E−007, 8.820E−005)	95.35 ± 0.63	94.17 ± 0.72(2.436E−012, 8.621E−005)	50.30 ± 0.74	51.69 ± 1.11(1.965E−007, 8.807E−005)
Wdbc	87.18 ± 2.11	88.40 ± 2.12(2.033E−004, 0.004)	93.11 ± 2.45	95.44 ± 1.09(7.662E−004, 4.743E−004)	91.80 ± 1.76	93.90 ± 1.65(0.002, 0.006)
Wholesale	90.19 ± 1.70	89.36 ± 2.29(0.013, 0.015)	82.03 ± 2.81	79.55 ± 2.01(3.143E−010, 8.795E−005)	82.59 ± 2.73	81.71 ± 2.50(0.789, 0.763)
Yeast	54.99 ± 2.14	60.00 ± 2.03(1.151E−009, 8.858E−005)	58.42 ± 1.82	60.37 ± 1.53(1.856E−005, 4.267E−004)	53.21 ± 2.17	56.35 ± 2.53(2.215E−007, 1.398E−004)

Note: In Table 5.19, Acc_{Train} indicates training accuracy rate, P_1 indicates P-value for paired t-test, and P_2 indicates P-value for Wilcoxon signed rank test. In Table 5.20, Acc_{Test} indicates testing accuracy rate.

From Table 5.20, one can observe that the fuzzy classifier ensemble with higher fuzziness achieves better generalization ability in comparison with the ensemble with lower fuzziness. This occurs on 14 data sets for fuzzy K-NN, 15 data sets for fuzzy ELM, and 16 data sets for fuzzy DT, respectively. Taking the average testing accuracy rate into consideration, the values of standard deviation in Table 5.20 show that the ensemble with higher fuzziness is more stable than the ensemble with lower fuzziness on most data sets. Moreover, the paired t-test shows that the difference between the ensemble with higher fuzziness and the ensemble with lower fuzziness is statistically significant on all the data sets except for two data sets. It is worth noting that the experimental results in Table 5.20 tell us that the fuzziness of base classifiers is important for constructing an ensemble, rather than telling us the fuzziness of a classifier is very important for its generalization power.

Also from Table 5.20, it is experimentally observed that the algorithms may be more suitable for tackling classification problems with complex boundaries than for those with simple boundaries. The boundaries estimated by fuzzy K-NN classifier are very difficult to exactly express and visualize for more than 4-dimensional data. We have not yet an effective way to estimate the complexity of boundaries acquired from K-NN on n-dimensional data when $n > 3$, but 3-dimensional feature subsets selected from the n-dimensional original data can provide some visualized impression about the K-NN estimated boundary. For example, we consider in Table 5.20 the Cleveland Heart data that do not support the conclusions (i.e., which does not show an improvement of testing accuracy for high-fuzziness K-NNs). In comparison with other data sets in Table 5.20, the Cleveland Heart data may have a relatively simpler boundary of K-NN, which can be partially verified via a projection of the original data in a 3-dimensional space. Figure 5.13 shows the projections in feature sets (3, 8, 10) and (3, 4, 9) of Cleveland Heart data. Although the two projection figures cannot reflect the entire characteristics of the K-NN estimated boundary, they partially indicate the less complexity of the boundary from different visualized profiles.

Reference [51] proposed data complexity framework that defined a number of measures to describe the difficulty of a classification problem and its boundary complexity. It is observed that based on the framework the behavior of a fuzzy rule–based classification system and its relationship to data complexity were discovered by Luengo and Herrera [52] and also based on this framework the performance of three classic neural network models and one SVM with respect to a series of data complexity measures was investigated by Luengo and Herrera [53]. We select two metrics F_1 and F_2 in the experiments to measure the boundary complexity of 2-class classification problems. For multiple class problems, we tentatively select two of them. Bigger F_1 for a data set indicates that its boundary is more of complexity. The experimental results are placed in Table 5.21, from which one can see that the better performance is achieved on data sets with bigger values of F_1.

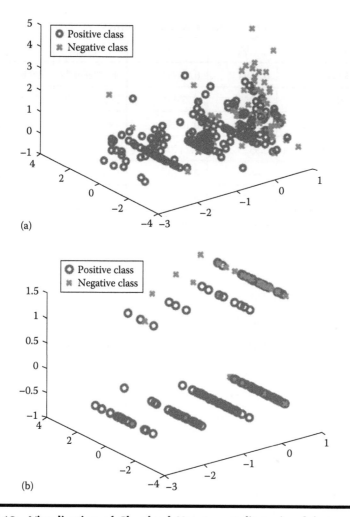

Figure 5.13 **Visualization of Cleveland Heart on 3-dimensional feature space.**
(a) 3-dimension F: 3 , F: 8, F: 10; (b) 3-dimension F: 3, F: 4, F: 9.

We now focus on the fuzzy K-NN classifier. As discussed in Section 5.5.2, the
fuzziness of fuzzy K-NN classifiers is greatly affected by its weighting exponent m.
In the following experiment, the impact of different values of m upon the algorithm
by Wang et al. [3] is examined. We first generate an ensemble of fuzzy K-NN base
classifiers by varying the value of l in (1, 15). The parameter m varies in (1, 2)
with step size 0.05 and in (2, 15) with step size 1, and the parameter K is fixed as
20 during the change of l. Therefore, 46 different fuzzy K-NNs can be constructed
on each data set. The average training and testing accuracy rates together with their
corresponding standard deviations are summarized in Table 5.22. The difference

Table 5.21 Boundary Complexity and Accuracy

Data Sets	F_1	F_2	Acc_{Train}	Acc_{Test}
Banknote	0.5894	0.1563	99.77 ± 0.22	99.66 ± 0.40
Blood	0.0049	0.2706	79.43 ± 0.76	474.27 ± 1.66
Breast Cancer	0.3088	0.1875	79.43 ± 1.11	72.50 ± 2.47
Cleveland Heart	0.9515	0.2120	93.33 ± 1.00	82.72 ± 2.20
Diabetes	0.6633	0.2516	81.86 ± 0.93	74.37 ± 2.16
Flare Solar	1.3786	0	66.20 ± 1.11	66.02 ± 0.90
German	0.4186	0.6619	89.57 ± 0.77	74.17 ± 1.28
Glass	42.2465	9.164E−004	100 ± 0.00	98.18 ± 1.36
Heart	1.0059	0.1959	91.14 ± 1.43	84.14 ± 3.50
Housing	44.8778	0.0144	100 ± 0.00	480.98 ± 2.75
Ionosphere	2.0177	0	85.08 ± 2.52	84.81 ± 2.51
New Thyroid	1.3481	6.998E−004	98.00 ± 0.61	87.08 ± 3.40
Parkinsons	3.957E+008	7.712E−010	100 ± 0.00	85.75 ± 3.13
Seeds	96.8723	0.0012	91.09 ± 1.43	91.90 ± 2.82
Sonar	1.932E+003	1.045E−006	81.22 ± 2.57	85.44 ± 3.61
Vowel	0.8790	0.0600	95.12 ± 0.84	93.45 ± 1.67
Wall-Following	9.8487	−6.669E−006	98.25 ± 0.12	98.91 ± 0.34
Wdbc	2.656E+003	0.0015	99.77 ± 0.18	88.40 ± 2.12
Wholesale	0.0158	4.814E−004	100 ± 0.00	89.36 ± 2.29
Yeast	13.0694	0	59.19 ± 0.86	60.00 ± 2.03

between Tables 5.21 and 5.19 together with 5.20 (fuzzy K-NN column) are worth noting. The difference is that the fuzzy K-NN ensemble in Tables 5.19 and 5.20 is generated by varying the value of K for fixed weighting exponent m, while the fuzzy K-NN ensemble in Table 5.22 is generated by varying the weighting exponent m for fixed K.

Table 5.22 shows an experimental result similar to those reported in Table 5.20. From Table 5.22, one still can note that the ensemble of fuzzy K-NNs with higher fuzziness produces better generalization performance and results in higher stability in comparison with the ensemble of fuzzy K-NNs with lower fuzziness. Moreover, the

Table 5.22 Training and Testing Accuracy of Fuzzy *K*-Nearest Neighbors (*K* = 20) Ensembles with Different Fuzziness Induced by Varying Weighting Exponent *m* (%)

Data Sets	Fuzzy K-NN(Low Fuzziness)		Fuzzy K-NN(High Fuzziness)	
	Acc_{Train}	Acc_{Test}	$Acc_{Train}(P_1, P_2)$	$Acc_{Test}(P_1, P_2)$
Banknote	100.00 ± 0.00	99.98 ± 0.07	99.64 ± 0.25(2.937E−006, 5.102E−005)	99.47 ± 0.53(6.722E−004, 0.002)
Blood	92.81 ± 0.73	72.20 ± 2.12	79.04 ± 0.83(1.086E−024, 8.858E−005)	75.62 ± 1.60(4.379E−006, 0.004)
Breast Cancer	85.11 ± 1.02	63.19 ± 2.61	77.87 ± 1.28(6.304E−019, 8.858E−005)	73.37 ± 3.27(2.525E−011, 5.167E−004)
Cleveland Heart	99.18 ± 0.45	72.67 ± 0.56	86.21 ± 1.40(5.720E−020, 8.845E−005)	81.89 ± 2.28(2.501E−013, 5.167E−004)
Diabetes	91.69 ± 0.64	62.34 ± 2.17	79.41 ± 1.14(1.690E−021, 8.845E−005)	74.13 ± 2.37(3.631E−013, 5.934E−004)
Flare Solar	66.05 ± 1.32	64.66 ± 1.56	67.60 ± 1.10(7.595E−004, 8.858E−005)	65.91 ± 0.00(0.002, 0.0002)
German	90.48 ± 0.53	53.11 ± 0.78	78.66 ± 0.89(1.178E−025, 8.832E−005)	74.70 ± 1.57(6.587E−028, 8.770E−005)
Glass	100.00 ± 0.00	98.86 ± 1.09	95.98 ± 0.71(4.149E−016, 8.807E−005)	94.62 ± 1.59(3.183E−010, 8.845E−005)
Heart	92.84 ± 0.78	65.43 ± 1.93	86.35 ± 1.56(2.455E−017, 8.795E−005)	83.77 ± 3.93(3.502E−019, 5.501E−004)
Housing	100.00 ± 0.00	79.64 ± 3.42	81.05 ± 1.37(2.202E−023, 8.858E−005)	86.57 ± 3.21(8.178E−004, 8.832E−005)
Ionosphere	98.90 ± 0.38	83.49 ± 2.42	83.22 ± 2.40(1.659E−017, 8.845E−005)	81.70 ± 2.78(0.002, 0.003)
New Thyroid	100.00 ± 0.00	85.00 ± 3.82	85.57 ± 1.50(2.179E−020, 8.845E−005)	91.15 ± 3.54(5.066E−008, 8.720E−005)

(Continued)

Table 5.22 (Continued) Training and Testing Accuracy of Fuzzy K-Nearest Neighbors (K = 20) Ensembles with Different Fuzziness Induced by Varying Weighting Exponent m (%)

Data Sets	Fuzzy K-NN(Low Fuzziness)		Fuzzy K-NN(High Fuzziness)	
	Acc_{Train}	Acc_{Test}	$Acc_{Train}(P_1, P_2)$	$Acc_{Test}(P_1, P_2)$
Parkinsons	100.00 ± 0.00	84.42 ± 3.64	$82.78 \pm 1.46(4.488E{-}022, 8.858E{-}005)$	$85.00 \pm 2.32(0.0016, 0.0023)$
Seeds	89.90 ± 1.78	90.79 ± 3.03	$90.85 \pm 1.64(0.0206, 0.0001)$	$91.19 \pm 3.19(0.5664, 0.0006)$
Sonar	90.52 ± 1.89	81.33 ± 3.88	$71.94 \pm 3.01(9.255E{-}019, 8.858E{-}005)$	$69.22 \pm 4.36(7.853E{-}011, 8.858E{-}005)$
Vowel	98.13 ± 0.58	93.86 ± 2.31	$78.52 \pm 1.51(1.056E{-}021, 8.845E{-}005)$	$95.07 \pm 2.89(2.817E{-}019, 8.820E{-}005)$
Wall-Following	97.55 ± 0.17	97.05 ± 0.90	$97.27 \pm 0.17(6.900E{-}012, 8.858E{-}005)$	$97.07 \pm 0.40(1.070E{-}006, 8.807E{-}005)$
Wdbc	99.80 ± 0.25	85.96 ± 2.34	$89.57 \pm 0.69(2.675E{-}024, 8.683E{-}005)$	$88.66 \pm 1.72(1.515E{-}006, 0.002)$
Wholesale	100.00 ± 0.00	88.83 ± 1.83	$92.69 \pm 0.92(7.319E{-}019, 8.820E{-}005)$	$89.59 \pm 2.27(0.0761, 0.135)$
Yeast	52.24 ± 1.19	52.75 ± 1.78	$60.59 \pm 0.78(4.680E{-}017, 8.858E{-}005)$	$59.69 \pm 1.77(5.839E{-}013, 8.858E{-}005)$

paired *t*-test demonstrates that the difference between the ensemble of fuzzy K-NNs with higher fuzziness and the ensembles of fuzzy K-NNs with higher fuzziness and with lower fuzziness is statistically significant on all the data sets. The experimental result indicates that the methodology by Wang et al. [3] is basically independent on the weighting exponent parameter m used in the classifier.

The fuzziness is strongly related to the number K of nearest neighbors. When we increase the number of K for points on the boundaries between classes, we can obtain a better generalization. It implicitly gives the relation between K and the classifiers selected with the highest fuzziness. That is, the classifiers with the highest fuzziness are also the classifiers obtained with the highest number of K. We experimentally verify this relation on the 20 selected data sets. Basically, most experimental results show a uniform trend, namely, both the fuzziness and the testing accuracy are increasing with the value of K for the single K-NN, low-fuzziness and high-fuzziness K-NN ensembles. For any given training set, K has a maximum value. When K exceeds the maximum value, the generalization no longer increases with change of K. So far we do not have any effective method to estimate the maximum value of K. As an illustration, Table 5.23 lists different fuzziness and testing accuracy of three models on the Breast Cancer data set induced by varying the parameter K values from 2 to 50.

Table 5.23 Different Fuzziness and Testing Accuracy (%) of Three Different Models on the Breast Cancer Data Set Induced by Varying the Parameter *K* Values

	Single Fuzzy K-NN		Low-Fuzziness Group		High-Fuzziness Group	
K	Fuzziness	Acc$_{Test}$	Fuzziness	Acc$_{Test}$	Fuzziness	Acc$_{Test}$
2	0.3013	65.23	0.2674	63.62	0.3412	68.38
5	0.5286	68.40	0.4884	67.63	0.5632	72.13
10	0.6402	70.63	0.6045	68.13	0.6756	72.63
15	0.6774	71.45	0.6426	69.75	0.7037	71.75
20	0.7038	73.18	0.6722	71.12	0.7335	74.25
25	0.7140	73.35	0.6827	72.50	0.7418	74.88
30	0.7269	73.18	0.6951	71.63	0.7621	74.00
35	0.7382	73.68	0.7074	72.75	0.7643	73.25
40	0.7397	73.40	0.7104	72.88	0.7628	74.75
45	0.7468	73.27	0.7224	72.12	0.7717	75.62
50	0.7468	73.55	0.7190	71.87	0.7703	74.12

Table 5.24 Testing Accuracy (%) and Diversity of Classifiers with Different Fuzziness

Data Sets	Fuzzy K-NN(Acc_{Test}/Q_{av})		Fuzzy ELM(Acc_{Test}/Q_{av})		Fuzzy DT(Acc_{Test}/Q_{av})	
	Low Fuzziness	High Fuzziness	Low Fuzziness	High Fuzziness	Low Fuzziness	High Fuzziness
Banknote	99.95 ± 0.10/1.00	99.66 ± 0.40/1.00	100 ± 0.00/1.00	100 ± 0.00/0.69	93.28 ± 1.08/0.93	95.66 ± 1.09/0.90
Blood	66.33 ± 2.66/0.89	74.27 ± 1.66/0.99	74.16 ± 2.12/0.99	77.67 ± 1.85/0.98	76.27 ± 0.34/0.99	77.09 ± 1.29/0.98
Breast Cancer	66.94 ± 3.79/0.97	72.50 ± 2.47/0.99	51.94 ± 6.58/0.96	72.06 ± 4.06/0.95	73.88 ± 2.66/0.99	75.75 ± 4.68/0.96
Cleveland Heart	85.22 ± 2.88/0.95	82.72 ± 2.20/0.99	83.67 ± 3.43/0.95	82.06 ± 2.82/0.83	81.83 ± 2.80/0.95	79.83 ± 3.33/0.03
Diabetes	72.51 ± 1.61/0.97	74.37 ± 2.16/0.99	73.27 ± 2.34/0.98	76.39 ± 2.64/0.91	73.77 ± 2.03/0.97	73.40 ± 2.12/0.89
Flare Solar	61.70 ± 3.85/0.95	66.02 ± 0.90/0.99	37.05 ± 7.19/0.86	39.66 ± 6.66/0.87	58.98 ± 4.92/0.94	63.98 ± 4.29/0.97
German	73.50 ± 2.13/0.97	74.17 ± 1.28/0.99	75.07 ± 1.80/0.95	75.83 ± 1.70/0.91	72.41 ± 1.34/0.97	72.89 ± 1.96/0.96
Glass	98.64 ± 1.19/1.00	98.18 ± 1.36/1.00	67.65 ± 6.82/0.93	86.29 ± 4.46/0.86	87.27 ± 5.02/0.87	88.56 ± 3.59/0.62
Heart	80.19 ± 3.91/0.97	84.14 ± 3.50/0.99	68.77 ± 5.82/0.95	79.57 ± 3.68/0.78	75.93 ± 3.89/0.72	77.47 ± 3.42/0.35
Housing	80.56 ± 3.33/1.00	80.98 ± 2.75/1.00	87.09 ± 2.02/0.97	86.70 ± 2.06/0.81	83.99 ± 2.65/0.98	86.21 ± 2.27/0.93
Ionosphere	84.29 ± 2.84/0.97	84.81 ± 2.51/0.99	85.43 ± 3.05/0.95	89.95 ± 2.69/0.88	84.34 ± 3.34/0.95	83.95 ± 3.88/0.91
New Thyroid	92.54 ± 4.21/1.00	87.08 ± 3.40/1.00	77.39 ± 5.07/0.99	86.00 ± 4.52/0.99	78.46 ± 4.53/0.93	92.62 ± 1.75/0.96

(Continued)

Table 5.24 (Continued)   Testing Accuracy (%) and Diversity of Classifiers with Different Fuzziness

Data Sets	Fuzzy K-NN (Acc_{Test}/Q_{av})		Fuzzy ELM (Acc_{Test}/Q_{av})		Fuzzy DT (Acc_{Test}/Q_{av})	
	Low Fuzziness	High Fuzziness	Low Fuzziness	High Fuzziness	Low Fuzziness	High Fuzziness
Parkinsons	85.33 ± 2.79/1.00	85.75 ± 3.13/1.00	72.42 ± 9.23/0.72	89.42 ± 2.93/0.97	84.75 ± 2.31/0.99	93.17 ± 2.96/0.54
Seeds	90.87 ± 2.41/0.99	91.90 ± 2.82/0.99	79.37 ± 4.89/0.99	76.43 ± 1.70/0.82	87.14 ± 3.13/0.98	92.78 ± 2.84/0.95
Sonar	81.41 ± 4.59/0.95	85.44 ± 3.61/0.99	72.27 ± 8.27/0.17	81.64 ± 4.44/0.41	75.28 ± 9.17/0.95	82.66 ± 4.67/0.27
Vowel	96.82 ± 1.19/0.99	93.45 ± 1.67/0.99	89.69 ± 1.59/0.90	90.36 ± 2.41/0.74	86.33 ± 2.13/0.79	89.06 ± 1.75/0.75
Wall-Following	98.66 ± 0.25/0.99	98.91 ± 0.34/0.99	95.35 ± 0.63/0.99	94.17 ± 0.72/0.90	50.30 ± 0.74/0.99	51.69 ± 1.11/0.99
Wdbc	87.18 ± 2.11/0.98	88.40 ± 2.12/1.00	93.11 ± 2.45/0.99	95.44 ± 1.09/0.95	91.80 ± 1.76/0.93	93.90 ± 1.65/0.98
Wholesale	90.19 ± 1.70/1.00	89.36 ± 2.29/1.00	82.03 ± 2.81/0.99	79.55 ± 2.01/0.95	82.59 ± 2.73/0.99	81.71 ± 2.50/0.98
Yeast	54.99 ± 2.14/0.94	60.00 ± 2.03/0.99	58.42 ± 1.82/0.99	60.37 ± 1.53/0.85	53.21 ± 2.17/0.93	56.35 ± 2.53/0.89

Finally, we check the impact of classifier ensemble diversity on the model by Wang et al. [3]. From references we can know that in ensemble learning the diversity of a classifier ensemble has a direct impact on the generalization ability of the classifier ensemble. In ensemble learning, the generalization of an ensemble system is closely related to the diversity of base classifiers, classification confidence of base classifiers, and approaches to generating base classifiers. Hu et al. [54] proposed a new methodology for generating base classifiers based on rough subspaces, which can lead to a powerful and compact classification system. Furthermore, Li et al. [55] explored the impact of classification confidence of base classifiers on voting mechanism in ensemble learning and obtained some interesting results.

It is interesting to observe the difference of diversity between two classifier ensembles with low and high fuzziness. There are several different definitions of diversity for a classifier ensemble. Here, we select a widely used form [11]. That is the Q statistic that can be used to compute the diversity between two classifiers based on the prediction correctness rate of both classifiers. The formula can be expressed as

$$Q_{ij} = \frac{N^{11}N^{00} - N^{01}N^{10}}{N^{11}N^{00} + N^{01}N^{10}}, \tag{5.33}$$

where N^{ab} denotes the number of samples for which the output of classifier C_i is a and simultaneously the output of classifier C_j is b. Moreover, if a given sample is correctly classified by $C_i(C_j)$, the value of $a(b)$ is taken as 1. Otherwise, the value of $a(b)$ is taken as 0. The averaged diversity for an ensemble is evaluated by

$$Q_{av} = \frac{1}{l(l-1)} \sum_{i=1}^{l-1} \sum_{j=i+1}^{l} Q_{ij}, \tag{5.34}$$

where l is the number of classifiers. Q statistic's value varies from -1 to $+1$ denoting negative and positive correlation. Experimental results on the 20 selected data sets for three kinds of classifiers are shown in Table 5.24. The testing accuracy rates of the three different methods are directly taken from Table 5.20.

It can be observed from Table 5.24 that the diversity of an ensemble of classifiers with high fuzziness is a little less than the diversity of an ensemble of classifiers with low fuzziness. From a new angle, it indicates that the diversity has a key impact on the ensemble learning performance, but it does not mean that the more diversity, the better performance.

References

1. X. Z. Wang, J. H. Zhai, S. X. Lu. Induction of multiple fuzzy decision trees based on rough set technique. *Information Sciences*, 2008, 178(16):3188–3202.
2. H. M. Feng, X. Z. Wang. Performance improvement of classifier fusion for batch samples based on upper integral. *Neural Networks*, 2015, 63:87–93.

3. X. Z. Wang, H. J. Xing, Y. Li et al. A study on relationship between generalization abilities and fuzziness of base classifiers in ensemble learning. *IEEE Transactions on Fuzzy Systems*, 2015, 23(5):1638–1654.

4. N. C. Oza, K. Tumer. Classifier ensembles: Select real-world applications. *Information Fusion*, 2008, 9(1):4–20.

5. N. J. Nilsson. *Learning Machines: Foundations of Trainable Pattern-Classifying Systems*. McGraw-Hill, New York, 1965.

6. D. H. Wolpert. Stacked generalization. *Neural Networks*, 1992, 5(2):241–259.

7. Y. Freund, R. Schapire. Experiments with a new boosting algorithm. In: *Proceeding of 13th International Conference on Machine Learning*, Bari, Italy. July 3–6, 1996, pp. 148–156.

8. L. Breiman. Bagging predictors. *Machine Learning*, 1996, 6(2):123–140.

9. A. S. Britto Jr, R. Sabourin, L. E. S. Oliveira. Dynamic selection of classifiers—A comprehensive review. *Pattern Recognition*, 2014, 47(11):3665–3680.

10. T. G. Dietterich. Ensemble methods in machine learning. In: *Multiple Classifier Systems, Lecture Notes in Computer Science*, 2000, Vol. 1857, Springer, Berlin, Germany, pp. 1–15.

11. L. I. Kuncheva, C. J. Whitaker. Measures of diversity in classifier ensembles and their relationship with the ensemble accuracy. *Machine Learning*, 2003, 51(2):181–207.

12. G. Brown, J. Wyatt, R. Harris, X. Yao. Diversity creation methods: A survey and categorisation. *Information Fusion*, 2005, 6(1):5–20.

13. L. Rokach. Taxonomy for characterizing ensemble methods in classification tasks: A review and annotated bibliography. *Computational Statistics and Data Analysis*, 2009, 53(12):4046–4072.

14. K. M. Ali, M. J. Pazzani. Error reduction through learning multiple descriptions. *Machine Learning*, 1996, 24(3):173–202.

15. R. Battiti, A. M. Colla. Democracy in neural nets: Voting schemes for classification. *Neural Networks*, 1994, 7(4):691–709.

16. E. Bauer, R. Kohavi. An empirical comparison of voting classification algorithms: bagging, boosting, and variants. *Machine Learning*, 1999, 36:105–139.

17. D. W. Opitz, J. W. Shavlik. Generating accurate and diverse members of a neural-network ensemble. In: *Advances in Neural Information Processing Systems*, Touretzky, D, Mozer, M., Hasselmo, M. E. et al. (Eds.), Massachusetts: MIT Press, pp. 535–541, 1996.

18. L. Xu, A. Krzyzak, C. Y. Suen. Methods for combining multiple classifiers and their applications to handwriting recognition. *IEEE Transactions on Systems, Man, and Cybernetics*, 1992, 22(3):418–435.

19. L. I. Kuncheva. Combining classifiers: Soft computing solutions. In: *Pattern Recognition: From Classical to Modern Approaches*. Pal, S.K. and Pal, A. (Eds.), Singapore: World Scientific, pp. 427–451, 2001.

20. M. Galar, A. Fernández, E. Barrenechea et al. A review on ensembles for the class imbalance problem: Bagging-, boosting-, and hybrid-based approaches. *IEEE Transactions on Systems Man and Cybernetics Part C Applications and Reviews*, 2012, 42(4): 463–484.

21. R. E. Schapire. The strength of weak learnability. *Machine Learning*, 1990, 5(2): 197–227.

22. Y. Freund, R. E. Schapire. A decision theoretic generalization of on-line learning and an application to boosting. *Journal of Computer and System Sciences*, 2010, 55(1):119–139.

23. Z. Pawlak. Rough sets. *International Journal of Information and Computer Sciences*, 1982, 11:341–356.

24. D. Dubois, H. Prade. Rough fuzzy sets and fuzzy rough sets. *International Journal of General Systems*, 1990, 17:191–208.

25. L. I. Kuncheva. Fuzzy rough sets: Application to feature selection. *Fuzzy Sets and Systems*, 1992, 51(2):147–153.

26. S. Nanda. Fuzzy rough sets. *Fuzzy Sets and Systems*, 1992, 45(2):157–160.

27. Y. Y. Yao. Combination of rough and fuzzy sets based on-level sets. In: *Rough Sets and Data Mining: Analysis for Imprecise Data*, Lin, T.Y. and Cercone, N. (Eds.), Kluwer Academic Publishers, Boston, MA, pp. 301–321, 1997.

28. R. Jensen, Q. Shen. Fuzzy-rough attribute reduction with application to web categorization. *Fuzzy Sets and Systems*, 2004, 141(3):469–485.

29. Y. Yuan, M. J. Shaw. Induction of fuzzy decision trees. *Fuzzy Sets and Systems*, 1995, 69(2):125–139.

30. G. B. Huang, Q. Y. Zhu, C.K. Siew. Extreme learning machine: A new learning scheme of feedforward neural networks. In: *Proceedings of International Joint Conference on Neural Networks (IJCNN2004)*, July 25–29, 2004, Vol. 2, Budapest, Hungary, pp. 985–990.

31. G. B. Huang, Q. Y. Zhu, C. K. Siew. Extreme learning machine: Theory and applications. *Neurocomputing*, 2006, 70(1–3):489–501.

32. C. Cortes, V. Vapnik. Support vector networks. *Machine Learning*, 1995, 20:273–297.

33. S. Haykin. *Neural Networks: A Comprehensive Foundation*. Prentice Hall, Upper Saddle River, NJ, pp. 178–228, 1999.

34. R. Battit. First and second order methods for learning: Between the steepest descent and Newton's method. *Neural Computation*, 1992, 2:141–166.

35. G. Golub, F. Charles, V. Loan. *Matrix Computations*. Johns Hopkins University Press, Baltimore, MD, 1983.

36. Z. Wang, W. Li, K. S. Leung. Lower integrals and upper integrals with respect to nonadditive set functions. *Fuzzy Sets and Systems*, 2008, 159(6):646–660.

37. A. Frank, A. Asuncion. UCI machine learning repository, http://archive.ics.uci.edu/ml, May 5, 2013.

38. G. B. Huang, H. Zhou, X. Ding et al. Extreme learning machine for regression and multiclass classification. *IEEE Transactions on Systems, Man and Cybernetics, Part B (Cybernetics)*, 2012, 42(2):513–529.

39. A. Verikas, A. Lipnickas, K. Malmqvist et al. Soft combination of neural classifiers: A comparative study. *Pattern Recognition Letters*, 1999, 20(4):429–444.

40. R. Yang, Z. Wang, P. A. Heng et al. Fuzzified Choquet integral with a fuzzy-valued integrand and its application on temperature prediction. *IEEE Transactions on Systems, Man and Cybernetics, Part B (Cybernetics)*, 2008, 38(2):367–380.

41. I. Kushchu. Genetic programming and evolutionary generalization. *IEEE Transaction on Evolutionary Computation*, 2002, 6(5):431–442.
42. O. D. Richard, P. E. Hart, D. G. Stork. *Pattern Classification*. New Jersey: John Wiley & Sons, 2012.
43. J. M. Keller, M. R. Gray, J. A. Givens. A fuzzy K-nearest neighbor algorithm. *IEEE Transactions on Systems, Man and Cybernetics*, 1985, 15(4):580–585.
44. C. Bishop. *Pattern Recognition and Machine Learning*. Springer-Verlag, Berlin, Germany, 2006.
45. A. D. Luca, S. Termini. A definition of a nonprobabilistic entropy in the setting of fuzzy sets theory. *Information and Control*, 1972, 20(4):301–312.
46. V. N. Vapnik. *Estimation of Dependences Based on Empirical Data*. Springer Verlag, New York, 1982.
47. X. Z. Wang, C. R. Dong. Improving generalization of fuzzy IF-THEN rules by maximizing fuzzy entropy. *IEEE Transactions on Fuzzy Systems*, 2009, 17(3):556–567.
48. J. G. Moreno-Torres. Study on the impact of partition-induced dataset shift on k-fold cross-validation. *IEEE Transactions on Neural Networks and Learning Systems*, 2012, 23(8):1304–1312.
49. D. Janez. Statistical comparisons of classifiers over multiple data sets. *Journal of Machine Learning Research*, 2006, 7(1):1–30.
50. S. Garca, A. Fernndez, J. Luengo, F. Herrera. Advanced nonparametric tests for multiple comparisons in the design of experiments in computational intelligence and data mining: Experimental analysis of power. *Information Sciences*, 2010, 180(10):2044–2064.
51. T. K. Ho, M. Basu. Complexity measures of supervised classification problems. *IEEE Transactions on Pattern Analysis and Machine Intelligence*, 2002, 24(3):289–300.
52. J. Luengo, F. Herrera. Domains of competence of fuzzy rule based classification systems with data complexity measures: A case of study using a fuzzy hybrid genetic based machine learning method. *Fuzzy Sets and Systems*, 2010, 161(1):3–19.
53. J. Luengo, F. Herrera. Shared domains of competence of approximate learning models using measures of separability of classes. *Information Sciences*, 2012, 185(1):43–65.
54. Q. H. Hu, D. R. Yu, Z. X. Xie et al. EROS: Ensemble rough subspaces. *Pattern Recognition*, 2007, 40(12):3728–3739.
55. L. Li, Q. H. Hu Q, X. Wu et al. Exploration of classification confidence in ensemble learning. *Pattern Recognition*, 2014, 47(9):3120–3131.

Index

For Product Safety Concerns and Information please contact our EU
representative GPSR@taylorandfrancis.com
Taylor & Francis Verlag GmbH, Kaufingerstraße 24, 80331 München, Germany

www.ingramcontent.com/pod-product-compliance
Ingram Content Group UK Ltd.
Pitfield, Milton Keynes, MK11 3LW, UK
UKHW021614240425
457818UK00018B/552